The Au Pair

The Au Pair is breaking moulds in the love genre and the gay love genre; it's a simply written story that is honest and beautiful.
– Elle magazine

The Au Pair bravely goes where no other book has gone, and tells the story which so many women have experienced, with complete honesty.
– Gay Pages

Written as it happened, one can feel the urgency and passion woven intricately through the pages of this jaw-dropping, and at times humorous, memoir.
– Exit magazine

Michele is in a relatively happy marriage and dotes on her three children. But when her eye disease worsens, she hires an au pair to help, the beautiful Marizette, who happens to be a lesbian. Soon, Michele finds herself falling for Marizette and we witness her turmoil firsthand as she admits to herself that she's a lesbian. A heart-warming read, filled with lots of explicit sex scenes. And it's a true South-African story! Yay!
– Heat magazine

The Au Pair

Michele Macfarlane

Published by Jacana Media (Pty) Ltd in 2010
First impression 2011
Second and third impressions 2011

10 Orange Street
Sunnyside
Auckland Park 2092
South Africa
+2711 628 3200
www.jacana.co.za

© Michele Macfarlane, 2010

All rights reserved.

ISBN 978-1-77009-908-1
Job No. 001541

Cover photo by Etienne Topham
Set in Sabon 10.5/15pt
Printed and bound by Ultra Litho (Pty) Limited, Johannesburg

See a complete list of Jacana titles at www.jacana.co.za

*To my mom for giving me courage and
my wife for giving me inspiration*

Chapter one

To: sara@naturalnurture.co.uk
Subject: Practise caution
Dearest Sara
Feeling a bit down today. The ophthalmologist said that with retinitis pigmentosa, you never know how fast you could lose your eyesight, but that my peripheral vision has definitely deteriorated. Luckily my forward vision is still good. Anyway, I've made the monumental decision to give up driving. I'm going to take on an au pair, rather than employing a driver. That way I'll also have someone to help out with the kids. I'm interviewing a woman tomorrow. Will keep you updated.

Enough about me. Prepare yourself for a lecture … OK, here goes: Sara, please, please be careful! I know I risk coming across as judgmental and prudish, but I'm allowed to because I love you, and I think you're making a big mistake fooling around with this Gael woman. In a London phone box of all places! Really? At thirty-eight you've decided that you're a lesbian!? Just like that? Please! I don't buy it. I know you better than that.

Here's what I think. You and Graeme have been together for a long time. You've spent the bulk of your relationship raising kids and you're a bit bored, understandably. Then a cute young lezzy comes along and shows an interest. And I'm sure it's all very flattering and exciting. But seriously?!

Look, I think you need to cut ties with Gael immediately and put your energies into your relationship with Graeme. Buy some sexy undies. Share a couple of bottles of wine together – add a bit of sparkle to things. I don't know. Fuck in a phone box if you must! Whatever it takes. Sara, you have so much to lose: a husband who adores you (worships you, actually); a loving family – just think of your kids. This affair with Gael could blow their world to smithereens.

It's your choice. Just be careful. And remember I love you and miss you. Give my love to Graeme and the kids. Take care. Love, Michele xxxxx

○

I press send, then log off, thinking back to when I first met Sara. It was on a weekend away in Cornwell, organised by the Natural Nurturing Network, a group that promotes gentle childrearing (long-term breastfeeding, no smacking, allowing babies to bed-share). There were about twenty families camping in the field with us, all with barefoot children running around, mothers carrying their babies in slings across their shoulders. Not a single pram or bottle in sight.

One woman stood out like a beacon. With her hair cut in a stylish, dark bob, wearing a strappy turquoise dress, Sara was nothing like the other mothers, who could be members of a drab cult, in their baggy tracksuits and faded, oversized T-shirts. The two of us hit it off straight away.

Sara is one of those rare friends you can speak to about absolutely anything, and saying goodbye to her was one of the hardest things about our move from England to South Africa. Over the last few years, our lives have been comfortingly similar, but now, with this crush of hers, I feel irrationally betrayed.

It's past midnight when I slip into bed with my sleeping husband and press my tummy and breasts into his warm back. He shifts slightly, snuggling in closer. I slide my fingers through his thick hair. I have always been simultaneously attracted to and jealous of Peter's lustrous locks, my own short hair being so fine and flyaway.

I try to sleep, but there are too many things playing on my mind. Most of all the fact that my retinitis pigmentosa is getting worse. What if I go completely blind? I picture myself grappling around for objects I can't see and walking into walls … Stop it! I need to sleep. I try deep breathing, counting sheep, meditating, but nothing's working, so I turn on to my back and reach down to touch myself. As my fingertip circles my clitoris, I conjure up a well-used fantasy …

I am standing at a dressing table looking at myself in the mirror. An androgynous figure comes up behind me, turns me around, and pushes me down on the dressing table, opening my legs … I concentrate on staying in the fantasy, rather than on my fingers, which are sliding over my ever-swelling clitoris. As I feel my climax building, I want to feel something inside me. I move my fingers faster, scared to slow down, I don't want to lose my orgasm. I shake Peter roughly with my free hand and gasp, 'Peter! Peter, quick!'

'Hey,' he says, sleepily, then quickly comes to attention as he takes in my shuddering body, my short gasps of breath. He doesn't want to miss an opportunity that comes up so rarely. I turn onto my hands and knees so that I can still play with myself, quite happy to skip all the kissing, which I've never really enjoyed that much anyway.

I'm not even sure how much I enjoy sex, but I still crave it. I'm tantalisingly close to orgasm but infuriatingly and predictably, my inner dialogue begins. Why can't I just open up and let go? Why aren't I enjoying this? This is my husband. Surely intimacy should come naturally? So why this wave of self-revulsion? And there he is, Steven, uninvited, wholly unwelcome, gatecrashing my orgasm. He is smirking and mocking, pleased with himself that after all these years he still has an effect on me. I am ten years old again. ' Go away you bastard. You have no place here,' I mutter to myself, squeezing my eyes shut, focusing all my attention on the dressing table until my anonymous lover comes back into focus. And that's where I stay until finally I orgasm.

As ever, I am well mannered. My husband has woken up past midnight to service me, so I push him onto his back and ride him until he climaxes.

'Thank you,' he whispers, placing his arms around me.

I snuggle into him, pressing my bum into his tummy; spooning companionably, enjoying the closeness, and trying desperately to shake off the post-sex yuckiness that clings to me like settled dust.

Peter has no idea of the ordeal I go through every time we make love. He knows about the abuse but I'm pretty sure he doesn't know the extent to which it still affects me. Ever the gentleman, he never pushes me, leaving it up to me to initiate, which I am both grateful for and insulted by. There is a fine line between being a gentleman and seeming disinterested.

○

To: sara@naturalnurture.co.uk
Subject: The joys of an au pair!
Dear Sara
We have an au pair! Her name is Marizette, and she's fantastic. The kids have taken to her already. She's done a lot of competitive sport so she's nicely built – tall, with broad shoulders, a flat tummy, and strong arms. She was raised on a farm in Venda (miles from anywhere) so she's super-competent, and has done all kinds of things by herself all her life. Unfortunately she won't be with us for long, as she wants to study again next year. But for now, for the first time in eleven years, I have some time on my hands. She does all the driving and helps tutor Max in the mornings.

Besides going blind (well, just about!), I love our new life in South Africa. Although I miss our friends in England, Cape Town feels like home to me. Whenever I go out onto the stoep and look out at our enormous garden (plus swimming pool!) and the surrounding mountains, I just can't believe my luck. It's certainly a far cry from the small mid-terrace where we lived in Milton Keynes. We even have a cleaning lady. O.K I know I said I would never have one, but after doing all my own domestics in England, I truly appreciate the extra help. Lebo is lovely, so I enjoy the extra company; being a full time mother can be a lonely business. And of course having my family close by but also in their own space is such a bonus. My brother, Ian, comes and goes as he pleases as the cottage has a separate entrance from the bottom of the garden, and the children love my mom and dad living upstairs in the flat. Peter loves finally having a space big enough to plant a vegetable garden. He's determined never to move again.

We're still teaching Max at home, but Chloe has decided to try a school, which so far she's loving. I was a bit disappointed to be honest, as I still feel passionately about the benefits of home education.

I must say, having Marizette around is a bonus as she's ready to try all kinds of activities I shy away from. We had Chloe's eighth birthday party over the weekend, which was a blast. Peter and I are a fantastic team when it comes to parties. Joshua and Ava were missed though. Lots and lots of love, Michi

PS: I think Marizette is gay! I know you can't really tell with these things, but her hair, which was carefully brushed down for the interview, is now spiked up into a trendy Mohican. She is also wearing seriously boyish clothes. But (don't laugh) she's actually really cute! I mean, really cute. In spite of the tomboy thing she has a pretty face. Especially her eyes. Anyway, I mentioned my suspicions to my mother. Mom, ever practical, replies: 'Well, if she is gay, that's a good thing. At least you won't have the problem of your husband running off with the au pair!'

PPS: I have decided to start judo again. Max has joined the senior class, so I'm going along to his next session. I know it seems insane at my age, but I've been reflecting on how little I've achieved. So I'm going back on the mat. I know it's not exactly some hot career, but judo is something I was good at. Marizette will drive us, obviously, and is even going to join in some classes. Can't wait!

Chapter two

'I know what you're like,' my husband lectures, as I pull on my old judo suit (dug out of a box of unsorted stuff in the garage). 'I'm a chiropractor, not a magician. If you injure yourself, I'm not necessarily going to able to fix it.'

'Uh-huh,' I grunt, half-listening.

'Just remember, you're not fit and you're not twenty anymore, so just take it easy. OK?'

'Sure, of course I'll be careful,' I reply reassuringly.

Half an hour later, I feel a frisson of excitement as I step onto the mat barefoot, bowing respectfully. Marizette, Max and I join the row of about twenty students standing in front of Sensei Lorraine, a short, stocky woman with a sharp shoulder-length blonde bob. There are a few pre-teens about Max's age, but most of the class look in their early twenties. I'm the oldest person by far. The judo hall is in a giant shed at the Wynberg military centre and the floor is covered wall to wall with mats. There's seating for spectators, which is occupied by a few parents, partners and … Marizette's girlfriend, a woman called Hilary, whom she has always referred to as her 'housemate'. Marizette mentioned her yesterday while I quizzed her on the way to collecting the kids from school.

'So, are you single then?' I casually dropped the question into our conversation.

She paused, 'No, I have a girlfriend.'

I felt a horrible, unfamiliar constriction in my throat. I knew it wasn't the gay thing. I don't care about anyone being gay. It's the bombshell about Marizette having a girlfriend. I really thought she was single.

In the judo hall, we take a bow as the sensei claps her hands and barks, 'Forward, run!' We dutifully circle the mat. 'Sideways, run! Backwards, run.' We continue at a brisk trot. And Peter was wrong; I am twenty! Or at least I feel twenty. I manage the warm-up with ease and agility, circling the mat with all the energy I can muster, proudly keeping up with the rest of the class.

OK, I'm showing off. Not for the sensei, not for Marizette, but for Hilary, who is parked off in the designated seating area. She's mostly reading, but whenever she glances over, I have a showy burst of energy. For some unfathomable reason, I feel childishly competitive with this young woman around. Earlier, when Marizette introduced us, I smugly noted that she's not that great; quite plain to be perfectly honest. Or is she? Marizette obviously sees something in her. I grudgingly admit she's extremely feminine, with long blonde hair and the flawless skin of a twenty-one-year-old. With a pang, I realise that's a full fifteen years younger than I am.

'OK,' the sensei claps her hands, 'time for some *randori*!'

I'm paired with Marizette. We begin with groundwork, which is my favourite part of judo. It makes me feel strong and capable, not clumsy and half-blind. A bit like wrestling, the purpose is to get your partner on her back and into a hold down. We sit back to back until the sensei barks, '*Hajime* (begin)!' Immediately I swing around and attack, grabbing Marizette by her lapels, trying to push her down. She's strong, and even though I decide to go easy on her in her first session, I realise I'll have to use all my strength if I want to get anywhere.

I'm quite put out that I'm struggling to wrestle Marizette onto her back or get her into an arm lock. And yet there is something about her strength that gives me a funny, fluttery feeling in my stomach. We shift about on the mat, both of us on our knees, grasping each other's jackets. I sense a moment of relaxation and take the gap, pushing her down with all my might. I throw myself on top of her, pinning her beneath me. I'm sure it's a complete fluke that I manage to get her down; she probably doesn't want to use all her strength against her boss, but I take full advantage of it. I squash myself on top of her, my arm around her neck, my face close to hers, my feet brought up towards my head; the classic shoulder hold.

Marizette struggles underneath me. Suddenly I'm acutely aware of her closeness, the heat from her wriggling body, her rapid breathing. My breasts pushed against her chest. I can actually feel her heart beating; or is it mine? And then I feel it, the pulling sensation above my pubic bone and I realise with horror that I'm turned on. Oh my God! Is this how the guys feel when they partner us in groundwork? I hope not! I shake my head and put the feeling down to endorphins released from all the physical exertion.

'OK, *matte!*' shouts the sensei. 'Change partners.'

I stand, flustered, and face Marizette for our bow. I

take in her flushed face and her dark, shining eyes, the fine nose and her full mouth, all set in pale skin. And it hits me. She is incredibly and undeniably beautiful.

By the end of the class, I feel invincible. We line up at the edge of the mat as Sensei Lorraine announces the upcoming nationals. I am so proud of myself. I managed to keep up with everyone for two hours, without taking a break. I also managed to hold my own in *randori* (free practice), even against the men. I'll bet they were surprised when they found they couldn't throw me around like a rag doll. I decide there and then, mid-bow, that I am going to enter nationals.

○

'Oh my God! Shit! Ow. Ow. Ow!'

I can't move. I'm in bed. It's 7am and I should be up by now, getting Chloe's breakfast ready. Peter is about to leave.

'Peter, you can't go. Please help me! Make me better,' I plead.

'Excuse me?' he laughs. 'I warned you. What part of "take it easy" didn't you understand?' He gives me a half-smile, 'If you come in later I'll give you a treatment.'

I try to get out of bed, an incredibly difficult task. Every muscle in my body is screaming in agony. My stomach muscles in particular are paying sorely for all the sit-ups I breezed through the night before.

'Look,' says Peter, softening, 'I'll quickly get Chloe ready for school. Marizette will be here soon, so you stay in bed for a bit.' He pauses, looking hopeful. 'I take it you won't be carrying on with judo?'

'Actually, I'm entering the nationals,' I mutter, my eyes closed.

◯

To: sara@naturalnurture.co.uk
Subject: Judo warrior
Dear Sara
Thank you so much for the e-mail. I miss you terribly. Wish I could be transported back to England for a couple of hours so we can chat and chat over multiple cups of tea. I'm happy Joshua and Ava are doing so well. Also extremely pleased to hear you're cooling things off with Gael, but what does that mean exactly? Does it mean you won't be seeing her again or that you'll be seeing less of her?

Things are going well on my side of the world. I'm training hard and have taken part in a couple of small judo competitions to qualify for the nationals. How cool does that sound? When friends ask how the judo's going, I casually say, 'Oh, I'm entering the nationals.' It sounds way more impressive than it is, as I'm only going to be fighting as a veteran (meaning I'll be fighting other women in their thirties, not the youngsters, who are beyond aggressive – trust me, I fought a couple in a competition last weekend).

I love judo, though. I love the fighting. I love being able to wrestle and sweat; the whole physical contact of the sport, which is the antithesis of the nurturing, gentle, motherly side of me. I also love how strong I'm becoming – I can really feel it from the inside and it feels great. Marizette is also doing really well, which is hardly a surprise, given her athletic background. She is gay, by the way, I was right. And she has a girlfriend called Hilary, a law student.

Anyway, must go. I miss you, and I miss the home-education group. Send me some gossip on everybody! Love, Michi

PS: I'm going to be thirty-seven tomorrow and I'm having a big party at my mom and dad's penthouse down at the Waterfront. It's normally rented out, but luckily available that weekend. My parents have said we can use it for the night. Marizette's babysitting, so I know the kids will be happy and I can relax. Wish you guys could join us. xxx

Chapter three

It's my party and so far it's going fantastically well. The penthouse is crowded with friends and family, laughing and chatting above the music. The setting couldn't be more perfect. We're on the top floor of a building in a sort of goldfish bowl; 360-degree windows with views spanning the harbour, the sparkly lights of the shopping centres and the silhouette of Table Mountain. Everyone is having a great time. Everyone except me, the party girl, who should be having the most fun. Instead, I'm sitting on the marble surface next to the sink in the main en-suite bathroom. And standing facing me (because I've dragged him here) is my long-suffering brother Ian, my number-one confidant. The person I trust most in the whole world; the person who will always hear me out and never mock me.

'Ian,' I begin urgently, 'I think I like the au pair.'

Ian looks past me, sighing at his handsome reflection in the mirror. And he really is handsome, even I can see that. Tall, with short, fair hair and Ken-like perfect features.

'Ian, are you listening to me?' I say impatiently. 'This is serious.'

He meets my eye, 'Yes, yes. You like the au pair. Um,

isn't that a good thing, considering she looks after your kids?'

'No, it's not a good thing! I mean, I really like her. I can't stop thinking about her; how brilliant she is with the kids; how competent and strong; and just generally fantastic …' my voice trails off.

'Wow,' says Ian, scratching his chin and smiling. 'It sounds like a crush. Ooh, my sister has a crush on her au pair!'

'Ian! This isn't funny,' I snap. I feel tears involuntarily spring to my eyes and I quickly wipe them away. 'It can't be a crush. I mean, I've only known her for two weeks.'

Ian's smile disappears. He looks confused, then concerned. 'Michele, come on. Don't be so serious! It's your birthday; all your friends are here to celebrate.' He reaches over and puts his arms around me. 'Hey, cheer up. Look, in my opinion, there's other stuff going on that's making you all emotional.'

'Yes, maybe you're right,' I concede. 'But you must admit, she's so gorgeous and sexy. God, Ian! What the fuck's the matter with me? I'm a normal woman, married with three kids. This is so unlike me!'

Ian looks at me with one eyebrow raised and an amused smile playing on his lips. 'Is it? Um, let's see …' He pauses, looking at me, chin in hand. 'OK, Oxford. My second year. You were up for the weekend to attend one of the balls. An after-party in my room, a few friends, my girlfriend, Angela?' Ian pauses again, still smiling, waiting for me to catch up.

As I realise where this is leading I open my mouth to protest, but he continues, 'You and Angela pulling into each other. God, Michele! It was like a floor show. I was so embarrassed I had to leave the room!'

'OK, I know, I know,' I blush. 'But come on, Ian, I was drunk, really drunk, so it doesn't count. I had reduced responsibility. I hardly ever drink, so when I do it doesn't count ...' I fade into silence. Did it count?

Suddenly I'm transported back to that room in Oxford. A handful of students, including Ian, lounging around, getting extremely stoned. A few of them sit around a lava lamp, completely transfixed by the floating globules of colour, moving slowly and changing shape. Angela, Ian's new girlfriend, is sitting close to me on the floor. Ian had already told me she thought I was gorgeous. I thought she was extremely attractive, with her long, thick hair, full, sensual mouth and big brown eyes. She was posh and clever, and as she edged closer to me, I suddenly found her incredibly sexy.

But then, I was drunk, which may explain my unnatural attraction to her, but is hardly an excuse for my actions. In my defence, I took my cue from her. She definitely initiated things, moving in closer to me, her leg touching mine. As Ian's Indian music twanged in the background, I moved my arm around her waist and we sat looking at each other, briefly, till she bought her hand to my cheek. I placed my hand over hers. Her face moved closer to mine ... then the kiss.

It's all so long ago and I was so drunk my memory is blurry. I remember getting more and more passionate. Me rolling on top of her; kissing, groping, touching her breasts, stroking between her legs, through her jeans. Ian left the room, shortly followed by everyone else. Everyone except Ian's friend Simon, whom I was dully aware of, sitting in a chair watching us, chain-smoking cigarette after cigarette. Eventually, Angela and I came apart. We never spoke of that night and Ian has never mentioned it, until now.

'Well,' says Ian, breaking into my reverie, 'I definitely think it counts.'

'Please,' I scoff, 'counts as what? It was fifteen years ago. I was young and experimental and clearly lacking in boundaries. And let's not forget I was very drunk.'

I jump off the basin and look in the mirror. Not bad. The judo classes have got me into pretty good shape. I rub the smudges of mascara off from under my eyes with my fingertip.

'Things are very different now. I'm celebrating my thirty-seventh birthday and I'm a responsible mother of three,' I say, just to convince myself, and down the rest of my glass of wine. I pour another glass from the bottle I brought into the bathroom, and decide that tonight, for once, I'm going to be irresponsible.

'Michele?' It's Peter. Everyone has gone quiet and I can see from the crack underneath the door that the lights have been turned off. Time for the birthday cake – yippee!

☾

The following day.

Dear God, please let the floor dry and please, please, take away this awful pounding in my head.

I'm on my hands and knees, aiming a hairdryer at the wet floorboards in my mom and dad's bedroom. The pale wood is darkened in patches where it's soaked through and I have no idea how, although I'm pretty sure it has something to do with Lucy, Brandy, Patricia and me being in the bath together. I remember the bathtub scene, but don't recall the water overflowing. Actually, there's quite a lot I don't remember. I stand up, abandoning my unsuccessful attempts to dry the floor, and am hit by a wave of dizziness and nausea. I stumble around the apartment surveying the mess while blurry images from the night before flash through my mind.

As the night wears on and guests begin to filter home, I realise I'm in no mood to stop partying. Being more than tipsy by that point, I shriek, 'Who wants to go to a strip club?' at the remaining guests. Shortly after, Peter and I are piled into a minibus with four other couples, heading for the bright lights of Cape Town. My dearest friend Lucy and her husband William (Peter's best friend) are with us, while the others are more recent friends I've made through Chloe's school.

They're all gorgeous in some way, I think, looking at each of the couples. Lucy is tall and leggy, with long red hair, while William has the classic good looks of a well-bred Englishman. Brandy is slim, with a sleek dark bob and full lips, sporting a dangerously low-cut top. Her husband Jack has dark hair and eyes; his handsome face friendly rather than brooding. Anne is curvaceous, with cascading curls, while her husband Ed is boyishly handsome. Patricia and Stan are the sexy couple. She has long, Farrah Fawcett hair and wears a crotch-skimming leather miniskirt, with not a hint of cellulite on her perfectly smooth, very exposed legs.

The vibe in the car is sparkly and electric, full of expectation. I suddenly feel young and carefree, and not just one of the school moms.

'Where to?' asks Jack, the dedicated driver for the evening.

'Moulin Rouge,' I shout back. I've no idea what to expect, but I've seen the sign in town, advertising dancing girls.

Later we pile through the club's entrance, laughing and happy, with the confidence that comes with being part of a group. Dark and smoky, the place has a dingy atmosphere. The patrons are sitting in front of a stage with a ramp protruding from it, catwalk style. Tables are packed, each promisingly fitted with a pole. An empty shower cubicle stands rather incongruously against the wall.

We order tequilas; salty tongue, the buzz as it goes down, sour lemon. We call for another round ... enjoying that fuzzy feeling. On stage, one woman after another is gyrating and dancing seductively. Each body a different shape with varying moves. More tequila. A sinewy, small-breasted dancer enters the shower and turns on the tap, her writhing body glistening wet. Peter and Jack are standing right next to the shower, their noses pressed up against the glass like schoolboys looking longingly into a sweet shop.

Next up is a strikingly beautiful girl, mixed race and exotic. Dressed like an Egyptian, she shimmies, tantalisingly peeling off her clothes, before leaping on to one of the tables and moving athletically around the pole before finally throwing herself upside down, clamping the pole between her thighs. By now, she's completely naked. I notice the details – the perfectly waxed bikini line, the caramel skin, her long, dark hair and perfect round breasts ...

Back in the penthouse I groan as I survey the mess of

empty bottles and dirty glasses which seems to have spread into every room in the apartment. I feel like a teenager who's trashed my parents' home after a wild party.

I don't even remember how long we stayed at the club. I know we stayed long enough to ask the Egyptian for a private dance, performed in a private room, with a pole. We cheer her on and I shriek loudly that it's my birthday so she gives me a bit of a lap dance.

I cringe at the memory. Moving into the lounge, I begin slowly, painstakingly, picking up empty bottles. How much more did we drink when we got back?

All of us, bar Jack, were already roaring drunk by the time we returned to the penthouse. Lucy, Patricia, Brandy and I are on the couch as I shout, 'Come on, guys! It's your turn – off with your clothes!'

The girls take up the chant, 'Strip! Strip! Strip!'

The music is pumping. The men dance mock-seductively and comically around the floor. William jumps up on to the coffee table, grinding his hips; a surprisingly good dancer. Peter, ever the clown once he's had a few drinks, pretends to get his jumper stuck and struggles to pull it over his head. Stan is the first to lose all his clothes. I laugh so much my cheeks hurt.

I shake off the image, massaging my temples. No wonder I feel so awful. I can't believe I drank so much. I head to the kitchen to find a plastic bag for the bottles. Peter is washing dishes.

'I think I'm going to die,' I say to him. 'And if I don't, then I want to die.'

His bloodshot eyes, underscored with black circles, tell me he doesn't feel much better. He just doesn't moan as much. 'You'll be fine tomorrow,' he says practically.

'Let's just get through today.'

I move heavily around the apartment as more scenes from the previous night unfold in my mind.

All the women in the bath together, naked. The men serving us Champagne, happy to do our bidding. Back in the lounge, the girls dressed in our undies and high-heeled shoes, dancing seductively, cheered on by our husbands. I dance with Patricia, holding on to her pert bum as we writhe up against each other. Brandy and Lucy dance with Anne sandwiched between them. And much later, finally falling asleep.

But not for nearly long enough as right now I feel so ill death would be welcome. I feel too horrible to even try to process what happened last night. And piercing my hangover is the image of my hands running up and down my friend's back, the roundness of Patricia's bum, her pelvis up against mine. For a brief moment I imagine my hands fondling Marizette's bum. I desperately and unsuccessfully try to banish the forbidden image from my pounding head. I must focus; I have to go home and look after the children. I decide on the spot that they'll definitely be having an afternoon of DVDs and takeaways.

○

To: sara@naturalnurture.co.uk
Subject: I'm too old to drink any more
Dear Sara
It's over a week since my party and I'm still recovering. A few of us went on to a strip club later that night and then back to the penthouse, where, let's just say things got a bit wild and some of my women friends and I ended

up doing a striptease for the guys. We discussed it over coffee the following Friday. We needed to touch base as we still have to face each other at school every day.

According to Brandy, Jack has been walking around with an erection all week just thinking of us all dirty dancing together. Then we got on to the discussion of the girl-on-girl thing and agreed we played up groping each other to impress the guys. Patricia admitted she finds girls sexy, but says that sexually, she'd never be able to go without a man.

To my shame, the floorboards of the bedroom at the penthouse need to be replaced. My parents are amazingly good-natured about it. My dad says if we ever have a party at the penthouse again, we need to remember the bath isn't designed for more than two people!

This whole wild party came after I confessed to Ian that I have a crush on Marizette. Yes, I'm sure you're laughing, but it is just that – a silly crush. And I have now extinguished it (or am working on extinguishing it). The extent of my crush dawned on me while I nursed my extreme hangover on Sunday: feeling jealous of Hilary, the fluttering in my belly when we do judo, being struck again and again by Marizette's beautiful face, being constantly impressed by how amazing she is, etc.

Naturally, I confided in my mom, who told me sensibly that little crushes are normal and will fade in time. But I must be careful not to give it any power by thinking about it too much. She reckons Peter and I have been so busy raising the kids that we haven't had much time for each other and that I need to nurture a bit of romance in my relationship.

I'm so relieved. Her advice means she's probably

harboured her own secret crushes over the thirty-odd years she's been married to my dad, and they're still happily married. So I've vowed to keep busy and focus on the kids, my husband and training for the nationals. That way I won't have any time to harbour a silly infatuation, and my feelings will just fade. Luckily, Peter is completely oblivious to my inner turmoil. He is so into his veggie garden that I don't think he'd notice if I posed naked in the kitchen when he gets home from work.

Anyway, I'm going to fight in the nationals in Durban and I can't wait. We've decided to make a family holiday of it. So the five of us and my mom (my dad will be in England at the time) are going to Durban together and then on to the Drakensberg. I am so excited – we haven't been on a family holiday for years.

Judo training is very demanding. I'm now going three times a week for two-hour sessions, with weight-training in between. You'd be completely impressed at how strong I've become. My arms are cut and I've even got a six pack! Peter says he prefers me a bit more rounded, but I'm delighted with my new look. I feel strong and confident and motivated. Think of me next weekend at the nationals! All my love, Michele

PS: They found a lump in my mom's breast and she has to go for tests. I'm trying not to worry about it, as these things are often benign.

Chapter four

Cape Town International Airport. I'm pleasantly surprised that we've got more than an hour to wait before our flight. Usually everything is such a rush, but this morning I was super-organised, and now my mom, Peter and I are at a coffee bar with the three children and some time to kill.

'Who wants a story?' I ask the kids.

'Me!' they chorus.

'Mom, can you please tell us how you and Dad met?' Chloe begs.

'Yes, please, please tell us,' the two boys add.

'OK, alright,' I concede. They must've heard this story a hundred times before, but it's still a favourite.

'Your dad and I met at college. I noticed him straight away on our first day there, because he looked like a rock star, with his long hair and ripped jeans. In fact, he was in a punk band called Bad Beach. Anyway, I flirted with him in class a little bit, and tried to give him the usual signals. But he didn't notice.'

'Like what, Mom?' Benjamin asks.

'Um, like trying to make eye contact, but then quickly looking away,' I demonstrate.

The kids laugh.

'Anyway, I realised the subtle approach wasn't working, so one day I approached him in the common room and asked him right out: "Peter, would you like to go out for a drink with me some time?" And he said: "Um, sure, sometime, yeah." He actually had a bead of sweat above his top lip. He was so nervous; like he was being interrogated by the police or something!'

'I was terrified,' Peter defends himself, laughing. 'Your mom was just so beautiful. It really scared me.'

'Well, I wasn't going to give up. The thing is, I wasn't used to being brushed off. I wasn't used to chasing a guy full stop. But your dad intrigued me. So I decided to hold a party at the house I shared with a couple of other students. I invited him, along with the rest of the class. Then I asked him to dance with me, which he did and then I kissed him! And after that we were together and we still are today.'

'Ah,' says Chloe, smiling, 'that's so romantic.'

Of course the story is highly censored. I did chase after Peter, but so did several of the other girls at college, and none of us had any luck. We all concluded he was probably gay. Then, at the party I organised, we all got trashed and Peter was one of the many students who slept over on a mattress on the floor in the passage. I jumped in next to him and took advantage of him, I guess. After that we kind of fell into going out with each other and had an amazing, crazy, fun student time together.

I didn't tell the kids about the time Peter started working and I was still studying and we broke up. Then I dated Noel, whom I was crazy about, and who was later murdered. The hole of grief after his death left me desperately wanting a baby. Basically, Peter offered me his services and by the time Max was born, Peter and I were firmly a couple again. I guess it was a strange start to our relationship, second time around. We only got married when Chloe was one and a half.

All in all, it's been good. The sex could be more regular, but I suppose it's normal with young children around for lovemaking to be thin on the ground. I'd say largely we're a good couple. Hell, everyone else says so. We hardly ever fight; we're sensitive to each other's needs, and we like one another, which counts for a lot. That huge passion thing never lasts anyway, from what I've seen. So I reckon we have a good thing, especially the children, whom we adore, and luckily agree on pretty much everything about their upbringing.

Peter reaches over and takes my hand, interrupting my train of thought. 'I'm just happy that things have turned out the way they did,' he says.

I squeeze his hand, 'Me too.'

◯

'Skip, skip, skip! Now go to the toilet, then spit in the sink. Then we'll weigh you again.'

It's the day of the fight and I'm at the weigh-in. The cloakroom is heaving with girls in judo suits or underwear. Girls from about eighteen years up, all shapes and sizes. A couple of serious-looking officials are standing at the scales. The girl who is skipping and spitting is being instructed by her mother, who's now berating her: 'I told you not to eat last night! I said have something to eat after the weigh-in. Now of course you're over and you'll have to fight in the next weight category.'

Honestly, can a bit of mucous, last-minute exercise and a poo really make that much difference to your weight? It must do, because there are several girls jumping around and rushing off to the toilet once they've stepped off the scales.

It's my turn to be weighed. Luckily I weigh in at sixty-one kilograms, which means I'm easily able to fight under sixty-three. I make my way to the sports hall, which is massive and crowded. My fight is at eleven and it's only nine-thirty now, so it's a bit of a wait. I hope the kids don't get bored. Peter and my mom know where to go to watch me but in the meantime I wait on a designated mat with the other women in my weight group. Being a veteran, I only have three fights. I check out my competition. Two of the women look like mommies – perfectly unthreatening. The third is another story. She has cropped hair and is a black belt! Focused, she's working through some stretches, and looks very intimidating.

Sensei Lorraine comes over to wish me luck. She catches my nervous look in Cropped Hair's direction.

'Oh yes, sorry about her. I forgot to tell you: she's actually the reigning SA champ in her weight group. She fights in the seniors as well. She just does the Vets as a bit of a warm-up.'

'Under sixty-three kilogram veterans to mat thirty-four!' booms the voice over the loud speaker.

My stomach lurches as I head for mat thirty-four.

Two fights later and I feel more confident. Sensei Lorraine was right; they were relatively easy. I managed to beat my first opponent in groundwork, holding her down for the required thirty seconds. My second opponent, being a bit stronger and more skilled than the first, took a little longer to defeat. I eventually won the fight by executing a clean hip throw.

But I can't be complacent. Standing before me is Cropped Hair. Unbeaten SA champ! My heart, which was beating wildly five minutes before, is now still. I feel very Zen and calm and focused. As I step on to the mat, I spot my children, who have pushed themselves to the front of the crowd. Chloe gives me the thumbs up and Max shouts, 'Go for it, Mom!' Peter is holding Benjamin up so he can see. I imagine the tears already welling up in my mom's eyes.

'*Rei*,' the order to bow. Then, '*Hajime*,' and we're off. Cropped Hair and I grab each other by the lapels. Everything happens so fast. She is extremely good, immediately attacking and tripping me. I manage to twist around mid-fall and drop to my knees. Cropped Hair launches herself at me, holding me down. I struggle to break free, writhing and bucking, but she is powerful and I can feel myself tiring fast.

Shit! This is it. A few seconds later and the fight will be over. I become aware of the shouting echoing around me, a solid mass of noise in the stadium and then, rising above it all, I can hear Max screaming full throttle: 'Come on, Mom! Get out! Go, Mom, go! Come on!' There is something in his voice that gives me strength and I draw on my last reserves. I relax for a second, then, knowing I have only one chance, give an almighty push and flip my opponent over, immediately executing a stranglehold as my fist grabs her lapel, my forearm pushed across her neck. Cropped Hair's face is going red, then blue. The veins on her forehead pop out. Her eyes are bulging. But I know I can't relent, or I'll lose the fight. Finally, she taps the floor with her hand, admitting defeat, and the fight is over. I can hear my family roar above the applause. Sensei Lorraine nods in approval from the sidelines as I stand up on wobbly legs. I've won gold. I am the reigning champion in my weight group (in the veterans' team, but still!).

Where to from here? This is but the beginning. At the end of the year is the World Cup in England, and I'm now eligible to fight. There's no reason why I can't go all the way to the Olympics. With my eyesight, I might even qualify for the Paralympics! I could even run motivational workshops: 'How To Overcome Adversity' or: 'Never Give Up On Your Dreams'. If I can do it; a partially sighted, almost middle-aged housewife, then anyone can!

We're in the rented car on the way to the Drakensberg. I've played this scene over and over in my head, wishing it to be true. If I think about it enough, I might be able to wipe out the humiliation of what really happened.

The reality is that Cropped Hair was my first opponent and she floored me in about two seconds. Then, a few minutes into my second fight, my knee gave way. So instead of glory, I ended up hobbling off to the physio room. And the only similarity between my fantasy and the real competition was Max's roaring support, which still brings a lump to my throat.

I look out the window, so my family can't see my eyes well up. I know I'm setting a terrible example to my children; my behaviour goes against everything I've taught them about losing graciously.

'Come on, Mom,' says Max, reaching forward to touch my shoulder. 'You did really well.'

'No I didn't,' I mutter, a tear finally escaping down my cheek. 'I lost both fights and didn't even make it to the third one.'

'Hey, at least you did it,' Peter says consolingly. 'At least you tried.'

'I think you're very brave,' my mom adds.

I look out of the window. Everything is so green, the mountains looming in the distance. It's such a beautiful day. All crisp and clear. I can already feel my mood lifting.

◯

I'm in bed and can't sleep. It's been an amazing day. In fact, the last four days have been idyllic. We've gone swimming, for long walks, and the children put on a play for us. We're so scattered at home as a family, all doing our own thing, that it's wonderful having time together. I should be happy but all I can think about is that my mom has cancer. And not just any cancer. Apparently, it's a really aggressive kind. My dad phoned earlier today to tell us the news. And I can't get his trembling voice out of my head.

'Mom has aggressive breast cancer and she'll have to have an operation as soon as she gets back to Cape Town,' his serious voice came down the line, shocking us.

I thought it was just a benign lump. 'Are they sure,' I ask, stupidly. 'Shit. She'll be OK, won't she?'

'I don't know,' he admits.

The fact that my dad didn't reassure me has sent me into a flat panic. I have an overwhelming urge to jump into bed with my mom, just to be near her; to make sure she's warm and breathing. I'm not ready to lose her; not now, not ever.

'Peter, wake up.'

He's snoring and I shake him gently until he stirs.

'What is it?' he mumbles.

'I can't sleep. This news, it's playing over and over in my head.'

He pulls me into his arms and I start to cry. 'Shhhh,' he soothes. But my sadness is a thick fog surrounding me.

Chapter five

To: sara@naturalnurture.co.uk
Subject: Frightening news
Dear Sara
We've just got back from the Drakensberg. I'm not going to elaborate on the nationals. Was completely humiliating, I was annihilated.

Truly awful thing is that my mom has cancer and it's bad. It's a really aggressive type, so she's going to have an op soon, to have the lump plus some lymph nodes under her arm removed. Then she's going to start chemo. We're all still in shock. What would I do without my mom? It doesn't bear thinking about.

I've told Marizette I want to be there for my mom when she goes through chemo and asked if she'd be willing to mostly take over the kids and the household. She's said she'll help in any way she can, as she's also grown close to my mother. I'm so lucky to have Marizette, she's so committed, and thank God the kids adore her, so I won't have to stress about leaving them with her for longer periods.

Sorry to hear you're not well. If you're exhausted the whole time and the doctors can't pinpoint the problem, it's probably stress. It can't help that Gael keeps trying to stay in your life. Or that you keep it a secret from Graeme. Please just tell her from me to take a flying leap. You don't need her damaging your family. Sorry for sounding harsh, I just care and worry about you. Love, Michi

☾

'OK, over to me. Pass the ball back,' Marizette shouts to Max.

She and the kids are playing rugby on the lawn. Max is running, the ball tucked under his arm. Chloe's chasing him and Benjamin is just behind Marizette. I'm in my bedroom, watching them through the window. I've just finished preparing lunch, but am suddenly transfixed by Marizette, unable to move away. She tackles Max; I'm impressed with her energy. I don't know what rules apply to their game (if there are any) or who is on whose team, but as soon as Marizette has the ball, the kids pile on top of her. The ball is discarded and Max half-heartedly wrestles Marizette, before giving up, and they all lie together in a pile on the grass. They're relaxed in each other's company. Benjamin's head rests on Marizette's shoulder, his arm around her neck.

I turn away from the window, irrationally jealous. Jealous for two reasons: One is that I can no longer run around with the kids the way I used to. The last time I tried, I ran into a low-hanging branch and nearly knocked myself out. The other, deeper, more burning jealousy is that my children can hug Marizette without restraint and they hug her all the time. I'm terrified of hugging her. Terrified that if I do, she'll somehow feel my attraction to her. I know I'm not meant to be, and I've been trying really, really hard not to be, but I am. And it's at times like this, when I secretly watch her from afar, that I realise how drawn to her I am. And I don't want her to find out. Ever.

I shake my head and call, 'Come in and eat! Lunch is ready.'

◯

'How was the salad,' I ask Marizette.

'It was good – thank you,' she smiles.

We're sitting on the balcony together, drinking coffee, part of a shared routine lately. We all have lunch together and then Marizette and I have a coffee on the balcony while the kids play or watch TV.

It's during this time alone with her that I've found out so much about Marizette and her life; her childhood, her first girlfriend. How her family disapproved when she confided in them that she was gay. How she came to Cape Town at nineteen and her parents withdrew all financial support, hoping she'd fold and have to come home where they can keep an eye on her. How she tried to support herself while volunteering at the Orthotics and Prosthetics Hospital, hoping to get a grant to go back to studying. But then realising she'd have to give up her dreams for a while and just save because she was too drained to work from seven to one in the morning every day, seven days a week. She was burning out and losing her zest, so she decided to look for a more stable job than waiting tables; one where she could rest and maybe save until one day she'd have enough go back to studying.

I'm horrified by what she's been through, but so

impressed at how she's managed to look after herself with no support from such a young age. Marizette has told me how close to her dad she used to be and how painful it was when he withdrew from her life. She also has three brothers; one older, who's always done the right thing, and then two younger brothers, whom she misses terribly. The youngest, Etienne, is only fourteen and she wants to get him down to Cape Town to visit her some time.

'So tell me, what is it exactly that Peter does at the MediSpa, while you're here at home with the kids?' Marizette asks.

'Well,' I begin, 'he's not just a regular chiropractor. He trained in England as a McThimony chiropractor, which is a far more gentle and effective approach. He's also got a couple of beauty therapists working for him. One girl claims to give the best Brazilian wax in Cape Town. Although, I wouldn't know, I've always been way too scared to have one.' Shit! Where did that come from? Is discussing Brazilians with my au pair inappropriate?

'Really?' Marizette is interested, her brown eyes sparkly with mischief. 'I should send Hilary there then.'

Oh shit. My stomach clenches with jealousy. I should just end the conversation right here and right now. I'm pretty sure discussing the removal of hair from one's nether regions is not what my mother meant when she advised me to limit my chats with Marizette to the children and safe topics. But I can't help myself, I'm burning with curiosity.

'So,' I begin casually, 'do lesbians go in for that sort of thing? I always thought they'd prefer the whole natural look.'

I've actually just assumed this, my opinions being

based, rather unfairly, on one lesbian. She was at drama college with us and didn't shave her legs or armpits. She also had a full head of manky-looking dreadlocks, so I'm pretty sure she sported a full-on bush.

'No way,' Marizette answers, shaking her head. 'The whole natural look? Hell no! It's so much better when everything's smooth.' She looks right at me, a naughty smile on her lips.

My stomach does a funny squeezy thing that reaches right down to above my pubic bone. Is she teasing me? 'Well,' I say hastily, 'I would never get waxed. I would never put myself through that pain, and I'd be cross if Peter expected me to.'

Marizette looks amused. She leans forward on her elbows and without taking her eyes off me, says, 'Well, if Hilary wants me to do what it is she wants me to do to her, then she knows to keep it smooth.'

A sudden, completely unwelcome image appears in my head of a naked Hilary reclining on a bed, her legs wide open, as Marizette licks her waxed, perfect vagina. Damn! Why do I have to have such a vivid imagination?

'Excuse me,' I say, grabbing our plates. 'I have things to do. Um ... my mom needs ... a cup of tea. Marizette, could you watch the kids for a bit?'

I storm into the kitchen, plonk the plates in the sink and make my way to the sanctuary of my bedroom. I'm thoroughly flustered. Was Marizette making fun of me? The way she was looking at me, I'm sure she was trying to get a rise out of me. Who does she think she is? I'm her boss for God's sake! Although, to be fair, I turned the conversation to Brazilian waxes. So why am I so pissed off? There's another, more urgent, nagging feeling tugging away at my insides. My mom didn't need a cup of tea, but I need release.

I lock the door, take off my shorts and panties and jump onto the bed. Thankfully it doesn't take long and as I come, an image of Marizette kissing Hilary's smooth vagina pops into my head, simultaneously arousing me and filling me with outraged jealousy.

○

The kids are finally asleep and I'm feeling a bit guilty about my illicit thoughts, so I've decided to surprise Peter. Earlier, I tackled my pubic hair with a pair of nail scissors and flushed the bits of hair down the toilet (some of it is still floating around on the surface). I then jumped into a hot bath, and with a fresh razor, shaved off the remaining hair. At the moment it looks terrible.

How I regret my impulsive actions! I feel all naked and vulnerable. I like the smoothness, but I hate how it looks. I stand in front of the mirror, criticising myself: My fanny lips actually poke out. And without hair it's even more obvious. Again I picture Hilary's fanny, which I've already decided is absolutely perfect. Like the ones in porn magazines, all neat and tucked in. Mine would probably only make the readers' wives section.

I'm so horribly self-conscious, even in front of my husband. How on earth would I feel showing off my vagina to another woman? Thank God I'm not gay because I don't think I could bear the shame of a woman seeing me down there. Especially Marizette. What would I do if I dated her and she expected me to wax? I wouldn't do it. I actually wouldn't even let her touch my vagina. I would just always have to be the doer in the relationship ... I pause. What am I thinking? Really! What the hell am I thinking?!

I hear Peter coming and quickly grab a towel from the floor to wrap around my waist.

Chapter six

To: sara@naturalnurture.co.uk
Subject: Trepidation and a rash (!) decision
Dear Sara
How are you? Hope you are doing better than I am. I'm sitting with a horrible rash on my nether regions at the moment. I shaved (everything off!) for Peter, to try to inject some romance into our lives. But it was a disaster. I felt so self-conscious that I couldn't relax and he didn't seem all that impressed by my efforts anyway, saying, 'I don't mind you being hairy.' So clearly I won't be doing that again.

On a more serious note, thank you so much for your support regarding my mom, your kindness means a lot to me and to her. She starts chemo after her operation, which is scheduled for Friday. I'm incredibly frightened. I don't know what to expect.

Marizette is going to look after the kids for the whole day as I want to be there for her as much as possible. She's been amazing and keeps telling me not to worry about any of the domestic stuff. And I trust her completely, which helps.

Dr Rene (Benjamin's best friend's mother) is a GP and a homeopath. She's prescribed my mom a whole load of stuff to help with the nausea and general side effects of the chemo, so I'm praying that'll make her more comfortable. Please think of us. All my love, Michi

○

'All right, love, just sit back and relax. Sister will come and put the needle in and fit you up in a minute.'

It's my mom's first chemo session. She's sitting in the reclining chair with an ice cap on her head. It looks like a biker's helmet and is stored in a freezer to keep the lining, which is filled with water, frozen. My mom's determined not to lose her hair so she's trying everything from frozen hair follicles to some of Dr Rene's alternative medicine.

There are about six other people in the room, all seated on comfy reclining chairs and fitted up to bags filled with stuff that's meant to kill cancer. They're mostly on their own. Only one elderly woman has someone – a man I presume to be her husband – with her. My mom's surrounded by my dad, Ian and me.

The sister arrives, clucking at us. 'My, aren't you lucky,' she says. 'All this attention! Could you move over please, so I can get this needle in?'

We move away while she finds a vein. Pushing the needle into my mom's arm, she fits the tube up to a bag filled with pink liquid. Ian and I glance at each other. I can see his eyes reddening and I feel mine welling up as well. My dad clenches his jaw. Shit, we can't cry now; we have to be strong for Mom.

We resume our positions as the sister leaves. Ian places his hands on Mom's shoulders, his eyes closed, in what I assume is deep meditation. I begin to massage her feet. Dad settles on a stool, reading the paper. Mom looks perfectly relaxed and at ease, leaning back in the comfy chair. I can feel my anxiety easing. Surely with the medication from Rene and all the love and positive energy she's receiving from us, things won't be so bad.

☽

A couple of hours later we are back home. I'm upstairs with Mom in her room. Dad and Ian have gone off to work for a few hours. I assured them I'd sit with Mom and we'd be fine. But I'm not fine. I'm traumatised. Mom has been heaving and vomiting into a bucket for about an hour now. Her face is pale and she can't even pretend to be OK. In between bouts of throwing up, she moans in pain, mumbling that everything hurts. I was totally unprepared for how bad this was going to be.

I kneel beside the bed, holding my mom's hand. Her hair is damp and sticking to her face, which is deathly pale.

'Mom,' I squeeze her hand.

She opens her eyes a fraction and looks at me. 'God, Michele. You look as if you've seen a ghost,' her words are slurred. 'Why don't you go downstairs and get yourself some tea or something?'

I watch as her eyes close. 'Oh, Mommy, don't send me away. I need to be here.' I can't leave her, as much as I can't bear to watch her suffering. Hot tears tumble down my cheeks.

'Oh!' Mom convulses.

I grab the bucket and she leans over, retching, before falling back on to the pillows, drained of energy. I sit quietly beside her. I can't believe she has to go through this again in six weeks' time. I can't bear it.

Chapter seven

To: sara@naturalnurture.co.uk
Subject: Sad and reflective – sorry
Dear Sara
I've decided to start seeing a therapist – can you believe it? The thing is, while I've made some good friends in South Africa, except for Lucy, none of them really knows me that well. So often the girls say how amazing my life is and how much they envy me. And from the outside it does look pretty damn good. Beautiful home; lovely husband and gorgeous children; supportive parents. But I'm depressed. And then I feel guilty about being depressed – especially in this country with all the poverty that surrounds us. I'm not myself at the moment, I'm extremely down about my mom, and frightened.

The chemo has been gruelling. She's having it every six weeks and as soon as she starts recovering from the one round, it's time to start the next one. Amazingly, she hasn't lost her hair. She wears this tortuous-looking ice cap every time she goes for a session.

I also find that with the all the caring I give her, I feel like a bit of nurturing myself, and I start picking holes in my relationship with Peter. I desperately want more affection from him. I want him to spontaneously hug me and hold me more. I've spoken to him, complaining that he doesn't give me enough attention but he insists he does. So I start keeping tabs. Seriously, I actually do this. I mentally calculate how many times he initiates holding my hand, hugging or whatever. And I came up with never; it's always me. He'll reciprocate, but never initiate and that's what I want right now. When I complain, it usually ends up with him saying I'm too needy. And maybe I am, but it's becoming a big issue for me. I wonder if maybe it's just men who don't do the affection thing, but you've often said Graeme is the opposite. In fact, I used to be jealous. You always say he can't leave you alone and you feel crowded by his continual hugging and kissing and touching.

God, sorry for being so self-indulgent. What else can I tell you? Marizette is being a complete superstar with the children. She almost single-handedly runs the household while I spend time with my mom. And at the moment I spend as much time with her as I possibly can. We go for coffee and when she's feeling up to it we take walks on the beach. I know it would be impossible to do this without Marizette. She often stays on later and never complains. She's taken on all Max's home-schooling, the grocery shopping and makes the kids' food.

I try to make time to catch up with her over a short coffee at home every day, usually after she's collected Chloe and given the kids lunch. That's when I find out what's happening in her personal life as she's started confiding in me. Right now, she and her girlfriend have been arguing a lot. Marizette complains that Hilary can be very hard. But you know what young lovers are like; one minute they're breaking up, the next they're completely in love again. I'm so relieved I don't have to go through all that bullshit any more. My relationship is stable, we understand each other, and have mostly sorted out our differences. I definitely don't want to go through any love dramas at this stage in my life. Can you imagine?! Love, Michi

○

'Then we moved to Cape Town, and that's kind of where the problems really began.'

I am about fifteen minutes into what has turned into a monologue. I'm sitting in the lounge of a therapist named Karen and I haven't stopped talking. I haven't even mentioned my mom's cancer or my eyesight yet, which is what I came in for in the first place. But Karen hasn't yet stopped me. I was so nervous about coming to see someone. What would I talk about? What if I spent the entire hour's session just sitting? But there have been no such worries. There's something about Karen that makes me feel incredibly relaxed. She's pretty, in a soft, gentle kind of way, which makes me realise how desperately I need a bit of nurturing.

I continue talking. I've already covered how often we moved around because of my dad's job and how unsettling that was.

'We moved to Cape Town where Steven lived with his family. He became one of my dad's business partners.'

My stomach starts knotting up as I mention his name and that familiar pang of anger and frustration starts coiling its way through my body. I pause. 'Anyway, as I said, it was in Cape Town that the problems really started. I hated my new school. As the new girl, I was targeted and bullied.

'And it was in Cape Town that Steven started abusing me. I didn't tell anyone for years because I was so scared of him. He was so authoritarian. And at school and home it was drummed into us to respect adults and never question what they did. The standard response if we ever questioned why we had to follow a command was: "Because I said so, and I know best because I'm an adult."

'I eventually told my parents and they didn't do anything about it. I know my mom wanted to, but my dad never has and that really hurts. However much my dad does for me, and he does a lot, I can't believe he actually loves me.'

At this point I suddenly start crying. Karen quietly passes over a box of tissues. I take several and wipe my face and blow my nose, but the tears keep coming.

'I'm so sorry,' I apologise.

'It's alright,' Karen soothes. 'It's good to cry.'

'Anyway,' I continue, 'I kind of accepted it, because I always understood how important the business was, and I knew if I made a fuss then it could jeopardise the business and everyone in the family would suffer. But nothing was said or done. My parents stopped me sleeping over at Steven's place, and they told my brother why. I know Ian is very angry with Steven and upset on my behalf. We're very close and have often spoken about Steven. Ian says he remembers feeling extremely helpless.

'I also stopped going to social gatherings to avoid Steven and that made me feel like an outcast. Then my family moved to England to expand the business and Steven stayed here with his family to run the South

African business. But one Christmas he and his wife Dolly were in England and I got into an argument with him in the lounge and swore at him, and he just went off at me. He ended up slapping me, which my mom saw because she was in the room and she lost it completely. All her pent-up anger came surging out and she literally flung him against the wall.'

I smile as I remember Steven's white face and my mom shrieking at him, 'Don't you dare hit my daughter, you bastard! You've done irreparable damage to her, you pervert!'

'The thing is, even after that incident, everything was swept under the carpet again. My dad somehow calmed everyone down and I know he's never said a single word to Steven since about the abuse. I always used to think it was because of the business that he didn't want to rock the boat, but the business is sold now and he still sees Steven and Dolly socially. They live in Cape Town and if I ever bump into them I don't greet them, but my parents still visit them.'

I feel a horrible toxic surge pump through my body as I discuss these long-hidden memories, but I can't stop now.

'It makes me so angry, because I have a really lovely husband who's been truly good to me and making love to him makes me feel so yucky. As much as I try, I can't get rid of that feeling. I can't be open to him and I know he feels that. It's not his fault, but it's getting worse as we get older. It seems that the closer he approaches the age Steven was when he started molesting me, the worse it gets.

'I've had quite a few boyfriends but there was only one I felt completely open with sexually. His name was

Noel and he was beautiful, with light, toffee-coloured skin, and the most gorgeous, slender, well-muscled body.'

I can still picture Noel perfectly. He had sensuous lips that I loved kissing, because somehow his face was always smooth.

'So what happened with Noel then?' Karen enquires, interrupting my thoughts.

I take a deep breath, my shoulders tensing. 'He was murdered. He was a bouncer at a nightclub in Coventry and he was stabbed after hours by some youngster.'

I start crying again and grab a handful of tissues. I'm totally overwhelmed and light-headed. I put my head in my hands, 'I can't talk any more.'

'OK,' says Karen softly. 'We've covered a lot today. There are obviously a lot of issues we need to deal with. I think we should make an appointment for next week.'

☽

To: sara@naturalnurture.co.uk
Subject: Cautiously hopeful
Dear Sara
What a can of worms I've opened by going to counselling! Ian joined in the sessions, followed by my mom, then finally my dad, but he was so reluctant it was like I put a gun to his head.

There's been endless drama. Karen said Steven's family must be confronted, as his daughter is having a baby girl soon. To cut a long story short, Karen phoned her and her husband and warned them to be careful not to allow Steven and Dolly to babysit and told them about the abuse. In the end Karen also got involved, and now, unbelievably, Steven and Dolly are joining us for the next therapy session.

Ian, in his eternal optimism, is quite excited about this turn of events and is hoping for some kind of mass family healing. Although in my opinion, I reckon the two of them are looking to absolve themselves more than anything else. I'm scared and stressed. Love, Michi

Chapter eight

'Good morning everybody,' begins Karen. 'Thank you all for being here. My colleague Belinda is joining me, as this is such a large group.'

I look around at the people gathered and I could just throw up I'm so nervous. I'm sure everyone in the room feels the same way. Steven and Dolly are sitting next to each other, their legs crossed. Steven has folded his hands over a notepad on his lap. He appears calm, his pale blue eyes expressionless, every bit the man about to conduct an important business meeting, trying to maintain control.

Dolly, on the other hand, is a bag of nerves. But she's desperate to hide her anxiety, and trying to maintain the same perceived calm that her husband exudes. She's wearing her signature make-up; tons of base, about an inch of black eye-liner, and lashes caked in thick mascara. Her lips are outlined in a dark maroon outside her lip line, then filled in with pink lipstick. Over the years I've come to realise that Dolly uses this excessive application of make-up as a mask to hide behind, rather than a tool to accentuate her looks.

My mom and dad are sitting on separate chairs, slightly apart from each other. My dad's clenching his jaw and his chin is twitching; a dead giveaway that he's stressed. And no wonder. The pressure is all on him. The outcome of today's meeting is uncertain, but much of it boils down to my dad's response. Will he finally stick up for me, or will he revert to being the peacemaker; feel sorry for Dolly and take the path of least resistance, where everything will go back to where it was, with all the pain and resentment simmering under the surface?

Finally, Ian and I are sitting next to each other on one of the couches. I don't think I could go through this without him. His presence gives me the strength to not flee the room. Perhaps, one way or another, things can finally be resolved. But for that Steven needs to acknowledge his wrongdoings and offer some form of apology.

My mom has warned this is wishful thinking, and that chances are Steven will never admit to what he's done. He'll continue to deny he ever abused me, will accuse me of being imaginative and dramatic. His reputation is everything to him and he desperately wants and needs to be respected.

Karen continues, 'I think we should all say what we're hoping to achieve from this meeting.'

Steven begins, authoritatively, 'I'm here to put these lies behind me once and for all.'

How dare he? I feel my breathing quicken and my shoulders tense, as anger courses through me. This toxic anger never goes anywhere, because it's never been fully expressed. Normally at rest, when it is triggered, my heartbeat quickens, every muscle in my body tenses, and I grind my teeth subconsciously. I urge myself to stay in control. Steven's opening is a blow, but not entirely unexpected.

Dolly pipes up, 'I just want to get to the bottom of everything.'

My mom already has tears in her eyes. 'I want the truth from Steven.'

'I'll take that further,' says Ian. 'I want the truth, and an apology, for the years of damage caused. Then, perhaps we can move forward as an extended family.'

'The thing is,' says Steven, jumping in quickly, 'what Michele accuses me of is entirely untrue.' He turns to me, 'Where is your proof of these supposed events?'

'Well,' I respond, 'I have my diary here, which I wrote from the age of eleven to thirteen. I've marked certain pages that'll indicate the times and dates.'

I can feel my anger rising, my hands are shaking. Get a grip, I command myself, nothing will be achieved if you lose your temper.

Karen turns to my dad. She knows that if nothing else, an admission from him in front of Steven will be of enormous healing value to me. 'Nigel, do you have anything to say?'

My dad pauses, and then starts talking, looking at Steven throughout. 'Steven, I want you to know that I believe my daughter. I believe you abused her and it has caused untold damage and unhappiness to her and our family.'

My heart leaps. I can't believe my dad is finally defending me. Ian squeezes my hand.

Unbelievably, Steven's face is still set and expressionless. 'Really, Nigel?' he replies sarcastically. 'So why did you never mention anything before? Michele has been accusing me of this for years, and you've never said a thing. Do you really believe her?'

The Au Pair

'I was wrong,' my dad admits. 'I was cowardly. I didn't want a huge fuss; I didn't want friendships to end. I didn't want the business to be affected. Whatever the reasons, I was wrong. I believe Michele, and looking at what you did to her, I think it needs to be acknowledged.'

I can't believe this is my father speaking – to Steven, in support of me! I'm so grateful. In that moment, my dad became the hero I always wanted him to be.

'Well,' says Steven, his expression giving nothing away. 'I won't give Michele what she wants. I continue to maintain that I never did anything to her. Our daughter had friends sleep over all the time. Has anyone else come forward to accuse me? No, because I've never done any such thing.'

Silence hangs in the air.

'It seems we've reached a deadlock,' says Karen. 'So, where do we go from here?'

'Yes, where?' asks my dad. 'Do we ignore each other in the street? Do we attend each other's funerals?'

My mom speaks up, 'From my side, I want nothing to do with your family until you can be honest, Steven.'

'I go along with that,' agrees Ian.

'Then it looks like we've reached a conclusion,' Steven says, every bit the businessman wrapping up a meeting. 'We agree to disagree, and no socialising between the two families.'

I can see my mom is furious. She stands up, 'Then we have nothing more to say to each other.' She beckons to us. Ian and I stand, but my dad is still seated. I have every intention of following my mom out of the room, but something in me snaps. Everything will be as it was before. Steven will carry on as normal, living the life of a respectable man and doting grandfather, while secretly …

It's less than a second before I flip. I turn to Steven, still seated, self-satisfied, and scream, 'You know you did it! You know!' I throw my diary at him. It hits him smack in the chest. I grab a large candle from the table and launch that at him as well, 'You fucking paedophile!'

Dolly moves in front of him to shield him from any further missiles, and even in my fury I find this gesture and her selfless love moving. I throw myself at him, planning to haul her out of the way and punch him. My fury has taken over to such an extent that I can't stop myself. I have a surge of superhuman strength. I could lift him above my head and toss him over the balcony.

Suddenly I'm stopped dead in my tracks. Ian has grabbed me by the arms and is holding me back. He can restrain me, but he can't stop me shouting, which I do, full throttle, 'You can lie to everyone else, but you can't lie to me, and you can't lie to yourself.'

I struggle to break free from Ian's grip, as Steven leaps up and makes a dash for the stairs, seeking refuge underneath them. His cool exterior has disappeared. His face is white, and he is shaking. I'm thrilled to see him like this. Thrilled, because for years I've been terrified of him and he held so much power over me. But not any more.

'Stuff not socialising! If I see you in the streets, I'll fucking kill you, you fucking paedophile!'

All the anger suppressed over so many years is unleashed, and I become the anger. Ian puts both his arms around me, completely enveloping me in his embrace. I'm so glad he's the one holding me back; if it was my dad, I'd have probably turned on him as well.

Steven has retreated further under the stairs to escape my mother, who has gone after him, shaking her fist threateningly, 'You did it. You did it.'

Dad has gone to her and is pulling her back. Then just as suddenly the drama is over. The shouting has stopped.

Karen comes up to me and puts her hand on my shoulder. 'You're going to be OK, Michele.'

'Oh Karen, I'm so sorry,' I apologise, as the extent of my actions dawns on me. 'Your candle …'

I want to leave. Right now I don't want to have to look at Steven and Dolly. I want to get far away and gather myself. I leave with Ian and my mom. Dad says he wants a word with Steven and Dolly, and will meet us in ten minutes.

It's a beautiful evening and the sun is setting as we drive past the beach. The long sands look so inviting. I need to get rid of some of the energy; I need to run. Seconds later, my mom pulls over and Ian and I run up and down the beach, whooping loudly at the tops of our voices, stopping every now and then to grab each other's hands and swing around in circles, as we did so often as children.

I should probably be in deep shock at what has just occurred. Maybe later I will be, but right now I feel an unbelievable and joyous sense of relief. I look up at the sky over the sea, a profusion of bright orange, pink and purple. Ian and I run back to our mother and wrap her up in a group hug. We sway quietly together for a moment, before heading off to meet my dad.

Chapter nine

To: sara@naturalnurture.co.uk
Subject: A turning point?

Dear Sara

Oh my God! I haven't told you about The Meeting with Steven and Dolly. As expected it was really emotional and ended with me having a complete meltdown and screaming and yelling at Steven, calling him a paedophile. Amazingly the whole experience was exhilarating. I spent so many years of my childhood terrified of that man and then even more of my adult years trying not to make too much fuss for my father's sake, that to finally let rip was truly empowering.

Talking of my dad, he finally confronted Steven and told him he believes me, which in itself has probably been the most healing aspect of all. Now I just have to come to terms with the fact that I will always feel weird when I have sex, because it seems no amount of therapy can make me feel alright in my own body, especially when my body is being entered by a man.

Anyway, I need to focus on the good, positive things in my life. I'm truly lucky to have a husband who is good to me and three wonderful children. Talking of which, we've just celebrated Max's birthday with a joint

Halloween party for him and Ian. As usual, it was a huge success, with a large group of friends. It was quite an eclectic mix: Ian's spiritual, didgeridoo-playing souls, old family friends and Peter and my couple friends, lots of kids, a big bonfire, scary decorations, some guests in costume. Marizette and Hilary turned up dressed for the occasion, and Maz still managed to look gorgeous, even with a fake piece of glass coming out of a very realistic-looking wound on her forehead. Can't remember what Hilary was wearing.

This weekend The Group is going to Treetops (a holiday place set on a farm). There are five wooden chalets on stilts among the trees. I'm so looking forward to it. We all get on so well and luckily our children do too. As always, wish you could join us. Know my friends would love you. Love, Michi

○

It's a beautiful night, complete with a clear sky dotted with stars and a full moon. Absolutely perfect. We're all sitting around a bonfire down at the river. The children are snuggled up in blankets, and either leaning against each other, or a parent. Benjamin is curled up in Peter's lap, with Max and Chloe snuggled on either side of him. The flickering firelight is casting a warm, dancing glow on everyone, and I think, not for the first time, how lucky I am to have such a great group of friends. It's been a lovely day so far with the younger kids running around collecting things, and the older ones spending most of the time in the river.

We've finished supper and with everyone fed and

settled, I'm coming to the end of a story. I'm always the official storyteller at these gatherings and am happy to comply.

'So,' I conclude, 'the fifty-two-tailed beast approached the village. He had the most beautiful eyes, the colour of sunshine. Everyone in the village who saw him fell to their knees, even the warrior who had wanted to slay him. And from that day forward, the beast was left in peace, as the chief forbade anyone to hunt him.' I pause to indicate the story is over.

'Please tell us another one,' the children beg.

'No,' I smile. 'No more stories, but if you go to bed now, I promise I'll tell you another one tomorrow.'

'I know,' says Lucy, 'why don't the dads put the kids to bed for a change, and we'll stay here and chat for a bit.'

The men reluctantly agree, leaving us behind at the fire.

'OK, girls,' I stretch and wink, 'who wants an adult story?'

'Yes, definitely,' they chorus.

'Once upon a time, there was a beautiful young woman. An Olympic sports star. She was the fastest female runner in the whole world. She had long, muscular legs, broad shoulders, and the most sparkly and mischievous eyes. Her name was Inka and she was everyone's darling. But Inka was harbouring a secret …'

'… So Inka and Tessa lay in each other's arms, next to the river. The moonlight cast a golden glow on their naked bodies. And finally Inka smiled, still tingling with delight,' I pause. 'The end.'

'Wow,' sighs Patricia, 'that was so sexy! Stan's definitely going to score tonight.'

'Jack too,' agrees Brandy. 'I'm so damn horny now. Michele, you should write erotica.'

Lucy's looking at me, her eyebrows raised. 'Am I the only one here who's noticed that Inka is an exact replica of Marizette?' she drawls.

Brandy puts her hand to her mouth, 'Oh my God! It's true – Inka is Marizette.'

'No she's not,' I protest. 'Inka's a star athlete.'

They all start laughing.

'Oh yes,' scoffs Lucy, 'that's about the only thing that's different.'

Brandy takes up the joke, saying breathily, 'And then Inka placed her strong arms around the woman's waist, kissing her ever so gently on her cheeks, then her neck …'

They all fall about laughing.

'Anyway, it's pretty obvious you like Marizette,' says Patricia.

'No!' I gasp, horrified. 'How?'

'Well, for a start, whenever we come to visit, it's like, "Ooh, Marizette's so great. She's so good with the kids. Isn't she fantastic? Don't you think she's amazing?"'

'It's true,' Anne agrees. 'And whenever you talk about her you sort of swoon and flutter your eyelashes.'

'I do not!'

'You do,' insists Lucy. 'In fact, I'm surprised Peter hasn't noticed.'

'Oh, come on,' says Patricia, 'Where's the harm? There are many men who enjoy having a pretty woman working for them.'

'As long as that's as far as it goes,' Lucy looks at me pointedly.

'Oh please,' I say, 'there's nothing to it. Yes, I do

have the tiniest bit of a crush on her, but it's nothing serious and nothing to worry about. Now let's talk about something else.'

Lucy doesn't look at all convinced and is still giving me a rather disapproving look. To be honest, I'm not sure I managed to convince myself either.

Chapter ten

To: sara@naturalnurture.co.uk
Subject: Good, old-fashioned holidays

Dear Sara

Sorry I haven't written for so long. It's been a really busy time, what with the holidays and New Year. Treetops was great, a good old-fashioned family holiday. Then of course there was Christmas, which I hosted. Still can't get used to celebrating in the sunshine. We had lunch outdoors and the kids spent most of the time in the pool. Then I threw a New Year's Eve party, with loads of friends and friends of friends. Again, lots of kids. So all in all, the season was very sociable, not to mention exhausting.

And yet, I've decided to go out clubbing this weekend! I'm really looking forward to it. Brandy's organised for The Group to go to dinner and then on to a nightclub. I asked Marizette to babysit, as Hilary is away and I assumed she wouldn't be going out. But she said no! She was planning on meeting Nico (my gay cousin) at Lush that night. I thought Lush was an all-girl party place, but Maz says guys can go as special guests. I begged until she agreed to babysit, as long as we're back by twelve so she can go out. Can't believe she's happy to start clubbing at midnight – when will she finish?! I'm so looking forward to a night out with Peter, carefree and fun. Much love, Michi

◯

'How do I look?' I ask Peter.

'Good,' he says, barely glancing at me.

My heart drops. I am so disappointed. Well, what did I expect? I suppose a 'Wow, you look beautiful!' or 'Very sexy!' would be nice. It would also be nice if he had a proper look at me; a good, long, appreciative up-and-down look. It's ages since I've been out and I want to look my best. The kids are fed and I'm itching to get going. I really need to go dancing and let my hair down a bit.

Twenty minutes later, I'm in the car.

'I meant it when I said you looked good, by the way,' Marizette casts an appreciative glance in my direction. 'Very good, actually.'

We are seated side by side in her car. Peter has decided at the last minute he doesn't want to go out after all. I could feel his enthusiasm waning all afternoon. By the time Maz and I were dressed and ready to go, he'd already had two beers and was settled on the stoep with his guitar.

'You can't get much better than this,' he said, looking at the mountain silhouetted against the inky sky. 'I would much rather spend the evening right here.'

Disappointment weighed down on me. Damn, I'd really wanted to go out! But Marizette was definitely not disappointed.

'Well, if you're not going out, then you won't need me to babysit, so I'll head off earlier then.'

I brightened up. 'Can I go with you?' I asked impulsively. 'Peter? Would you mind looking after the kids?'

I wasn't sure how either of them would respond. I expected Marizette to be less than thrilled to have her boss tag along and that Peter wouldn't be that keen on the idea of taking care of the children by himself. So I was surprised when they both agreed. Marizette even seemed pleased, although that could be my imagination.

Half an hour later we're heading into the city centre. The sea ebbs and flows on our left and the mountain towers on our right. The road is dark and my excitement builds as we approach the lights of the CBD. I'm so excited but nervous at the same time. I don't want Marizette to feel tied down by me, so I decide to stick with Nico.

Nico is much younger than me and gay. We get on really well and it's a treat to be out with him again. I can't help smiling. I'm going clubbing. And not just any club; a gay club! I wonder if anyone will chat me up; a bit of harmless flirting could be fun. Then my insecurities kick in. Will anyone even find me attractive? I'll be so much older than anyone there. What if I'm overdressed? Underdressed? Is my make-up OK? Maz says I look good, but did she just say it to be polite? My insecurities and confidence wrestle each other all the way to the club.

Thankfully Nico meets us at the entrance otherwise I think I would've lost my nerve. He looks gorgeous as usual; tall, dark and immaculately dressed. There are several women standing at the door, one issuing stamps to everyone who comes in.

Marizette hugs her and turns to me, 'Michele, this is

Myrna,' she says. 'Myrna organises all the Lush parties. Myrna, this is my boss.'

Myrna is striking, with short, red hair. She smiles at me, 'Hello, Michele, welcome to Lush. I hope you have a lovely time tonight.'

I grab Nico's hand as we enter the already heaving club, partly for courage and partly because with my eyes, the dark room and strobe lights are even more disorientating. I do notice though that Lush is filled with women. Lots and lots and lots of them. I don't think I've been in a confined space with so many women since my days at an all-girls' school. Back then though, it was drab uniforms, and aging, sour-faced teachers. Now I can't stop gawping. I just stand there, hanging on to Nico's arm, scanning the room. There are women standing at the bar ordering drinks, women chatting and laughing in groups, women moving rhythmically on the dance floor. There are women of all shapes and sizes, ages and styles.

Admittedly there is a prevalent 'look'; a uniform of sorts, I suppose, especially among the younger girls. Many sport intricate tattoos and facial piercings. The more boyish girls have short, spiky haircuts and wear tight T-shirts, with thick buckled belts and trousers hanging halfway down their bums, exposing boxer-style underwear. Possibly stereotyped, but it all looks incredibly sexy to me. Interestingly, there are also many girls who don't fit the stereotype at all – pretty, feminine girls with long hair wearing dresses or sparkly tops. There are so many women! And Marizette seems to know all of them; she's been greeted and hugged by seemingly hundreds of women since we arrived.

Nico pulls me to the bar and orders us each a drink,

which I desperately need to calm my nerves. I love everything about Lush! The vibe is electric; the music is pumping, calling me to the dance floor.

'Come on, Nico,' I shout above the music. 'Let's dance!'

Nico is such fun to dance with, high camp, pulling lots of fancy moves. We bump and grind, completely over the top, laughing at each other. We dance to about three songs before joining Marizette at the bar. She insists on buying me a tequila which I down immediately. Nico has bought me another cider and we clink bottles and take a swig.

He leans over and yells into my ear so I can hear him above the bass. 'So, Cuz, how are you enjoying yourself?'

'I'm great!' I enthuse, then cover my mouth to half-whisper, half-yell in his ear, 'Isn't Marizette looking gorgeous? She's so damn sexy!'

'Whoa, Cuzzie,' he exclaims, laughing. 'Did I hear you right? You fancy your au pair?'

Before I have a chance to reply, a girl advances on us, calling out, 'Nico! Oh my God, I don't believe it! What are you doing here?'

Nico turns around and throws himself at her. 'Lynette! What are you doing here? I didn't know you were …'

They do a quick information exchange; who's doing what to whom, etc. She lives in Joburg, is working as a dentist, and has a girlfriend. I lose interest and turn to Marizette. My heart lurches; she's staring at Lynette, watching her intently, with shiny, hungry eyes.

'Listen, I'm here with friends. I'll join you in a bit,' Lynette apologises, and retreats into the crowd, Marizette's eyes following her.

'Wow! She is fucking gorgeous!' Marizette enthuses.

'Nico, how do you know her?'

I churn with jealousy. 'She's completely ordinary,' I state sourly.

'Nah, Marizette's right, there's something about her,' Nico agrees.

Irrationally, I feel betrayed by Nico.

'Yup,' continues Marizette, 'and later on, I'm going to get her phone number.'

I'm filled with moral indignation; Marizette is with Hilary, even if they are having a bad time at the moment. I need to get rid of some energy. 'Come on, Nico,' I say, grabbing him. 'Let's dance.' Marizette follows and several dances and drinks later, much to Marizette's delight, Lynette joins us.

Then something happens. It's so subtle that I'm probably the only person who has noticed. It's a look I get from Lynette, and in that moment I know without a fraction of doubt that she's interested in me. Something takes over. I start dancing in an exaggerated, sexy manner, with lots of hip thrusts and suggestive moves. All the while I look straight into Lynette's eyes. She takes the bait, grabbing my belt and pulling me towards her.

Why am I doing this? Because I want to make sure Marizette doesn't stand a chance with her. Because I know I won't be able to bear it if Maz and Lynette get off with each other. I'm desperate to keep them apart. By the time the song is over I'm pretty sure I've diverted any potential interest Lynette might have had for Marizette.

'I'm going to sit down for a bit,' I gasp, making my way to a vacant seat.

'I'll get some drinks,' Marizette says, heading for the bar.

The Au Pair

Exhilarated, I lower myself down, and lean against the wall. Lynette is upon me before I'm even aware she's followed me. She leans over me, one knee resting on my leg, and takes my face in her hands. What follows is the most passionate kiss I've ever had in my entire life. It takes my breath away. Her lips graze my face and neck, before settling on my mouth, where she devours me with a deep, longing kiss. Instinctively, I respond in kind, pulling her head towards me, completely taken up in the moment. Then as quickly as it starts, it's over. Lynette tears herself away, looking at me, holding my hand as she backs away.

She shakes her head as though it's an effort to leave me, 'My friends are here,' she says regretfully. 'I can't; I'm sorry. I have a girlfriend in Joburg.' Then she's gone.

Nico arrives with the drinks. 'Hey Cuz, you look dazed. Lynette asked me to say bye to my super-hot cousin.' He laughs, 'Michi, you are a naughty, naughty girl!'

'Oh my God! Did you see?'

'Everything. So did Marizette.'

'Shit ...'

My cellphone rings; a very irate Peter. 'Michele, when are you coming home? Do you know what time it is?'

'It's not that late, is it?' I stammer.

'It's two-thirty in the morning. I don't want the dogs waking up the kids when you come in. Can you hurry up and come home please?'

I look at the time; he's right, it's nearly two-thirty. I find Marizette outside and tell her we need to leave. On the way home, she's very upbeat about my experience with Lynette, 'Way to go, Michele!'

I'm disappointed, but I don't know what I hoping for

– a little jealousy perhaps? I desperately want Marizette to be attracted to me. And yet it would be so dangerous if she was. At least if the feelings are one-sided and unrequited, everything's safe and manageable. Besides, now I have a distraction: Lynette. And as a relationship that can never be, it's a safe and welcome diversion. For now, it can hopefully direct my increasingly intense feelings away from Marizette.

○

Three days later, Peter still isn't speaking to me unless he has to. He's angry and withdrawn, making the atmosphere at home heavy and electric with tension. I've never seen him like this and I'm not quite sure what it is that's made him so angry. He can't know about Lynette. I've already decided to tell him, but haven't found the right time.

One night after supper, when the children are in bed, he says he wants to speak to me. We sit opposite each other in the kitchen.

'I finally know what's bothering me so much,' he says. 'I've thought about it a lot, and I've worked it out. It's Marizette. I think you have strong feelings for her. To the point where it's making me paranoid.' Peter's eyes are ringed with dark circles from lack of sleep. 'I'm so scared of losing you, Michele. I love you so much.'

'Oh God, Peter,' I take his hand in mine, half-smiling. 'You never have to worry about that. I'll never leave you; you're my husband. I'm sorry, but you're stuck with me forever.' I take a deep breath and continue, 'Look, something did happen at the club. There was a friend of Nico's called Lynette, who kissed me. I wanted to tell you, I promise. I don't want to keep secrets from you. I was just too scared.'

Instead of angry, Peter seems relieved. 'So that's why you've been acting so strangely?'

'Have I been?' If I think about it, I probably have. The whole Lynette incident has shaken me up. Why did that kiss feel so good? Why can't I feel like that when I kiss my husband? What's the matter with me?

'Look,' Peter continues, 'I don't know what I'd do if we split up. Besides the fact that I would hate to be without you, I've just started on the vegetable garden and I don't want to carry on if I'm going to have to move out.'

'That's not going to happen,' I reassure him, 'ever. This is your home and I'm your wife. Nothing's going to change that.'

I squeeze Peter's hand, glad I finally told him about Lynette. I mean it when I say I don't want to leave him. I must get a grip; stop all this silliness and get back on track.

Chapter eleven

To: sara@naturalnurture.co.uk
Subject: I kissed a girl and I liked it ...
Dear Sara
OK, need to tell you something. A while back I kissed a girl at a nightclub. It was just a kiss, but it shook me up for ages; I couldn't stop thinking about it and I didn't feel myself any more. It was all a bit weird. But things are fine now. I've been focusing a lot on the kids and Peter, and we're spending a lot of time together as a family.

Joy of joys, Peter and I are off to Italy soon for his brother Jason's wedding. In a way it'll be like a honeymoon for us, as with two children on the scene when we eventually got married, you know we didn't have the time or the money to go away. I'm so looking forward to rekindling a bit of romance with my husband.

My counsellor's opinion of my girl-on-girl kiss is that I'm having a mid-life crisis. She's suggested I try to be more romantic with Peter; find a bit of private time together, away from the kids. And Italy will be just that, as we're leaving the kids with my mom for two whole weeks! She's finished with her chemo now and is having a break before starting the radiation treatment. After that she'll be on a drug called Tamoxifan for about five years.

Marizette and Hilary have broken up, so Marizette is staying at our place to help out, which will take a lot of the pressure off my mom. Luckily they get on really well. In fact, my mom went as far as saying she loves Marizette. Either way, I have no worries about the kids' well-being, as they're in the best of hands. Love you lots, Michi

◯

Rome.

'Peter, please,' I beg. 'I can't walk another step. My feet are killing me and I'm exhausted.'

Peter grabs my hand. 'Come on,' he urges, 'not far to go. We're nearly at the hotel.'

I stop in my tracks, 'I'm not walking another step. I can't.'

He laughs, 'We can't stop here and I'm not going to be able to carry you. I know, there's a coffee shop literally three steps away. I think a double espresso and ice cream are in order.'

Ten minutes later I'm walking cheerfully back to our hotel, hand in hand with my husband. Rome is everything I could've wished for and more. We've only three days left and want to see as much as possible; leaving the hotel straight after breakfast and returning well after supper time, exhausted but happy. The wonderful thing about Rome is the attractions are all so near to each other. We've used the hop-on-hop-off bus thing, to cram in as much as possible, stopping only to eat or grab an espresso. My highlight so far is the Palatine Hill. Peter and I wandered around there for hours before finally settling, lying side by side on our backs among the ruins.

I'm not sure why, but a wonderful sense of peace washes through me when ever I'm near ancient structures. And here at the Palatine Hill are layers of history, dating all the way back to the ancient Egyptians.

'Do you feel it?' Peter asked after several minutes.

'Feel what?'

'The ghosts or energy or whatever you want to call it.'

What I did feel was an incredible feeling of contentment. I reach for Peter's hand, smiling. I want to keep this time in Rome in my heart forever and ever.

Chapter twelve

To: sara@naturalnurture.co.uk
Subject: Back on track again
Dear Sara
Just arrived back from Italy after having the most wonderful time. Rome was awesome and Ravello was postcard perfect. It was wonderful seeing Peter's brother get married and I enjoyed catching up with his sisters and their families, especially my little nieces and nephews. I'm truly lucky to have such a good relationship with my in-laws. I miss them terribly and wish we saw one another more often.

Although Ravello is one of the most romantic places in the world, Peter and I only made love once, not the ten times a day we predicted. But I enjoyed myself so much that the lack of sex didn't bother me one bit, and Peter didn't complain either. It was a magical time. Being in Italy confirmed for me that he and I are right for each other. We enjoy each other's company so much and are true friends; we didn't fight once. The holiday has made me reflect on how much I would lose if we broke up. I must be careful not to jeopardise what we have.

It's wonderful to be with the children again and tomorrow night my parents are taking us all out for supper at a pizza restaurant to treat us before they leave for the UK.

Hope all is going well on your side of the world. Love, Michi

☾

Friday night, a busy pizza restaurant in town. It turns out quite a big group of us is gathered around the table. As well as my mom and dad, Ian, and the five of us, my parents have invited Marizette and Tammy, a family friend. Right now, my holiday resolve to give up my feelings for Marizette is overcome by the most horrible jealousy. Ian is sitting between Tammy and Maz, and there's a major three-way flirtation going on, which I can witness clearly from my seat directly opposite them. Ian is in his element, sitting between two beautiful women, and they, in turn, are playing their parts; all teasing, with suggestive body language and conversation, fuelling Ian's well-known lesbian fantasies.

Opposite, I'm between Max and Chloe, straining to hear their conversation while simultaneously answering the kids' questions.

Max tugs on my arm, 'Mom, can I have a large pizza?'

'Yes,' I reply, distracted.

Tammy turns to Marizette, smiling. 'So, what's sex between lesbians like then?'

Max leans over again, 'Can I have a Coke?'

Marizette smiles suggestively, 'Well, we're both single. Maybe I can show you later …'

Max raises his voice, 'Mom? Can I have a Coke? Please,' he remembers to add.

'Uh, yes ... Coke ... sure.'

Tammy laughs raucously and my head snaps up. I can see from Ian's satisfied smirk exactly what he has in mind. I'm furious. My brother and my friend are flirting madly with Marizette, in front of me. They know how I feel!

Max pushes his luck, 'And an ice cream after?'

The evening wraps up quite successfully. I managed to not knock over any drinks and the kids are thrilled they got me to agree to a fizzy drink and a pudding. We put on our jackets, grab our bags and check under the table for anything left behind. As I herd the kids to the door, I see Ian and the two girls clustered together, scheming.

'Why not,' Tammy laughs. 'It could be fun. Ian, are you joining us?'

'At a lesbian night? Definitely.' My brother is practically salivating.

'Ian,' I call over to him, 'could I have a quick word with you outside?'

Peter sighs. He's carrying a sleepy Benjamin. 'Must you? We need to get the kids home.'

'I'll be quick,' I promise. 'Get the kids to the car in the meantime.'

'What's up?' Ian asks. 'You sound intense.'

'Ian,' I begin earnestly but sternly. 'Don't you dare get off with Marizette. I know exactly what you're planning tonight.'

He looks crestfallen. 'Michele, this could be my chance. These are two willing and very beautiful women!'

I look him in the eyes. 'Please. Don't do it. If you love me, don't do it.'

'Hey,' Ian jokes, 'remember Angela? It's payback time!'

But I don't laugh. 'If you do anything with Marizette, I'll never forgive you.'

Ian whistles quietly. 'Wow, Mich. That's pretty serious. Damn you! This was my one and only opportunity …' he sighs, shaking his head in mock sorrow.

'Thanks,' I say, kissing him on the cheek. 'Oh, and one more thing. You must make sure nothing happens between Tammy and Maz either.'

'How am I meant to do that?'

I think for a second. 'Get off with Tammy,' I command. 'Make a play for her and keep her away from Marizette.' My plan is foolproof and I know Tammy will go for it.

'I'll do my best,' Ian promises, 'but only because you asked so nicely.'

'Do whatever it takes.'

Tammy and Marizette emerge from the restaurant, and join us on the pavement, each taking Ian by the arm.

'Bye guys,' I say sweetly, 'have a great time.'

Ian looks back and winks at me mischievously as they walk away. I point two fingers at my eyes and then at him. 'I'm watching you,' I mouth, glaring.

He laughs and as they head off down the street and I join Peter and the children in the car, a knot of anxiety heavy in my stomach.

○

Ian has lost his resolve. Despite every intention of being loyal to me he's now in the Jacuzzi at the penthouse; the very bathroom I confided to him in almost two years ago. Sitting on the edge of the tub, he's watching Tammy and Marizette soaping down one another. Until this moment, he's stuck to his promise. But watching their glistening bodies writhing up and down, Maz's hand sliding sensually over Tammy's buttocks, he thinks, 'Fuck it!', throws caution to the wind and …

I force myself to stop thinking at this point. I have no idea what they're up to, but I know if Ian had his way, they'd be up to no good. I have never felt jealousy so powerful. It's hot and raging and I don't know what to do with myself. The kids are asleep and Peter is lying peacefully beside me. I've tried phoning Ian but his cellphone is off, and with no way of communicating with him, my imagination runs wild.

On our way home, Peter asked me what was wrong, as I was uncharacteristically snappy. I pleaded ignorance and claimed I was just tired. I'm far too restless to sleep. I slip out of bed and pad into the kitchen. The kitchen clock shows ten o'clock, which is probably too late to phone Lucy. She's probably in bed by now, with the twins being so little and having to be up early for work in the morning. I decide to phone anyway. I desperately need to speak to someone. We've been friends since we were teenagers. I know Lucy loves me and will always have my best interests at heart.

'Hello?' her voice is foggy with sleep.
'Did I wake you?'
'Mich? No, I was just falling asleep. Are you OK?'
'Yes. Well, no,' I admit.
'What's the matter?' she says, concerned.
'Ian's gone out with Maz and Tammy, and you know what he's like. He says he won't, but he'll probably land up sleeping with Maz and I won't be able to stand it …' I pause for breath. 'And I can't get hold of him to find out

what's going on and it's driving me crazy.' Silence. 'Lucy? Are you still there?'

'Now, listen to me, Michele,' she begins. 'Firstly, if Ian does sleep with Maz he's a major arsehole, because I'm pretty sure he knows you feel something for her. But it's how much you feel that's scaring me. She's not your girlfriend, Mich, and your jealousy is inappropriate. I knew you had a little crush, but this is something else. Just think carefully. Do you want to jeopardise your marriage with Peter? We're talking a long relationship here, with the father of your three children. Look, having Marizette around all the time, with the feelings you have for her, is risking everything you and Peter have built together. Is that what you want?'

'No,' I reply meekly. Lucy used to be a teacher and has a way of delivering a lecture that puts you firmly in your place.

'Well then, this is what you need to do. You must get rid of her. She can't carry on working for you any more. And you must do it soon; give her three months' wages and find someone else to do your driving in the meantime.'

'What do I tell the children?' I protest. 'They really love Maz.'

'You'll think of something.'

I climb into bed with a heavy heart. I know Lucy's right and that I must get rid of Marizette. I just need to think up a good reason to tell her why I'm doing it.

I feel so sad. The kids adore her; they'll be disappointed. And I'll miss her so much. I know Maz was never going to stay forever. And if she does stay on it could be dangerous. Even if she feels nothing for me, my feelings for her are driving me crazy. I'll have to speak to her; she'll have to leave.

Chapter thirteen

To: sara@naturalnurture.co.uk
Subject: It's all for the best
Dear Sara
I've decided to get rid of Marizette (my feelings were getting dangerously out of control) and guess what? She beat me to it! Says she's moving back to Pretoria as she wants to be near her family and start studying again. I was so relieved I wouldn't have to go through the awkwardness of sacking her, so I told her it was fantastic and I was delighted for her. I think I may have been a little too enthusiastic as she looked slightly crestfallen.

The thing is, now that the relief is over, I'm gutted. Pretoria is so far away! Once she's moved, chances are I might never see her again. I know that would solve my problem, but I'm surprisingly sad. I thought even when Maz stopped working for us she'd still be a part of our lives somehow. When I confided in Lucy, she said it was all the more reason for Maz to get as far away as possible. By now, all my close friends know how I feel. Well, they know I have a crush on Maz; I'm not sure they know how strongly I feel.

I certainly don't think Marizette knows, although I very nearly told her this morning. We were sitting at the kitchen table and she said: 'You seem so happy about me leaving. I was worried about you being disappointed. But you're just pleased, right?' Maybe she was just fishing for compliments, wanting me to say, 'Oh, Marizette, I've no idea how we're going to cope without you!' Actually, I don't know and will have to cross that bridge when I come to it. I looked into her eyes, all serious, and said: 'Do you really want to know the answer to that?' I think my intensity frightened her, because she looked at me for a few seconds, then said: 'No. No, I don't.' I felt like a right twit. I was so close to telling her. It's probably just as well she's leaving. I need to get over this feeling of loss.

So now I'm on safe ground. I can't afford to jeopardise my marriage – I know you'll understand that. It's just not worth it. For what? A silly infatuation about a hot young woman who I'm sure doesn't share the same feelings for me, and even if she did, we come from such different situations that we'd literally have nothing to offer each other.

Anyway, Maz has invited us to the all-girl party at Lush this weekend; it's going to be a karaoke night and sounds like a heap of fun. I will never sing, but I'd love to watch a bunch of lesbians do their thing. Ian's going, as Maz managed to persuade him to sponsor some prizes. Peter's sponsored some too (vouchers for facials and manicures, etc.), but as much as I've tried to persuade him to join us he's said there's no way he'll be going. I've made Ian promise to not allow me to sing, no matter how drunk I get.

It sounds like you and Graeme are definitely back on track. Although I think you should try to inject a bit more passion into your love life. Graeme's way too highly sexed to endure this drought of yours without getting frustrated …! Big hugs to your whole family. Love, Michi

☾

I'm inexplicably excited about going out. Peter has told me that if I'm going to be out later than midnight then I'm to stay over at Ian's place. He doesn't want me coming in at ungodly hours and setting off the dogs, who'll then wake the kids. So no pressure to be back early. I can stay out all night if I want to, and I already know it's going to be a late one.

Ian's been given the dubious title of honorary lesbian for the night. Next to him in the front seat of the car is a pretty redhead, whom he's introduced as Sally.

'So, how do you feel about going to a gay club?' I ask her.

'No problem,' she smiles. 'I've got gay friends so it doesn't bother me. How about you?'

'Oh, I don't mind either. I'm mainly going because Ian's going,' I say, then immediately question myself. Is that true? I know Maz will be there. Would I have come if she wasn't? I'm pretty sure I wouldn't have made the same effort when getting ready. I'm wearing tight jeans with heels and a lacy purple top that's practically see-through. OK, it is see-through, but it's paired with a fabulous bra that's giving me a very sexy cleavage.

The club is already quite full by the time we arrive and luckily Ian is let through without the usual grilling at the door. Marizette spots us and makes her way over. 'What do you want to drink?' she asks.

'You don't have to buy us drinks,' I reply, suddenly awkward.

'Come on, please. I want to buy you a drink.'

'OK, well, what are you having?'

'Hunter's Dry.'

'I'll have the same.'

'A Hunter's Dry it is,' she smiles. 'Come with me,' she grabs my arm and steers me towards the bar.

'Two Hunter's Dry and two tequilas,' Marizette orders.

I open my mouth to protest; I get drunk far too quickly on shots, but she insists, pressing the tot glass into my hand.

'You have the night off,' she argues, 'and anyway, it's too late, I've already paid for them.'

We clink glasses, silently toasting each other and down the tequila in one go. Nice, I think, enjoying the taste and the instant buzz.

One hour, two Hunter's, and one tequila later, I'm happily tipsy. I've danced to almost every song so far, mostly with Ian and his girlfriend, or on my own. Marizette is here and there, flitting between her friends, occasionally coming over to say hello. Then, suddenly, the music comes to an abrupt halt, leaving the dancers awkwardly mid-step.

'Good evening, ladies,' Myrna purrs into the microphone. 'I hope you're all having a fabulous time and that you've got your songs all lined up. There are some wonderful prizes to be won tonight, so get ready to sing!' The crowd cheers enthusiastically and Myrna waits for the noise to die down before continuing. 'We've got a panel of judges but the audience is free to weigh in as well. Enjoy the night!'

Marizette is standing beside me. 'I'm on fourth,' she mutters. 'I'm so nervous.'

Any nerves should've been eased by the first singer, who is unspeakably awful, singing horribly out of tune, with a grating voice that rises to a piercing shriek on the high notes. She seems oblivious to the laughter and continues good-naturedly all the way to the end, much to the delight of the crowd. In comparison, the next two singers are pretty good.

'And next up is Marizette,' announces Myrna, 'singing Katie Melua's "The Closest Thing To Crazy".'

'Good luck,' I say, squeezing her arm as the crowd cheers for her.

Marizette takes her place at the front. The opening bars are slow, melodious. The crowd surrounding me melts away, and suddenly I'm standing alone, watching Maz highlighted by a single spotlight.

She begins to sing. What a voice – so beautiful it gives me goose bumps. I've heard the song before, but never really listened to the words. But now, every single word holds meaning for me and rings true.

Heartfelt emotion pours from Marizette, and I'm fairly sure she keeps looking in my direction.

As I stand watching her, I'm hit with the sudden realisation that I don't have a crush on Maz; I'm in love with her! So in love that it hurts, and as I watch her I ache for her. I'm overcome with a longing so deep I can barely stand it. I can feel my heart constrict. Tears in my eyes, I reach for Ian's hand. 'Oh, Ian … it's so painful.'

'She feels for you too,' he says. 'Look.'

And Marizette is indeed looking at me, straight at me, while she sings. Our eyes are locked on one another.

She's singing for me! Or is she? Am I reading this wrong? All I know is that right now, I feel crazy. And all the contradictions of the song resonate deeply in me.

There's no mistaking it. She's looking right at me for the closing line. The music trails off as the crowd erupts in whoops and cheers. Maz bows and walks straight over to me. We hug, a proper, tight hug.

'You were brilliant! You have such a beautiful voice,' I babble.

She squeezes me back. My heart is beating insanely fast. I don't want to let her go, but I can't just keep hanging on. We're still hugging and it feels so right. We pull apart.

'I need a drink,' she says. Then to Ian and Sally, 'What do you guys want?'

'We won't have anything, thanks,' Ian says. 'We're going home. Mich, are you coming with us or staying on?'

'I can take you home later,' Marizette says quickly. 'Come on, stay. It's still early.'

I should go home with Ian. I know I should. I really, really should go home. I know this with every fibre of my body.

'OK,' I say, 'I'll stay. See you guys back at the cottage.'

But I'll behave. I won't drink much more. I must get a grip. My emotions are threatening to spill over. Maz and I are seated at the end of the bar where it's a little quieter. She's dragged me here, telling me we need to talk. Sounds ominous. We're each perched on a stool facing one another, so close our knees are touching. I must be fairly drunk by now, as I haven't shifted or moved my leg away.

'So tell me,' I begin, 'what is it you want to talk

about?' I sound formal. Not a bad way to keep things.

Marizette pauses, 'Michele, have you been happy with me working for you?'

'Of course, yes! You've been an amazing help to me. The kids love you ...'

She doesn't let me finish, 'Then why have you been so pleased about me leaving?'

'I'm just being supportive. I want you to finish your studies ... and do well.'

She presses on, 'But how do you feel? Are you happy I'm leaving?'

Her face is close to mine so we don't have to raise our voices. She's looking at me intensely, her eyes boring into me, waiting for an answer. What does she want from me? To say we'll miss her? That we don't want her to leave? Does she want me to beg her to stay on? I must choose my words carefully. And then it comes out. I can't keep it in any longer. I look her straight in the eye.

'Marizette, I'm in love with you.'

She exhales and moves away.

Shit! What is she thinking? She probably regrets questioning me. I'm filled with doubt. Then she puts her hand on my knee. I can feel its heat; even though it's touching only a small part of my body, its energy travels through me, spreading into my veins, filling me with an excruciating longing.

This is where I should stop. Call it a day, apologise for my confession. Firmly remove her hand from my leg. Go home, jump into bed with my husband, stuff waking the dogs and children. Let him be irritated. Irritation is far preferable to the other possible outcome. I know Maz and I are moving into dangerous territory and the further we enter the harder it'll be to return. I know all this and yet I remain seated.

'Michi,' Marizette begins, 'I've had dreams. In the dreams we're together. We're doing normal stuff that any couple would do. Like holding hands or walking with our arms around each other. And it feels so comfortable and right. No awkwardness.'

She is so close. She leans forward and brushes her lips against my neck. From the corner of my eye I can see Myrna walking past. She looks straight at us and shakes her head ever so slightly. That slight movement, coupled with her disapproving expression, makes me pull away slightly.

Marizette continues: 'In my dreams Peter is never there. He never has been, so there are no complications. The kids are there, but he isn't.'

I reel with all this information. Till now, I've assumed my feelings were unrequited. If the feelings flowed in one direction alone, everything would be safe. Now I know nothing will be the same ever again. I down the last of my drink and realise that I'm both unsteadily drunk and stone-cold sober at the same time. The music is too loud, the club too smoky.

'Let's go,' I say, sliding off my stool.

Marizette takes my hand in hers and leads me out of the club. The cool night air is a welcome relief. We cross the road, still holding hands, and it feels so intimate and so right. We drive home, the car hugging the coast. Marizette keeps one hand on the wheel, the other on my knee.

It's an enormous relief being back at Ian's. Thankfully, they're still up. As we sit drinking hot cups of organic ginger tea, some sense of normality is restored, for the time being at least. We chat about the evening; who should've won the karaoke competition; how awful yet brave the first singer was, and how the sexiest legs belonged to a gorgeous cross-dresser.

However, Ian has brought a girl home and doesn't want to chat all night. 'I've made up a bed for you in the spare room,' he says, getting up and grabbing Sally's hand to pull her up off the couch. 'See you in the morning.'

Sally follows him to the bedroom, 'Goodnight, guys. Lovely to meet you.'

And suddenly we are left alone. Marizette looks at me. Her beautiful, brown eyes are sparkling, filled with intent. She moves towards me but instinctively I pull away before her face reaches mine. She places her hand gently behind my head, making it difficult to for me to withdraw. Never in my wildest dreams did I imagine I would actually kiss Marizette. And yet here we are. She's insistent; I'm trying to resist. My hands are shaking.

'Marizette, please …'

She pulls me to her and places her mouth on mine. I've always found first kisses awkward. The uncertainty of how it's going to turn out. Will it be too wet; too much tongue? There's so much to worry about. And this kiss is so natural and perfect. And Marizette's lips! They're soft, and she commands the kiss with such confidence and expertise. I've never really enjoyed kissing but I'd be happy for this kiss to go on and on. Forever and ever.

My heart is racing – this is Marizette! All my suppressed longing is suddenly released, and it's terrifying. I can feel her hands cupping my face. And I know what frightens me; she wants me too. When I thought my love was unrequited, it was still safe. But now, knowing Marizette wants me as much as I want her, this thing, this need, is gaining power. I know I should stop, that I can still turn back, but my desire overcomes any sense.

Marizette pulls away from me and, taking my hand, leads me into Ian's spare bedroom. At this point I know Marizette and I are going to make love and I know it goes against my very moral fibre and I know there are going to be terrible and dramatic consequences. But I have wanted to make love to her so badly and for so long that it's bordered on obsession. I thought I'd never have the chance, and now that it's offered to me, I am powerless to resist. I don't know if it'll ever happen again so I grasp the opportunity with both hands, and take full advantage.

We begin kissing and I pull off my top hurriedly, and then tear off hers as well. I'm suddenly impatient. Not wanting to waste any more time, I push Marizette onto the bed and pull off her trousers, taking her knickers with them. Wow.

'Please,' I gasp, 'just lie there so I can look at you.'

I want to take her in. Remember the image forever. Marizette obliges, spreading herself on her back with one arm behind her head, her legs slightly open. Her head is tilted slightly and she looks at me seductively through dark brown eyes set in a pale face. Her lips are so red – my own naked Snow White lying before me. I'm so privileged to see her naked like this; so often imagined and yet till now never seen. And what a vision lies before me. Long legs and broad shoulders; small boobs. But unexpectedly, large protruding nipples; tasty-looking, like two Jelly Tots.

I push her legs open slightly and there is the biggest surprise of all. Marizette has trimmed her pubic hair.

And underneath, she's shaved off all the hair on her labia majora (Did she know she'd be in this position? Did she prepare herself for me?), revealing the most beautiful little vagina I could ever have imagined. No description could do justice to its sheer gorgeousness. A soft shade of pink with lippies so small they're completely hidden. That is until I push her legs open a little wider and her neat little lips are revealed.

I undo my jeans and step out of them, leaving my panties on. I am incredibly shy about Marizette seeing or touching my vagina, which in contrast to hers, I perceive to be so much less than perfect. Primarily because I didn't expect any action tonight and am hairy and unkempt. But more importantly because of my long-standing self-consciousness about my vagina.

Faced with Marizette's perfection, I am doubly aware of how awful it must look and feel. I don't want to put her off me, and I'm convinced that if she sees or touches me she'll be repulsed. Imagine if that's what she remembers of me after tonight! So I decide to keep my knickers on. She can explore any other part of my body, but my vagina is out of bounds. Instead, I'm going to make beautiful love to her. Slow and sensual, exploring each part of her body with my hands and mouth.

Well, that's the plan, but as I kiss her on the lips and feel my nipples brush against hers, all the desire I've suppressed for so long explodes. I want Marizette; need her. I'm hungry and greedy. I want to feel her all over, inside and out. I feel her with my fingers, taste her with my tongue, and I can't do it all fast enough. Desire overpowers my anxiety to please. I kiss Marizette furiously; grabbing her hair, pulling her head back and kissing her neck. I move down her body, pausing to take her nipples in my mouth; first one, then the other. Enjoying their hardness on my tongue, so hard and yet soft. I resist the urge to bite them.

I move further down, still kissing and nibbling; down the smooth length of her belly, past her belly button. Impatient to reach that smoothly shaved exquisiteness. I force myself to be patient and kiss her gently on the soft skin of each inner thigh. She starts moaning. Unable to wait any longer, I finally place my mouth over her vagina. I part her vulva with my tongue and suck gently on the lips hidden inside; so little, but rapidly swelling.

'Please direct me,' I ask, suddenly self-conscious.

'Oh God, you're doing just fine,' she moans.

I feel her hands on my head, her fingers playing with my hair. I explore her whole vagina with my mouth. Sliding my tongue over and around her clitoris; kissing, licking, sucking. Oh, the heavenly softness. I slide my tongue in between her lips, then push it deep inside her, as far as it can go, and I'm overcome with a heady mix of glorious sensations. The taste, scent, wetness – her cocktail fills me. I could stay down here forever, but Marizette pulls at my head, grabs me by the shoulders and pulls me down on top of her.

'Didn't you like what I was doing?' I ask, worried.

'Of course I did!'

'Then why ...'

'Shhh,' she silences me with a finger to my mouth then turns me over and pulls at my knickers.

I grab hold of them. 'Please don't,' I plead. 'I don't feel comfortable.'

'Trust me,' Marizette insists, pulling off my panties

in one move, 'you'll feel a lot more comfortable without these on.'

I put my hand over my vagina. I feel tears welling up. I'm so frightened she'll be repulsed by me. 'Please don't,' I beg.

'Why?'

'It's my lips. They stick out. Well, they're different from yours and …'

Marizette grabs my hand and pulls it away. I gasp as her fingers slip inside me, moving rhythmically, coming out to rub my clitoris, then sliding back in again.

'You're no different from anyone else,' she whispers, her face close to mine; the softness of her cheek rubbing against me. 'In fact, you feel beautiful.' She repeats this over and over again, while moving her fingers in and out; in and out. And I'm overwhelmed; these are Marizette's fingers!

I realise what I feel – joy. Really and truly! Without any resistance my body welcomes in Marizette. There are no yucky feelings; no zoning out; no diversions or fantasies. I want to experience each and every sensation. The friction of her fingers against my skin; her body moving against mine; her tongue against my teeth. This is what lovemaking is meant to feel like. How ironic: making love within the context of marriage is permissible, and yet over the years, on a very deep level, my body has protested. Now here I am, committing adultery; wrong by anyone's standard, and yet it feels so right.

Marizette slips her fingers out of me and moves down to kiss me between my legs. And I don't stop her. She is experienced, taking her time, slipping her fingers in me as she licks my clitoris. Tears well up in my eyes and begin to slide down my cheeks. I am in heaven but at the same time exhaustion descends on me. I can feel the alcohol circulating in my system, making me nauseous. Nausea and desire mixed with tiredness and from the edges anxiety creeps in. Time passes as Marizette holds me. I long to sleep; panic rises inside me. How am I going to cope with the children later? What about Peter? I moan as another wave of nausea surges through me.

Marizette tries to comfort me; touches my cheek; strokes my hair, 'I wish I could make you feel better,' she whispers.

She sleeps intermittently, kissing me every time she wakes up, kisses I accept, in spite of feeling so incredibly ill. Eventually I sleep. Far too briefly though, and wake up to sunlight pouring through the window. It's going to be a beautiful day but my heart is filled with dread. Everything in my life has changed and it can never be the same again. Churning with anxiety, I picture Peter storming across the piece of lawn that separates our house from Ian's cottage. He enters the house and finds me in bed with Marizette. I have to get out of here. I sit up and swing my legs off the bed, fighting the desire to throw up. What am I going to tell Peter? I have to tell him something. But what and when and where? For starters, I'll have to tell him I'm insanely hung over. I'll never be able to hide feeling this bad.

○

By eleven it's turned into a beautiful day, as expected. Sunny, blue skies, birds singing – that sort of thing. All of which is unusually lost on me, although I'm trying desperately to act normal in front of Peter and the kids. We're all sitting under the trees, down near the trampoline. Benjamin has begged Chloe to bounce with him and their laughter pierces the morning. Marizette makes her way over from Ian's and grabs a seat at one of the tables.

'Hi guys,' she greets us, casually, lighting a cigarette.

'Marizette,' Benjamin shouts from the trampoline, 'look at me! I can do a somersault!'

Marizette acts suitably impressed but too soon looks over at me and catches my eye. Damn, I don't want Peter to suspect anything. Not yet, anyway. Just act normal, the mantra goes round and round in my head. My nerves and the two coffees I gulped down earlier are making me hyper in spite of feeling so hung over. I snuggle up next to Peter, and kiss him on the cheek. Then, idiotically, decide to do a handstand, 'Hey kids, look at me!'

Whoa! That was stupid. My head starts spinning and I crawl over to Peter, who's spread out on the grass, and lie on top of him, ruffling his hair. What am I doing? I'm not acting normal. But Peter seems oblivious to any of the massive shifts that have taken place overnight. In fact, he seems quite glad of the attention I'm lavishing on him. Guiltily I glance at Marizette, but she's left.

◯

It's night time. The kids are in bed asleep and I have no idea how I got through this day. After lunch I felt so ill that I went to lie down for a few hours, leaving a reluctant Peter to look after the kids. Next to me in bed, Peter is also still awake, completely unaware of the turmoil going on inside me. I must stop thinking. I'll phone my mom when Peter is at work tomorrow. She'll know what to do.

I roll on top of Peter and begin to kiss his face, something I never normally do. I decide to try to make love to him with as much passion as I can muster. I need to know for sure; maybe I just haven't tried hard enough over the years. Maybe if I act passionately, then I'll feel passionate. A bit like smiling, even if you feel sad and then eventually feeling happy, because you're acting it (surely I've read that somewhere?). In spite of my incredible experience with Marizette – or maybe because of that passion – my husband still deserves to be loved properly. And, I think guiltily, until last night I didn't even know what that meant. Maybe things can be retrieved; maybe I can transfer some of last night's passion to my husband.

Two hours later I'm still lying awake, frustrated. Peter's finally dozed off after what he said was the best sex he's ever experienced. I wish I could share his enthusiasm. It just felt wrong; like a betrayal to myself. I can't wait, I need to speak to my mom. I reach over and grab my cellphone. It's two in the morning already, with England an hour behind us. I slip quietly out of bed and grab my nightgown from behind the door, pulling it on as I pad down the silent passage. Sitting in the half-lit kitchen, I dial my mom's number, wishing I'd brought my slippers. My fingers shake as they dial the numbers.

'Michele,' my mom answers sleepily on the second ring.

On hearing her voice, my throat constricts and suddenly I can't speak. Hot tears slide down my cheeks.

'Michele, are you there? Is everything alright?' Her voice is filled with motherly concern and I know if I keep sniffing and don't speak soon she'll assume the worst. But whatever worst-case scenarios are going through her head, nothing will prepare her for what I'm about to say.

'Oh Mommy,' I begin, speaking through my tears, 'last night we went to that Lush party. Remember I told you about it? Marizette and I got talking and I told her I was in love with her and she said she had feelings for me too. So we went back to Ian's place and kissed and … and more …' I pause, but there's no response from my mom.

'And I haven't told Peter, but I know I have to and I don't know what's going to happen. You know I have feelings for Marizette and now that I know she has feelings back, it's like … I love her. And I have done for a long, long time. I just didn't realise how much,' my voice trails off as fresh tears break out.

There is silence as my mom processes this monologue.

'Michele, listen,' she begins slowly. 'You do need to tell Peter, but just know that when you do, the outcome is going to be explosive – for all of you. For Peter, Marizette and the children, but most of all for you,' she says seriously.

'I know,' I whisper.

'I know you, Michi, you always want to keep everyone happy. But you're not going to be able to do that in this situation, whatever decisions you make. What I'm saying is wait until I get there before you speak to Peter. You're going to need me. I'll be on the first flight I can get.'

'What about Dad?' I ask, my heart sinking. I can't begin to imagine how my father will respond to this.

She pauses. 'He still has a lot to do here, he'll probably stay on.'

Relief washes over me. I'm far too brittle to cope with my dad right now. 'Thanks, Mom. I love you so much.'

'I love you too,' she says. 'Now go to bed, I'll speak to you in the morning. And try to get some sleep.'

Chapter fourteen

To: sara@naturalnurture.co.uk
Subject: Caution: X-rated content
Dear Sara
The night before last I slept with Marizette. And now I have no idea what to do. I'm so scared and so in love with her. Yes, love – I now know what you and the girls have gone on and on about over the years. The very same friends I mocked for being childish. And now I have all the symptoms: racing heart, wild abandonment, fluttering stomach. I'm like a schoolgirl. But it's not as simple as happily ever after, obviously. I have all these conflicting emotions colliding with each other. For example:
a) Elation – Marizette loves me! When she made love to me it felt so unbelievably beautiful and sacred. As if all the love I've suppressed for so long could burst out of me. I feel so free – nothing she did to me made me feel dirty. This is actually the most profoundly powerful thing of all: it's like I've been freed from the shackles of my abuse. She could enter me however she chose and I could never be invaded. I didn't know I could feel this good in my body after making love.
b) Sadness – I don't know what the outcome of the night's events is going to be, but whatever happens,

I'm going to be devastated.

c) Fear – I don't want to change my life. I desperately want peace and a nice family life, free of drama. But the idea of losing Marizette terrifies me.

d) Confusion – What the fuck is going on?! I'm not gay! So why did that night feel so right? And yet it was so wrong on so many levels.

e) Guilt – Huge and all-encompassing guilt. I'm an adulterer. I've been unfaithful to my husband, who trustingly allowed me to go out without him. I have jeopardised everything in my life; everyone who means something to me. My family, my children, being a good person.

I've crossed the line. I am no longer good. I don't even know who I am any more. All the tragedy or drama that's happened so far in my life has been unfortunate, but this is of my own doing. I'll phone you soon, but things are very screwed up right now. My mom is cutting her trip short. Can't wait till she gets here. Love, Michi

◯

The following morning. Chloe is at school, Benjamin's playing outside and Max is doing schoolwork with Marizette. I've skipped gym and am lying in the bath, enjoying the warmth, trying to unravel my frazzled nerves.

A knock on the door; Marizette's voice, 'Can I come in?'

'Yes,' I call, 'come in.'

We haven't been alone together since The Night.

'Oh, sorry,' she apologises, 'I didn't know you were in the bath.'

'It's fine, don't leave. Please. It's not as though you haven't seen me naked.'

She comes in and crouches down next to the bath, trailing her hand in the water, then touching my stomach, 'You're so beautiful.'

My heart does a triple-somersault as I feel her fingers on my skin. Marizette is looking at me, with her gorgeous brown eyes. I take her hands and kiss her fingertips. The same fingers that were doing such incredible things to me just two nights ago.

Marizette draws her hand away, 'Michele, what are we going to do?'

I sigh. 'I don't know,' I say honestly. 'I really don't know. I do know I have to tell Peter. I can't keep this a secret from him. I'm going to tell him when my mom gets back next week. She's managed to book an earlier flight.'

'Look, just do me one favour,' Marizette says seriously, 'if you do tell Peter before your mom gets here, then let me know straight away. I don't want any surprises.'

'I promise.' I pause, then take a deep breath and say, 'Did you mean all those things you said to me?'

She squeezes my hand. 'Absolutely everything. And I'll tell you something else. I hated the way you were carrying on with Peter yesterday. That's why I left.'

'I'm sorry,' I reply, looking away. 'I just didn't want him getting suspicious.'

'Well, it really upset me. Did you sleep with him?'

I quickly weigh up the situation; everything is so complicated already. 'No. Now come give me a kiss.'

Marizette is just leaning in to kiss me when Max calls for her from the schoolroom.

'Damn! I thought I set him enough work. Sorry,' she

says ruefully, giving me a quick kiss, 'got to go.'

I watch her leave and sink back down into the lukewarm water, filled with frustration and longing.

Chapter fifteen

To: sara@naturalnurture.co.uk
Subject: Emotional roller coasters
Dear Sara
This is the most stressful, surreal, terrifying, joyful emotional roller coaster of a week. I have no idea what's going to happen, I just know the shit will hit the fan very soon. Can't wait for my mom to return so I can tell Peter. But what do I tell him exactly? I'll have to censor things. I won't tell him I've slept with Marizette, just that we've kissed. Which we're currently doing at every opportunity; as soon as Peter's left for work, in between teaching Max and picking Chloe up from school. I can't help myself! It's like a magnetic force, I can't keep away from her. I grab her for kisses in the laundry room, in the lounge when no one is around, even up in the tree house like naughty teenagers. All unbelievably stressful and I'm terrified of getting caught. There are so many people in our household! Don't know how people conduct long-term affairs. My already frazzled nerves could never take it.

    I badly want to tell Peter and get it out of the way, but I'm dreading the actual moment. It's like waiting for an awful and inevitable punishment. I keep imagining the different scenarios. Favourite, most-hoped-for option:

Peter hears me out, but takes the news calmly: 'I love you, Michele. I want to understand you. Whatever happens, nothing will change the way I feel about you. One way or another we'll work it out. Look, I've always had my suspicions. Tell me, when did you first have feelings for Marizette?' Then I tell him and he cries, then I cry and we comfort each other and he says we'll always be the best of friends. Or something.

My optimistic imaginings sort of evaporate at this point. It's highly unlikely. He could be so outraged that he never wants to see me again. Or Marizette might decide it's all too much and go to Pretoria after all, leaving me heartbroken. Wish I could fast forward my life past the next few months or even sleep through it all. Peter must suspect something, though. I'm edgy and am consciously finding fault with him. Everything that's ever bugged me about our relationship has now expanded into much bigger issues, and I'm speaking up instead of keeping quiet like I used to. Stuff like: 'Peter, do you realise you're going into the garden without greeting me properly? A kiss on the cheek might be nice.' Or: 'You never show me any affection.' And: 'Nice you get to go for a two-hour run every Saturday while I stay home with the kids.'

And I'm so angry – angry at God for making me this way (although I don't necessarily believe in Him); angry with Steven, it's probably his fault anyway. Angry at Marizette for coming into my life and making me fall in love with her. Just plain angry. Why can't I be normal? Then my life wouldn't be such a mess. But on the other hand, I'm ridiculously grateful to be given the opportunity to feel as good as Marizette makes me feel; to have the chance to be loved by such an incredible woman.

On one hand my sexuality is finally emerging and, like a love-sick teenager, I feel all those coming-of-age emotions I was denied back in puberty. The wheels are turning and I can't go back now, I can't change what's already happened. I'm so sad and overcome some days I feel as though I am going to drown. I must make a decision one way or another, and once I've chosen, I need to stick to it. I don't want to split up with Peter, but I never want to be without Marizette – ever.

Throughout all of this it amazes me how parallel our lives have turned out. I never thought I'd be e-mailing you with the same kind of situation that you had with Gael. It seemed so foreign to me when you first told me about falling for her. Please know I fully understand and respect your choices, but I can't handle my situation the way you've chosen to handle yours. I feel like I'd be suppressing who I am by keeping my relationship with Maz a secret love affair. Plus, I don't think I could stand the strain. I don't mean to be judgmental; you have very clear reasons why you've never said anything to Graeme and the kids, and your choices have worked out well for you. No one is any the wiser, no one gets hurt, you get what you need and still have the security of your husband and family – I'm envious.

You are the one person who truly understands what I'm going through. Don't know how I would cope without being able to write to you. Sorry for such a long rant. Love, Michi

The Au Pair

'Oh my God, Michi! What's going on?' Brandy settles herself on the couch opposite me. Outside, her daughter Rose is playing in the garden with Benjamin. Marizette is making us some coffee.

'Uh, why?' I stall, as I haven't told her anything yet.

'Well, you're positively glowing. And something else, but I can't quite put my finger on it.'

I smile impulsively, but before I start explaining, Marizette enters the lounge with the coffees. She puts the tray on the table and sits down next to me.

'Wow,' says Brandy, her eyes sparkling with delight, 'Tell me everything! When did the two of you get together?'

I'm shocked, 'How do you know?'

'Oh please, it's obvious just looking at you together. And you'll never be able to keep it to yourselves. Does Peter know? I can't believe he doesn't suspect something.'

'Is it that obvious?' I ask, horrified.

'Hello? Yes! As long as you two are in the same room people are going to notice.'

Outside, Benjamin starts crying and Chloe calls for me, 'Mom! Benjamin hurt himself on the trampoline.'

Marizette stands up, 'I'll go,' she calls over her shoulder as she heads outside.

Brandy turns to me, 'Quick – tell me everything.'

I look outside. Marizette has kissed Benjamin's ouch better and is coaxing him back on to the trampoline with Rose. I don't know how long they'll be, so I talk quickly. Somehow I manage to cram all the events of the last few days into about five minutes.

'So,' I conclude, 'I don't know what the fuck I'm going to do.'

'Well, Michi, I just want you to know that whatever happens, whatever happens,' she repeats for emphasis, 'I'm here for you. If you decide to be with Marizette you're going to get a lot of criticism. People can be very judgmental. But if I hear anything nasty, I will so stick up for you.'

I'm so grateful to hear Brandy's staunch loyalty, but also terrified by her words. I haven't thought as far as telling friends yet, or even that I need to tell them anything, never mind how they'll react. Right now, I'm just taking it one day at a time. It's comforting to hear that whatever the outcome, I'll have at least one truly supportive friend. I swallow, fighting back tears.

Chapter sixteen

'Michele?' Marizette looks serious, and slightly uncomfortable.

I nod at her to carry on.

She takes a drag of her cigarette and exhales before continuing. 'Look, this girl Ellen invited me on a date this coming Saturday. I met her a few weeks ago. We actually set the date before anything happened between you and me,' she pauses and looks at me. 'Now I don't know what to do. I haven't spoken to her this week; I could cancel. What do you think?'

She wants me to decide for her? Shit! What do I think? Rather, what do I feel? Insanely jealous, actually. And completely petrified at the mere thought of Marizette going on a date with this woman. Although we've expressed our love for each other we haven't actually made any promises or formulated any concrete plans. I haven't even told Peter yet! I desperately don't want her to go, but we aren't even dating, so officially I have no hold over her.

'I think you should go,' I say determinedly, full of false cheerfulness.

'Really?' Marizette sounds uncertain.

'Yes, go, I think you need to. You know, get away

from here for a bit. See what you really want. Go on the date; I don't want you to skip it and regret it at a later stage,' I urge, really meaning it. As unhappy as I am about Marizette meeting Ellen, I don't want her to be playing out what-if scenarios in her head further down the line.

○

Saturday night. Max and Chloe are watching a movie and Benjamin is sitting in the lounge with Peter, playing with his Lego. It's a beautiful spring evening and we're planning to have supper on the veranda later, by candlelight (Chloe's idea). Theoretically a magical family scene that will probably wrap up with Peter playing his guitar as all of us sing along to well-known Irish love songs. An evening that would normally fill me with warm satisfaction, but right now, I sit tensely, with the knot in my stomach tightening as Marizette pops in to say goodbye before she leaves for her date.

Fuck it. She's made an effort and looks absolutely gorgeous: spiky hair, smoky eyes, snug Diesel jeans and a white shirt. Jealousy and anxiety have a gleeful stabbing session in my chest. She obviously wants to impress Ellen. So what is that supposed to mean? Do her feelings for Ellen run deeper than she's let on? Frustratingly, I can't put any of these questions to her.

Benjamin jumps up to give Marizette a hug and Peter looks up briefly from their Lego city. At least he knows she's going on a date, so for now he won't be suspicious of all the happenings between us over the past week.

'Enjoy your evening,' I manage to force out, hoping upon hope that she won't.

The Au Pair

◯

A lazy Sunday afternoon. Peter and I are spread out on a picnic blanket in the garden, basking in the sunshine. The kids and dogs are bustling around us. Bees buzz in and out of the lavender maze. This is what I've worked so hard to build.

But instead of the peace and contentment the moment would normally induce, I feel totally and utterly wretched, and am struggling to conceal the fact. Marizette did not return last night, which was totally unexpected. I was prepared for her to be home late but never considered that she wouldn't come back at all. By now, we would've discussed her date already. Instead, the day has dragged by and I have no idea what's going on or any way of finding out without looking pathetic. She hasn't contacted me and I don't want to phone her. What if she's in bed with Ellen when she gets a desperate phone call from me? Because that's how I feel right now – desperate.

I try to clear my mind, focus on the pottery classes I'm thinking of starting. I've always loved the feeling of cold wet clay between my fingers. Maybe Marizette …

Dammit! I bet they've slept together. I just know it. And as much as I try to chase the images of their naked bodies entwined, the more they persist. Marizette touching Ellen the way she touches me; whispering in her ear, 'Oh God, Ellen, you're so beautiful.' That would be a betrayal far worse than her just fucking Ellen. What if all those things she whispered to me were just sweet nothings? Signature lovemaking moves … No! I shake my head firmly and change position, turning away from

Peter. I have to get a grip. This is ridiculous.

'Mom! Mom, wrestle me. Come on, please!' Max pleads, tugging at my top.

Normally, I would throw myself into the game and launch into a hold down, before allowing him to work himself free. But I'm not in the mood for games.

'Go wrestle Dad,' I say shortly.

'Yeah, Dad, come on,' Max shouts, diving on top of his father.

'Ouch, Max! My neck is still stiff. Rather fight your mom, she's the judo expert.'

Suddenly I can't take any more. 'For Christ's sake, Peter!' I explode. 'Can't you make an effort? Why does it always have to be me?' And with that I storm off.

My mood worsens as the hours drag on but I can't help myself. By the time we're in bed, the tense silence lying heavily between us, I've worked out how perfect Ellen and Marizette will be together. For a start, Ellen is available. Already a major plus – I'm married. She has no children – I have three. She probably has a successful career – I've been a full-time mom for twelve years. She compares so favourably with me that I become convinced Marizette has also seen the light by now and is just wondering how to break the news to me.

○

Monday morning. I pedal furiously on the stationary bike, going nowhere, wondering if Marizette is ever going to speak to me again. She didn't come home last night, so Peter dropped me at the gym after taking the kids to school. By now I've worked out she's decided to leave her job and never see me again. She's realised she's made a big mistake and that she'd be far better off with Ellen.

I've been cycling flat out for over an hour now, but thanks to some kind of manic energy I'm still going strong, waiting for the endorphins to kick in.

'I hope you feel better after your workout,' Peter called after me earlier; I'm sure he suspects something.

I wish I could feel better. I wish I could sweat out all these torturous feelings. I wish … And then I see her – Marizette – at the gym! I rip out my earphones as she reaches me. Overcome with relief, I don't care what's passed between her and Ellen over the weekend.

She puts her hand over mine. I can feel tears gathering in my eyes but I don't care who sees.

'Oh God, Marizette! I thought I'd never see you again. Why didn't you phone to say what was happening? I've been so frightened. Were you with her the whole weekend? Do you want to be with her?' It all comes out in a flood and then just as suddenly, my wild energy deserts me and I slow down my pedalling to a stop.

Marizette takes my hand in both of hers, 'It's OK, Michi, calm down. I love you. I spent the weekend with friends. I told Ellen I'm in love with my boss,' she smiles.

Chapter seventeen

To: sara@naturalnurture.co.uk
Subject: Just a quickie
Dear Sara
This week is just crazy. I'm trying super hard to hold things together on the domestic front. Mom is back the day after tomorrow, and then I can tell Peter the truth. Don't know how I'm gong to make it through all of this – it's so stressful. But there's one thing I do know and that's that I can't let Marizette go. We had a long discussion. We want to be together, but we're not sure of the practicalities. Where will Peter stay? How will I explain the situation to the children? I just hope that whatever the outcome, Peter understands and isn't too heartbroken. I also hope we can remain friends. I don't want to hurt him or the kids in all of this. Don't want to hurt anyone. Badly wish you were here. Love, Michi

○

Saturday morning. Peter and I are outside in the driveway, cleaning out the car; no small task, given the amount of clutter that's built up. My mom arrives tomorrow. Luckily, Peter isn't at all suspicious that she's cut her trip short. Tomorrow, I'll have to tell him I'm in love with Marizette. Tomorrow, I'll be breaking his heart.

'Mich,' Peter calls from the other side of the car, 'pass me the bucket, will you?'

Lost in my thoughts, I don't respond.

'Mich,' he repeats, louder this time, 'are you listening to me? Could you pass me the bucket?'

Silence.

'Don't worry, I'll get it,' he snaps.

'Sorry,' I mumble, shaking my head, 'I was just about to pass it to you.'

Peter dunks a sponge into the bucket and begins washing the car. 'You're in a world of your own today. Are you OK?' He pauses, 'In fact, you've been in a weird space for a while. What's the matter, Michele?'

I can't find the words to answer him, so I say nothing.

He drops the sponge and walks round the car, looking intently at me. His own eyes are full of concern and worry. 'Michele, please. Tell me what's wrong. You've been so out of character lately, all cross and grumpy. It's not like you.'

Oh God, I don't want this conversation. Not here. Not now. Not ever. But I can't put it off forever. Etched in Peter's face is the fear my silence is causing.

'Michele,' he says quietly, 'do you love me?'

'Yes,' I answer truthfully, 'I love you.'

'Will you love me always?'

I feel the beginnings of my heart breaking. 'Yes, Peter I will. I'll always love you.'

He takes me by the shoulders and looks straight into my eyes; his face pleading and fearful. 'Will you be with me forever?'

I inhale and pause, 'I don't know.'

Peter reacts so instantly and so unexpectedly to this final admission that I'm completely thrown. He starts to cry – huge, heaving, uncontrollable sobs. With three words his world has fallen apart. Helpless, I watch him sob. There's nothing I can do, because I can offer no words of comfort, no gesture of affection to make things right again. Nothing that is true and honest, anyway. I could say, 'Sorry, Peter. Of course I'll be with you always. Nothing can change that.' Words, in fact, that I said and meant just weeks ago. Before everything was turned upside down.

'Why?' he asks between jagged breaths. 'Michele? What's happened?'

I can't avoid the question, my mom here or not. 'I'm in love with Marizette.'

Peter sinks to his knees and howls. No lead-up, just instant, unabated grief. I feel terrible. I wish there was some way to make him feel better; to soothe his sorrow. But I'm the cause of his pain. All I can do is stand, horrified and impotent, as I watch the man I love bawling his eyes out like a child. A man whom I've only once witnessed crying in the eighteen years I've known him. I'm rooted to the spot. Then suddenly, everything goes quiet inside my head, and I shut down, I step out of myself, and watch the terrible scene from a distance, like it's a movie. Here in the driveway, I feel nothing. But elsewhere, there's another Michele; a Michele torn to shreds with pity and sadness and raging guilt.

At some point, unnoticed, Benjamin has wandered outside. He stands over Peter, patting his shoulder, his little face pale with worry. 'Daddy, what's wrong?'

Peter tries, but he can't stop crying.

Unsure of what to do, Benjamin continues to rub his father's shoulder, 'Daddy, please don't cry. Please don't be so sad.' He kneels down next to Peter and puts his arms around him.

Suddenly, Peter gets up. Still sobbing, he staggers to the car and climbs in. I reach the window as the engine revs. 'Please, Peter. Don't drive now,' I plead. 'Come inside.'

'I can't,' he says, refusing to look at me. 'I need to be away for a bit.' The window slides up. His face is puffy with tears; his eyes red.

Oh Mom, I wish you were here, I pray.

Benjamin takes my hand, his eyes widen as Peter screeches away. My heart fills with dread. This is just the beginning.

Inside I settle the kids in front of a DVD and make my way blindly to the upstairs flat. I take the stairs two at a time as a sense of urgency overcomes me. I have to speak to Marizette before Peter returns. I need to keep my promise to her so she can be prepared for his reaction.

Marizette can see the panic written all over my face as I burst in without knocking.

'Michi, what is it?'

'Peter knows,' I begin. 'I couldn't not tell him. He was asking too many questions. I either had to tell him or lie to him.'

'OK,' says Marizette, taking a deep breath. I can see the tension in her shoulders. 'Now what?'

'Fuck, I don't know. I have to take care of the children – Benjamin saw him crying. I'd better go downstairs.'

Marizette wraps her long arms around me, enveloping me completely. I take temporary refuge in the warmth of her body, the strength in her shoulders. I squash myself into her, pressing my cheek into her chest. I don't want to let go.

'We're going to be alright,' she whispers in my ear. 'We'll get through this.'

The rest of the afternoon passes in surreal peace. Peter returns, Marizette comes downstairs and the three of us sit around the fireplace. Everything is in limbo. None of the major events or decisions is raised; just idle chitchat. The kids have been in and out of the house, begging us to make a fire, which Marizette did, even though it's only four o'clock and still light outside. Anyone watching would think we're a regular family enjoying their Saturday afternoon together. But all is far from well. The tension is palpable. We don't look at one another properly when we speak. Peter and Marizette are chain-smoking.

Later we braai food that only the kids eat. My beautiful children, so carefree and unaware. I want to freeze this moment for them. It's only a matter of time before I drop a bombshell on their perfect world.

Chapter eighteen

At last my mom is here. We're in the lounge in Ian's cottage; just the two of us, for now. She's staying with him for the time being, so Marizette can stay in the flat. We're both holding large mugs of tea. Taking a sip, Mom gets straight to the point.

'So, Michele, what is it you want?'

I shrug, unsure.

'What does Marizette want? Where do the two of you want to go from here?'

'Christ, Mom! I don't know. All I know is that I want to be with her. I want her so badly that the thought of not being able to see her again fills me with a crushing pain.'

After playing this conversation over and over in my mind, and the agonising wait for my mom to arrive, it's a relief to be able to say these words aloud to her.

'Other than that, I don't know. We haven't really discussed the practicalities.'

'Well, everything has happened rather fast,' she concedes.

'I know, and I'm so scared for Peter. I'm more worried about him than I am about the kids at the moment. And the worst is that I have the power to make everything alright again, for the whole family. But I can't. I can't cut ties with Marizette. You'd have to lock me up, or section me,' I say dramatically, 'like they did with errant wives a hundred years ago. Or even more recently, probably ...'

'Michele, you don't have to ...'

'Oh God, Mom! What's going to happen? I'm so scared and so guilty. Am I doing the right thing? What is the right thing? End it with Marizette and get on with my life, leaving our family intact?'

Mom takes my hand, 'But Michele, what about you? Would that be the right thing for you?' She pauses, 'I can see all the unhappiness and pain this situation is causing, and we both know if you decide to be with Marizette there'll be difficult times ahead.'

I nod miserably.

'But I look at you and see a light in your eyes that I haven't seen since ... well, since you were a child.' She looks down and swallows. Her lips wobble and her eyes well up. 'Listen, Michele. I haven't always been there for you in the right way. I've compromised your happiness to keep the peace.' Tears slide down her cheeks and splash into her tea. 'Or for what I thought was the greater good of everyone involved.' She's crying freely now. 'This time, I'm here for you, however hard things are for everyone else.' She squeezes my hand for emphasis.

I reach over and hug her. 'Oh, Mommy, thank you so much for being here for me. I'm so glad that Dad's still in England for another month. He'd never understand ...'

'Ah, yes,' she pulls away. 'Your dad phoned this morning. He's arriving on Tuesday.'

'Damn!' I exclaim. 'That's all I need; Dad coming to sort things out.'

My parents have always stood by each other on any

decisions, especially those regarding me and Ian. But somehow I doubt my dad will be too supportive of his only daughter running off with the au pair.

Mom squeezes my hand again. 'I'm here for you,' she emphasises. 'But you're going to have to be strong. You'll have to face huge challenges; far bigger than you can imagine.'

○

'I want her out this house!' Peter shouts.

We're in the kitchen and the children are watching TV in the next room.

'Peter, please,' I urge, 'keep your voice down.'

'Why should I? The kids are going to find out. They're going to find out that their mom's an adulterer,' he yells, relishing the impact of his words. 'And with the au pair! That's disgusting – what the hell are you thinking? She's so much younger than you. It's sick! Do you know how old she would've been when you were her age?'

She would've been eight. I know this because our age gap bothers me immensely. I've worked it all out. The age gap between her and Chloe is the same as the gap between us. When I started college she was four. When I moved to England at fourteen she was only just born. When I gave birth to Max, she was ten years old. I torment myself endlessly with all these different interpretations. It's pointless, I know, but I can't help it.

Still ranting, Peter paces up and down the kitchen. 'And what do you think a court will say if you decide to leave me? They're not going to want to let a mother practising as a lesbian look after children,' he sneers.

'Oh please, Peter!' I scoff. 'There are plenty of gay parents, even in this country. Being gay isn't a reason to take someone's kids away.'

'Except you're not gay, Michele, I know you're not. I don't know what you're playing at, but I know you're not gay. I think you're just bored and want to spice things up a bit.'

'Oh my God, Peter!' I can't believe him, 'Have you any idea how hard this is? I would never put us all through this heartache just to spice up my life!'

'Well, I want her out. I can't take seeing her here every day. It's still my home.'

'It's my home too …' I start, but he cuts me off.

'You end this now or get her out.' His voice is rising, 'If you want to continue your relationship with her, then she must be gone by the time I get back tomorrow. She doesn't work here any more.'

'Where's she meant to go?' I ask desperately. 'She doesn't have family in Cape Town. And who's going to help me with the driving?'

Peter shrugs, 'You should've thought about all that. If she wants to continue working here then you must put an end to this. Otherwise she's out.'

The children know that something is going on. Max is lying in bed, reading a *Mad* magazine, when I come in to say goodnight.

'I heard you and Dad shouting,' he says. 'What's going on? You guys never fight.'

I ignore his questioning look and change the subject. 'Do you enjoy *Mad*? I used to love them when I was your age.'

'Yeah, this one's got this really funny bit about the

pros and cons of having gay parents,' he smiles.

I'm gob-smacked at the timing. 'Really? Let me have a look.'

He shows me the article, pointing out his favourite bits. 'It's silly stuff. Like with two moms you have two women wanting to pick your spots but when you become a teenager, all your friends imagine your moms in bed together, you know.'

'Max, Dad and I will speak to you tomorrow.' I kiss him on the cheek, completely unnerved. Has he picked up on something?

○

Later on that night, the kids are all asleep and Marizette has gone out to visit friends. She says being at the house is too stressful and she doesn't want to sit on her own upstairs in the flat. Peter and I are in the kitchen, chatting.

'Michele, I'm sorry I shouted at you earlier. The thought of losing you terrifies me. There must be a way around this.'

'How?' I ask wearily.

'We're so good together. What if we don't split up?'

'But, I'm in love with ...'

'Michele, hear me out. We stay together, keep the family intact and you and Marizette can still see each other. Just think about it.'

Could this work, I wonder.

'If Marizette moves out, I'd let you see her twice a week, say. And I'll look after the children ...' his voice trails off.

'Peter, are you serious?'

'I don't want to lose you, Michele.' His eyes fill with tears again and he has to look away.

Now it's almost midnight. The children and Peter are in bed and Marizette and I are facing each other through the bathroom window. I presented Peter's ultimatum to Marizette when she returned home about an hour ago, but she won't even contemplate it.

'Michele,' she says, reaching through the burglar bars to take my hands, 'I could never do it. As much as I want you, I could never share you. If you want to be with me, then you have to leave Peter.'

'But, Mazzie, I have so little to offer you. The kids take up all my time, and Peter's accepted that because he's their dad. We're partners, raising the kids together,' I try to explain. 'Peter and I bought into that from the very beginning. But you're still young. You'll want lots of time alone with me, and for us to go out partying all night together, and I can't do that with …'

Marizette cuts in, 'Michi, do you want to be with me?'

'Yes, so much. But I'm married, I made vows …'

Marizette puts her finger to my lips and leans in for a kiss, which is rather awkward given the burglar bars.

The door bangs behind me and we leap apart. It's only the dog. My heart is racing; I thought it was Peter.

'Maz, you'd better go. I'll speak to you tomorrow.'

Chapter nineteen

To: sara@naturalnurture.co.uk
Subject: Peter's ultimatum
Dear Sara
What a day. It's two in the morning and I can't sleep. Had a horrible fight with Peter earlier, where he said Maz has to move out immediately if I want to be with her. He then did an about-turn and suggested a scenario where I could still stay married and see her on the side. The fact that I even considered this as a real option is a reflection on how crazy things are at the moment.

Of course, there's no way that it could work out long term, so now I have to speak to Maz tomorrow and tell her that if she still wants to be with me, then she has to move out immediately. My mom will come with me for moral support. Thank God for mothers.

Ian's sympathies definitely lie with Peter, which is hard as he's always been my rock. Mom says Ian feels responsible, because Maz and I got together at his place. He's also trying to be as supportive of Peter as possible.

My guilt is consuming me. I've always tried to behave so I'd never have to deal with guilt. I didn't give in to peer pressure at school; never spread malicious gossip. I don't hit my children. I've done all I can to build a comfortable home for my family. And now, despite never meaning to hurt anybody, my actions are causing so much pain. I'm having thoughts I haven't had since my late teens. I want to cut myself as a means of release for this overpowering guilt. I fight images of tearing myself to shreds; of walking into the road and being hit by an oncoming car.

And yet unbelievably, all this drama is doing nothing to diminish my desire for Marizette. I want her all the time. I never knew I could feel so strongly about anyone. I've always silently mocked friends who go on and on about how in love they are with their boyfriends (and you with Gael, to be honest). I thought it was childish and silly. And now here I am, my heart doing somersaults just thinking about Marizette. All the clichés – butterflies when she catches my eye and winks, legs turning to jelly if she brushes my skin, my head light and frothy. Just one touch and I'm instantly orgasmic.

I miss her terribly. It's driving me crazy being here in bed, alone, knowing she's so close by. But I'm dreading telling her about Peter's ultimatum. What if she decides to end the relationship? We've expressed our love but never talked about the future, or said we want to be together as a couple.

Either way I let someone down. If I leave Peter I'll be hurting my children and they'll never trust me again. I've always told them I'll never leave their dad, will never get a divorce. So by choosing to be with Marizette I will have lied. But when I made that promise to them I meant it.

Oh God, Sara, everything is moving so fast.

Anyway, enough for now. Thank you for being so understanding and non-judgmental. It helps so much being able to write to you. I must try to get some sleep.

I'm overtired and frazzled, but every night I struggle to fall asleep. Think I'll play some sudoku. Much love, Michi

◯

One, two, three, four, I mouth silently, climbing the stairs up to the flat where Marizette is waiting for us. There are fourteen steps in all. I know this because with my eyes, it's a way of orientating my self to avoid accidents. Thirteen, fourteen … I stand at the door, terrified of what I'm about to do. My mom comes up behind me. She's going to put Peter's ultimatum to Marizette. I can't bear to; I don't want to seem as though I'm throwing her out.

Marizette opens the door for us, looking pale and nervous. My mom and I follow her into the bedroom and sit on the bed, facing one another.

'Marizette,' my mom begins, her words slow and deliberate, 'Michele and Peter spoke yesterday. I'm going to get straight to it. If you want to be with Michele, then you need to move out for now and leave this job.' My mom pauses, 'But you need to do it today. If you two are going to be together it'll be unbearable for Peter to have you around, and at this point we can't just kick Peter out overnight,' she pauses again, giving Marizette the chance to respond. But Marizette remains silent, staring intensely at my mom.

'Nico says you can stay with him for the time being and I'll give you a month's pay to cover you while you look for another job. If, on the other hand, you want to carry on living here and working for Michele, then you two need to end your relationship.'

There's another pause, then Marizette exhales loudly and I realise she's hardly taken a breath in all the time my mom's been speaking.

'Is that it?' she asks, visibly relieved.

My mom nods, still looking serious.

Marizette jumps up off the bed, 'OK, I'm leaving. I'll start packing now. I'll find a different job.'

'Is this what you want?' I ask, standing up uncertainly. 'Does this mean we're going to be together?'

'Yes and yes,' she says, taking me in her arms.

I'm astounded, she wants to be with me! She's leaving her secure job and home overnight so we can be together.

'And you,' she asks, looking at me hopefully, 'do you want to be with me?'

I don't hesitate, 'Yes, I do.' I have no other choice. I can't face the possibility of making a life without her any more. I have to be with her. Which means I'll have to tell Peter our marriage is over. And then talk to the children. At this last thought, my stomach clenches with dread.

While Marizette and I hold each other tightly, my mom slips out, quietly closing the door behind her to give us some time alone.

'Oh Michi, I was so scared!' Marizette pulls me closer. 'I really thought you were going to tell me things were over.' Her relief is tangible.

'Never,' I say, breathing in the familiar scent of her skin. 'I could never be without you. I love you, Marizette, and I know it's crazy, but I want to be with you.'

'Michi, you do know we're going to have so much against us, right?' she pushes me away slightly so she can look at me.

'I know.' My mom's words come back to me: *You've*

got huge obstacles and challenges ahead of you; bigger than you can imagine. I meet Marizette's eyes, 'But I'm prepared to face anything to be with you.'

Chapter twenty

To: sara@naturalnurture.co.uk
Subject: I have a girlfriend!
Dear Sara

Marizette and I are officially a couple! I now have a girlfriend, which feels incredibly weird; like I'm playing a part. Maz has moved in with Nico, and we're all living in limbo, not sure who will live where. Peter's not doing well at all, and is losing weight frighteningly fast. He's still going in to work every day, saying he's got clients. When he gets home in the afternoons we've been doing a lot of talking in the garden. He's convinced I'm not gay, and that I'm having some kind of mid-life crisis. Or that it's an emotional reaction to the shock of Mom's cancer or the abuse coming up again.

We went to see my therapist together, but I don't find Karen particularly helpful or understanding. She thinks I'm 'self-sabotaging', whatever that means. When I told her I wanted to break up with Peter she said I needed to tell him directly, to his face. So I turned to him and said, 'Peter, I want to break up with you.' And as I spoke, it felt a knife plunging into my heart. Then he started crying and I started crying; even Karen looked like she was going to cry.

We're planning to speak to the kids this Friday when Peter gets back from work. Midweek isn't good timing. At least this way they'll have the weekend to try to process everything. They are very confused by Marizette's sudden and unexplained departure. Especially Max. He's taking it very badly and feels a bit abandoned, I think. Maz bought three fluffy toys (hippo for Max, elephant for Chloe and a rhino for Benjamin) and asked me to give them to the kids on the day she left. She wrote a note with each one saying: 'Please always remember that I love you.'

Spoke to a child psychologist today and she recommends telling the kids the truth from the start. But the truth is, I don't really want to break up with Peter, but I can't imagine being without Marizette. What's that saying about having your cake and eating it? Peter's so desperate he said if I ever change my mind, even if it's years down the line, then he'll be there for me. Which breaks me.

I'm dreading having to tell the kids. I really don't want to put them through all this. And I can't turn to Marizette for comfort as she's at Nico's, so I'm constantly filled with an unbearable longing. In a perfect world I could be with Marizette, somehow the kids' lives would carry on exactly as it is, and Peter and I would always be together. I want to keep the kids' world safe, to protect them. And I know it's still within my power to turn things around, but I don't feel like I have any power. This thing is stronger than me. Now that I've discovered this side of myself, it's grown too large to contain. I don't want to go back to feeling yucky ever again. God! Does that make me selfish? How can I sacrifice my children's well-being to feel OK in myself? Feel like I'm going crazy, with so many clashing thoughts and emotions.

Anyway, sorry for going on so much, but you're one person who really understands what I'm going through. I'm going to play sudoku; the only thing that gives me temporary calm. All my love, (a wretched) Michi

○

It's four in the afternoon. We are gathered on our giant bed; the heart of our family. One king-size bed with a single attached to create a big enough space for any of the children to join us if they wake up frightened or lonely. Peter and I are sitting side by side against the pillows, with Max and Chloe wedged between us. My mom is perched at the foot of the bed and Benjamin is playing with his Lego on the floor. I think back to the countless times we've all cuddled under the duvet for stories, breakfast in bed, videos and naps. All three children were born at home and each of them spent their very first night out in the world in this bed. It was the one item I insisted on shipping over from England. And it seemed the safest place to break such devastating news to them.

Peter's jaw is clenched and my mom's already a little teary, dabbing at her eyes and blowing her nose. I don't know where to begin.

Chloe's face is pinched with anxiety, and yet she is the one to break the ice. 'So, Mom', she says seriously, 'what do you want to talk to us about?'

'Well,' I begin, 'um …' Shit! How to put it … I've spent hours thinking of the exact phrasing and yet now in the moment I can't find the right words.

'You know how Dad and I have been fighting lately?' I begin slowly, and look to Peter. But he remains stonily silent, so I'm on my own. 'Well, there's a reason for it.'

I pause. Max and Chloe look at me expectantly. Benjamin carries on playing with his Lego, giving no sign he's even listening.

I take another deep breath. 'Well, you know Marizette?'

The kids look at me as though I'm stupid. 'Of course we know Marizette, duh,' Max says sarcastically.

This is going badly, it's all stilted and coming out wrong, but I plough on, 'Well, you know Marizette left suddenly this week?'

'Yes, Mom,' sighs Max, 'we know that too. I thought we were here to speak about you and Dad?'

'We are, but it's also about Marizette ...' my voice trails off.

'Mom, please,' says Max nervously. 'Just tell us what's going on.'

I take a deep breath and it all comes out in a rush. 'OK. I've fallen in love with Marizette. I love Daddy very much and I love you three more than you know, but I want to be with Marizette and that means not being with Daddy.'

Silence.

Then Max and Chloe look at each other and nod. Chloe takes Max's hand and pulls him off the bed, whispering in his ear.

'OK,' Max announces, 'children's conference. We're just going out for a bit. We'll be back.' And with that he and Chloe run out of the room, slamming the door behind them. My mom, Peter, Benjamin and I don't move. Horrible expectancy.

Suddenly, from the other side of the bedroom door,

we hear raucous, laughter, first Chloe, then Max joins in.

'Oh my God! She must be!' shrieks Chloe. More laughter.

'They don't seem that upset,' mutters Peter, disappointed.

'They're in shock,' my mom offers. 'It's a huge thing for them to process.'

The door opens and Max and Chloe come bounding back into the bedroom. Chloe speaks, putting her hand in front of her mouth, trying to stifle a laugh. 'Mom, does this mean you're a … lesbian?' She emphasises the word.

'Yes, Chloe,' I answer. 'I'm a lesbian.'

And it sounds so weird coming from me; words I could never have imagined using to describe myself. I repeat the phrase silently. *I'm a lesbian.* A few weeks ago I wasn't, but, hey, now I am. Everything is very surreal and comical all of a sudden. I feel a giggle rise in my throat, and although I know how inappropriate it is to start laughing at this point, I can't stifle it. Like my daughter before me, I put my hand over my mouth to keep it in.

Peter gives me a hard, disapproving look that suggests I'm not grasping the seriousness of the situation. 'I'm sorry,' he chokes, 'I just can't …' he hurriedly leaves the room, heading into the garden. Max follows him.

Chloe has curled up in my mom's arms. The laughter is gone now and her eyes are wide as saucers. Benjamin, still oblivious, is playing with his Lego.

I flee, locking myself into the children's bathroom. Everything is so absurd. I'm laughing and crying simultaneously. Hysterical now, I can't stop. I sound like a mad woman. Get a grip, I command myself, taking deep breaths, the children need you. I splash my face with cold water, sobered by the thought of my kids and how horribly confusing and painful this must be for them. Calmer, I am just about to go back to the bedroom when the words *I'm a lesbian* pop into my head again. I start laughing, first through my nose, and then out loud, as hot tears stream down my cheeks. That I seem unable to control this hysteria scares me, but I have no choice but to let it run its course.

By the time I finally bring my emotions under control and, subdued, return to the bedroom, only my mom and Benjamin are still there. Through the window, I can see Peter and the two older children sitting at the garden table down near the trampoline. They're howling, huddled together in shared grief. The group sobbing session is so poignant I'm filled with a dull ache that starts in the base of my tummy and rises up my chest to my throat, suffocating me. I have that same weird splitting sensation that I felt when I told Peter that I was in love with Marizette, and I couldn't bear to witness his sadness. It's like I'm stepping out of myself, leaving me oddly disconnected.

Suddenly I desperately want to, need to, see Marizette.

'Mom,' I say, 'I badly want to see Marizette. I need to get away, but I feel so guilty leaving the children after all this drama. I'm sure that they need me.'

My mom is practical, 'Michele, they probably need Peter more at the moment and I don't think he wants to be with you right now.' She touches my hand, 'You're going to have a lot to deal with for a long time, so go and take a breather. Let Marizette pick you up; I'll stay here with Peter and the kids. We can get a pizza and a video tonight.'

☾

Later that afternoon, Max is in the garden with Peter. My mom and Benjamin are watching TV, and Chloe and I are in the lounge, talking. Chloe's on the sofa, her arms are wrapped around her legs, which are tucked under her T-shirt. Hot tears spill unchecked down her cheeks and drip off her chin. She is crying silently, staring straight ahead with bloodshot eyes. I move over to her, placing my arm around her shoulder. She shifts away, but I persist, again trying to pull her into a hug.

'Mom, please. Don't,' Chloe sobs.

'I'm so sorry. I understand if you're angry with me.'

'It's not that,' she says, more tears overflowing. 'I just don't feel comfortable with you. I don't want you to touch me. I don't know who you are any more.'

This last bit comes out as a choke and she places head face down on her knees, sobbing quietly, shoulders shaking.

I picture Chloe as a five-year-old, running across the garden towards me, long hair flowing out behind her, blue eyes sparkling. Chloe launching herself at me, trusting me to catch her; then wrapping her arms and legs around my torso like a monkey, burying her face in my neck. Will she ever forgive me? Will our relationship survive? This is the price I'll have to pay. I start doubting my choices. I can still turn back; I can change things. No! I must be firm in my resolve. I've made up my mind. I knew this was coming. If I waver now and stay with

Peter, I could end up like Sara; unhappy, periodically falling in love with different women. Peter would always be suspicious. I'd be unfulfilled, resentful. Our marriage would become toxic and the resentment would bleed into the fabric of our family. No, I can't do that. I have to stay strong. I just have to.

Marizette has arrived and is waiting for me at the gate. I seek out the kids one by one to say goodbye. Max is on the computer.

'Goodbye, my darling,' I say, kissing him on the cheek. 'I'll see you tomorrow.'

'Whatever,' he doesn't look at me.

'Max, if you don't want me to leave, I'll stay.'

'Actually, I don't care. I don't want to see you anyway.'

I watch him a little longer but he refuses to look up from his game so I give up. Benjamin and Chloe are jumping on the trampoline.

'Bye guys!' I shout, waving at them.

Chloe yells back between jumps, 'Bye Mom, and don't worry! All this madness will come to an end. It won't be like this forever.'

She sounds far older than her eleven years, it's frightening.

Chapter twenty-one

'What would you like to drink?'

Marizette is sitting opposite me in Café Manhattan, a gay restaurant in Green Point. After she picked me up we went back to Nico's place, where she's staying for the moment. As she drove, I filled Marizette in on the afternoon's dramas.

'But please,' I begged, 'let's not talk about it any more. I need a break.'

'I know,' I brightened suddenly. 'Let's go on a date. We haven't been on one yet.'

'OK,' Marizette smiled. 'Where would you like to go?'

'I don't know. How about somewhere gay? Do you know of somewhere like that in Cape Town?'

'Yes, as a matter of fact I do,' said Marizette. 'I know just the place. Young lady, tonight I'm taking you on a date.'

I'm childishly excited: I'm going on a date with Marizette, to a gay restaurant! What a weird start to a relationship. We are officially together already, I'm leaving my husband and yet this will be our first date.

'I'll have some dry white wine,' I say, looking at Marizette. I haven't been able to take my eyes off her. She's so beautiful; her dark brown eyes twinkling in the candlelight. We've already made love at Nico's place. I tore off my clothes as soon as we stepped through the door; couldn't get enough of her. And now we are in this gay restaurant, as a couple, which is so surreal. It feels as though I've stepped into someone else's shoes and I'm playing out her part in a story. The story of a lesbian on a date with her girlfriend. My own story, with my part as wife and mother, ended too quickly, too unexpectedly and I'm struggling to catch up in this new situation.

But for now it's a relief to be here, away from traumatised children and a devastated husband. It's also great to be in a space where I can openly reach out and hold Marizette's hand without causing pointed looks and raised eyebrows.

'Michi,' Marizette says, holding her glass up to mine, 'I know it's been a hectic day, but this is our first date. Tonight, let's try to put everything to one side and just enjoy ourselves.' We toast each other, smiling.

○

After dinner it's on to Lush, as a couple this time. I'm ridiculously nervous. All of Marizette's friends know I was her boss and I've no idea how we'll be treated as an item. But Marizette is very keen to go out clubbing tonight.

'You're so beautiful,' she whispers in my ear as I stand in front of the mirror, applying my lipstick. 'I want to show you off.'

I'm flattered, having always thought she saw me as her 'old boss', I'm thrilled she isn't ashamed of me. However, my heart is still pounding and I feel about ready to throw up as we arrive at the club. Myrna is at the entrance, greeting guests by name as they arrive. She kisses me on the cheek, a welcome I'm grateful for, but hugs Marizette and whispers something in her ear.

'What did she say?' I interrogate Marizette, as we move through the crowd.

'She said Hilary's going to be here later and to be sensitive.'

Two hours and several drinks later, I'm on the dance floor with Marizette, in the middle of an over-exaggerated display of sexy dancing. Leaving very little to the imagination, I writhe up against her to the beat of the music, kissing her at every opportunity. The reason behind my behaviour is twofold. One is my very real attraction to Marizette, but the other, more pressing reason is Hilary, who's standing nearby, glancing in our direction every now and then. I wonder for a moment who this jealous, possessive woman is, and what happened to the sensitive person I've always believed myself to be. Marizette, unaware of my internal battles, is responsive to my dirty dancing, holding me close and kissing me passionately, a combination that makes me incredibly horny.

'Come on,' I whisper into her ear, 'let's go home.'

Once we're in the car I casually broach the subject of Hilary. 'So, were you alright with seeing Hilary?'

'Yeah, it's a bit sad she's so angry and isn't speaking to me.'

This, of course, is not what I want to hear. I don't want to know Marizette still has feelings for her ex-girlfriend, but before I can stop myself I speak up. 'Are you still sad about her then?' I ask, ignoring my instincts to leave the subject alone.

'Of course I am! We only broke up about three months ago.'

'Well,' I retort, 'I only broke up with Peter about … let's see, just over three days ago. And I was with him for over fifteen years. You were with Hilary for what?'

'Nearly three. I don't think you can compare your sadness to mine, Michi,' she says quietly, keeping her eyes on the dark road. 'I don't think you can undermine what I felt or feel for Hilary, or how painful the break-up was. Just because we weren't together for as long doesn't make it any less painful than your break-up with Peter.'

'How can you even compare the two?' I snap, shocked. 'You have no idea what breaking up a long marriage feels like. Not just the pain, but the guilt. And watching Peter and the children cracking up.'

Moments ago, we were moving sexily with each other at a nightclub, but now the atmosphere in the car is confrontational and heated. I'm overemotional and upset, and it looks like Marizette feels the same way.

She tries to make amends. 'I'm just saying it's relative. I'm a lot younger than you, so for me, three years is a long time.'

'Well, I'm just saying you don't know anything,' I say staring out of the window away from her.

'Just tell me, Michele, exactly how long have we been together?'

'I don't know. We kissed about three weeks ago.'

'And how upset would you be if we were to split up now?'

OK, clever little shit, but I'm still not going to bow down to that wisdom, I think stubbornly.

'So, come on,' she presses.

'Yes, Marizette, I would be devastated. But that's because I'm madly, crazy in love with you. So? What are you saying? Are you saying that you were madly in love with Hilary when the two of you split up, because that's not what you told me,' I say accusingly. 'You told me it was by mutual agreement, and you weren't in love any more.'

I realise I'm working myself into a state, but I can't help it. The atmosphere between us crackles with anger.

Suddenly Marizette pulls over and turns off the engine. 'I'm just saying it was also painful, OK?' She gets out the car.

We're back at Nico's. I am so lost in my anger I didn't realise where we were. I get out and slam the car door. What am I becoming? Who is this confrontational woman? I've always done my best to avoid an argument, not fuel one. And I realise that irrationally, a part of me is furious at Marizette for coming into my life and making me fall in love with her.

Out on the balcony of Nico's flat, Marizette is smoking a cigarette. I'm sitting apart from her and we're both visibly upset.

Marizette sighs and reaches over to squeeze my hand. 'I'm sorry, Michi,' she says. 'I don't want us to fight.' Tears start welling up in her eyes. 'I just find all this very difficult. Being with you goes against everything I believe in. I would never choose to break up a marriage, especially where children are involved. I was raised to view marriage and family as sacred,' Marizette starts crying openly.

I shift closer and put my arm around her shaking shoulders. It's a warm evening and the seagulls are squawking nearby. Thankfully, Nico is still out and we're alone at the flat. For the first time it occurs to me how much my split with Peter has been weighing on Marizette's conscience. I've been so caught up in my own feelings of guilt and grief and shock that I haven't even thought about the impact all of this would have on her. We are two women, trying to deal with extraordinary circumstances, and already we're both highly emotional. Will our relationship survive?

One of the things I've always valued is the peace and ease of my marriage to Peter. Now on my first official date with Marizette we've had an evening charged with a volatile mix of emotions, and I don't know if I can cope with it all. We're both emotionally drained. What the fuck am I doing?

Subconsciously sensing my doubt, Marizette reaches over and touches my face. Ever so gently, she kisses my cheek, then my neck, and then my lips. All my uncertainties dissolve, replaced by the desperate physical longing I feel whenever Marizette touches me. It's so powerful that I just know, with cast-iron certainty, that whatever adversity is ahead, I will overcome it rather than have to live without this woman.

○

Later, I lie naked on the bed, as waves of ecstasy wash over me, filling my entire body with warmth and joy. An equally naked Marizette is lying on her stomach, her head between my legs, her tongue working its magic on me. And my God she's good, I think dreamily; unbelievably so. She knows exactly what to do, almost as if the tip of her tongue is reading my ever-swelling clitoris. I begin groaning and then gasp as Marizette slides her fingers into me, expertly building up a rhythm and flicking her tongue over my clitoris at the same time.

I love the way she handles me. I am in heaven: the contractions in my vagina; the surging heat rising into my chest and my face; the tingling of my lips; the tears gathering behind my eyes. Most of all, I'm filled with wonder that it's Marizette who makes me feel this way. The same Marizette I've wanted for so long. Never in all my wildest imaginings did I think this scene would become reality. I am powerless to resist her and am willingly rendered her slave.

○

The following evening the kids and I are in the video shop in Hout Bay, while my mom waits in the car. The store is full of families choosing DVDs for the weekend. Nice, normal families, I think. I recognise a few and say hello. Hout Bay is small and it doesn't take long before you're on greeting terms with most people. If only they knew, I think … Actually, rather not. Not yet, anyway.

'Mom, can I choose a DVD of my own?' Chloe pleads.

I was up for most of the night making love to Marizette, and being desperately tired, my resistance is low. 'Yes, love. You can each choose your own movie.'

Normally, we'll only get DVDs out once a week, but in such desperate times I've given in and allowed them to hire movies two nights in a row. Finally they make their selections. I pay and we're about to leave, when Max decides to look at some PlayStation games.

'Come on, Max,' I urge, 'we need to get home.'

'Don't you tell me what to do!' he suddenly screams. 'You … you woman being a lesbian with the au pair!'

Mortified, I have no idea how to respond and I can feel the heat rush to my face as several people turn to stare at the commotion. I turn on my heel and head for the car. 'Mom,' I say, climbing in and sliding down as far as I can in the front seat, 'don't ask any questions and I'll explain later. But can you please, please go get the kids from the video store?'

She can't help laughing when I relay the story to her later. 'Well,' she smiles, 'that's one way of letting people know what's going on.'

Now it's after midnight again and I'm still awake. Lying on the bed, I'm reading through Marizette's letter to me for the second time. She pressed the folded page into my hand before dropping me back at home earlier.

To Michele, my darling angel, my queen,
I know the past few weeks haven't been easy for you, and that you've had to endure so much. I've been volatile towards you at times and not the most understanding person in the world. What I'm going through is probably the hardest time I've experienced in my whole life, and trust me, I've had some hard times. I fended for myself for the past six years and there were times I couldn't feed myself and had to rely on friends to lend me money for rent.

When I get angry and frustrated it's only because of the guilt I feel and the fact that I struggle to forgive myself for breaking up your family. As much as I would like to just walk away and never turn back, I can't. I can't turn my back on what I feel for you. I never thought I'd have someone love me the way you do. It's so surprising someone loves me for me and for being the person I am.

It may sound stupid, but after my parents cut me off I was so broken it was easy to believe I'd ruined everyone's hopes and dreams and that my family wouldn't love me any more. I never thought I'd heal from that until I met you. You've helped me believe in myself and you've given me hope.

I want to be so good to you; make you feel special and fulfil your every desire. I'm in love with you, and I promise to try my best to support you and love you the way you deserve to be loved. I hope your three beautiful children will forgive me and love me and accept me in their lives.

Please understand I don't always know how to control what I feel and it's normal for us to have bad days and good days. I only want what's best for you. If that means you feel you've made a mistake and want your life back, then even though I'll be heartbroken, I'll leave.

Sorry this letter doesn't make sense. I'm just writing to get everything out. I love you and want you so very much. All my love, Mazzie xxxxxxxxxxx

PS: Meet me in my dreams tonight.

I fold the letter and place it beside my bed, filled with tenderness for Marizette. I'm so caught up in how raw I feel that I forget how stressful everything is for her. I switch off the bedside light, vowing silently to be more understanding.

Chapter twenty-two

To: sara@naturalnurture.co.uk
Subject: Roller coaster emotions: round 2
Dear Sara

Our household is in a very weird transition phase. Right now, I'm not sure what the outcome will be, who will live where. For the time being, the kids and I are all camped out in Max's room together, while Peter has the main bedroom. I feel too guilty to chase him out of our room. It's been two weeks since I told him about Marizette and it has been an unbelievably eventful roller coaster of a time.

I've booked the kids to see a child psychologist who will work with me, guiding me in how to handle them. They're each dealing with things differently. Max is outraged and upset. He feels especially betrayed by Marizette, whom he loved. He's kept the hippo toy she gave him, but it's been launched against the wall several times. While he was on the computer yesterday (the hippo next to the mouse pad), I asked him how he felt about Marizette. Without looking at me he said: 'Well, I'll hate her with a passionate hatred for as long as she lives, which won't be long because she's going to kill herself smoking.' He empathises with his father to a huge degree and feels sorry for him.

Chloe's hanging on in the hope Peter and I will get back together. He bought me flowers when he went shopping the other day, and from the expectant look on her face when he handed them to me, I know it was her idea. A few days later, Peter and I were chatting in the kitchen, saying how we would always be friends, no matter what. He started to cry and I reached over to hold him, at which point Chloe walked in. Her face was radiant when she saw the two of us hugging. She gave Peter an excited thumbs up, which just broke my heart.

And then Benjamin. I don't think he really grasps any of what's going on. Chloe watched him playing the other day and remarked how pleased she was that Benjamin is too young to understand any of this. I don't know how long his youth and ignorance will protect him, though. The truth will come crashing down eventually.

Oh Sara, as much as I want Marizette, I can't believe I'm capable of hurting my kids. And the worst part is I know we're still at a stage where I could turn around and stay with Peter, and we could go back to being a family again. But there will come a point when that's too late.

My dad has arrived and you have no idea how awkward this is for me. You know what he's like; remember Graeme saying my dad scared the shit out of him? The funny thing is I don't remember my dad ever hitting me, but he's such an imposing man. In fairness, he's a total softy underneath, very compassionate. I've never worked out what it is about him that demands respect. He's always managed to be authoritarian without being violent, and although he'd probably deny it, I would say he's a bit of a patriarch.

So of course it's extremely frustrating for him that he

can't 'sort things out', which is exactly what he planned to do when he rushed back here from England. When my dad puts his mind to something, he usually achieves it. Now he wants a meeting with me and Maz. Oh, the dread! I won't blame Marizette if she runs for the hills. I look forward to things settling down, but right now it feels like they never will. Love you lots, Michi

○

Supper time. Usually the evening meal is a chatty and cheerful affair, where we're almost always joined by my parents and/or Ian. Sometimes the whole extended family thing can be a bit overwhelming, but mostly I enjoy it.

Right now, however, I'm not enjoying it. I have a huge knot in my stomach and an almighty lump in my throat. I feel as though I can't swallow; no wonder I'm losing weight. Peter and the children are subdued and my father and brother are glaring at me from the other side of the table. I'm not imagining it; disapproval is emanating from every fibre of their bodies. My dad has pointedly ignored me since he arrived. Well, not really ignored, because he glares at me at every opportunity. The tension is almost unbearable; I'm dealing with enough as it is. Most people have the luxury of conducting their break-ups without a disapproving parent living on the property.

I look down at my plate. In ten seconds' time I'm going to look up and see if they're still glaring at me. One, two, three ... nine and ten. I look up. One set of green and one set of blue eyes bore into me.

Something snaps. I can't take it any more. I shove back my chair, 'I'm done. Max and Chloe, can you put your plates in the sink once you're finished eating. Mom, please help Benjamin when he's done.'

And with that, I'm gone.

In the bedroom I throw myself on to my bed, grab my phone and dial Marizette's number.

She answers almost immediately, 'Hey, my angel.'

'Marizette, I don't know how I'm going survive. Dad and Ian are bad-vibing me the whole time. I'm going crazy!'

Her voice in my ear is soothing. 'Come on, we're going to see each other tomorrow night when your mom babysits. Just get through the next twenty-four hours.'

'I don't know if I can. I honestly don't.'

'Hey, Michi, come on. You're going to be alright. We'll get through this together.'

'My dad hates me,' I mutter.

'No, he doesn't. He might hate me at the moment, but he'll never hate you.'

'He does. I know he'll never come around,' I say sulkily.

Marizette sighs. 'I don't know if he'll come around, but I know he'll always love you.' She changes tack, 'Now just picture my mouth on that beautiful vagina of yours …'

Immediately said vagina gathers moisture. I can't believe how Marizette turns me on to such a degree that it penetrates all my stress and grief. And it's so damn frustrating that my sexual awakening and the whole honeymoon period of our relationship (which I know instinctively will never be quite as intense again) is so tainted by stress and anxiety.

That night I'm lying on the mattress on Max's bedroom floor. The kids are fast asleep and although I'm exhausted, I'm too restless to sleep. I reach over to grab my cellphone and begin texting: *Looking forward to kissing your body all over, then slipping my fingers into your smooth vagina. xxx*

I hit the send button. Seconds later my phone beeps with a response: *I can't wait to suck those fingers one by one.*

I smile to myself in the dark and text back: *Oh God, you're getting me all horny. Now what am I meant to do???*

Phone beeps: *Till tomorrow. Love you. Love you. Love you. Your Marizette xxxxx*

Further from sleep than ever, I put my phone on the floor and pick up my sudoku book.

Chapter twenty-three

To: sara@naturalnurture.co.uk
Subject: Sudoku queen and other stories
Dear Sara
Damn, I'm becoming good at sudoku! I've moved onto Fiendish now. I love the fact that it takes my mind off things. All I have to do is eliminate numbers.

It's been a few weeks since I got together with Marizette and things are still surreal. It's strange and wonderful and unbearably stressful all at the same time. Pretty much all our close friends know by now. I decided to be as open as possible about the whole story. In fact, to avoid confusion and gossip, I wrote a letter to all my family members and friends explaining the full story. It also means I don't have to repeat myself over and over again.

I've also met with Chloe and Benjamin's teachers to let them know what's happening. It was actually Chloe's idea. She wants her teacher to know what's going on so he knows why she may be upset at school, and for support if anyone teases her about her mother being a lesbian. Both teachers were amazing. Neither passed judgment (not to me anyway), and both said their priority was to be there for the kids. I'm extremely grateful.

So much has happened over the last two weeks it's

hard to know where to begin. I'll start with Peter. He's lost a huge amount of weight in a very short space of time. He could afford to lose a few kilos and everyone says how good he looks, but I know there's nothing healthy about it. He is devastated. And the worst thing is there's nothing I can do to comfort him. When I went to the toilet earlier I could hear him crying again. It took so much to stop myself from going to him. He's already asked me to stop apologising and wants no physical comfort from me (no hugs or shoulder squeezes) at all, unless I want him back. He says it's too difficult otherwise.

The two of us went to see the child psychologist a few days ago to discuss damage control for the kids. She wants to see the kids individually, but asked to see Peter and me together first. When the therapist asked about our plans for future living arrangements, Peter broke down and started crying and didn't seem able to stop. He just kept sobbing, 'You told me you loved me. You said we'd always be together. You promised me …'

Thankfully the woman was very practical and just passed him tissue after tissue. With his skinny frame and swollen red eyes, underlined with black rings, I saw Little Peter. A lost boy I want to pick up in my arms and soothe. Let him bury his head in my chest. The problem is there are no ways of comforting him; I just have to watch him crumble before my eyes.

My dad is still heavily disapproving of us. He empathises with Peter to such a degree that my mom says it's almost as though he's going through the break-up. I told my dad not to bother joining us for supper if he's going to glare at me the whole way through the meal, because my nerves can't take it. So he's said he'll eat alone for now, as he can't promise not to.

Anyway, I'll have a break from it all soon as we're going away. A bad idea maybe, but Peter and the kids and I are going on a family holiday next week. I've thought and thought about it and eventually decided to go. We booked it a year ago and the kids have been looking forward to it for ages. The Group is also going to be there, so our kids are looking forward to spending time with their friends.

Of course, Marizette is less than happy with things, but I'm going anyway. It'll be our last holiday together as a family. In fact, it will be our last time together as a family full stop, as Peter is moving out as soon as we get home (his decision). He's going to stay at a flat in Sea Point. What can I say? It's so sad. Much love, Michi.

○

'I spy with my little eye something beginning with ... T,' says Chloe in a singsong voice.

'I know,' Max pipes up, 'it's tree.'

'No,' she says smugly.

'Tyre?'

'Nope.'

'OK, I give up. What is it?'

Chloe is triumphant, 'Treetops!'

'That's cheating!' shouts Max. 'I think I should get that one.'

'No you don't!' Chloe yells back.

I sense a full-scale war brewing in the back seat of the car and quickly intervene. 'OK, Max, you can have that one. Now your turn.'

The Au Pair

We are on our way to De Hoop Nature Reserve, with all the ingredients for a perfect family holiday: a mom and dad; three kids strapped in the back, mostly behaving themselves; promising weather and breathtaking scenery. I've made Peter his usual flask of coffee for the drive and despite the view and the promise of the upcoming break, we all know it's our last family holiday together. And my own role in the course of events leaves me feeling impossibly sad.

Marizette is understandably unhappy about us going away together as a family. But the children have been so looking forward to this holiday that I couldn't bear to cancel our plans, especially with the recent upheavals in their lives. Maybe I'm doing the wrong thing, but Peter and I aren't even sharing a room at De Hoop. Marizette is unconvinced.

'Maz,' I pointed out, 'right now Peter and I are sleeping in different rooms in the same house back home in Hout Bay. This will be no different.'

'What if your friends persuade you to go back to him?' she complained. 'What if you have such a good time with him that you decide to leave me?'

I've given her all the assurance I can, but she's still not happy.

'I promise I'll phone you all the time,' I said when I kissed her goodbye.

○

That evening all the adults have gathered around the fire after dinner. The children are off playing and the sounds of their laughter echo in the clear night air.

'So, Michele, you're looking as sexy as ever. Man, what a bummer! I was hanging on for the day when you and me, you know,' Stan says suggestively, pressing up against me.

I laugh, putting my arms around him. I'm so grateful he's being his normal, lecherous self.

Sipping on the last of our wine, we're sitting companionably around the fire, a carpet of stars sparkling above us. It's been a glorious day. We went to the beach, en masse, spreading out on multicoloured blankets, with various picnic food, and buckets and spades for the children. We were the only people on that particular beach and could clearly see the whales frolicking in the calm ocean.

Chloe and Tessa, Patricia's daughter, went for a long walk together, which pleased me as she's been very withdrawn. Patricia, Anna, Brandy and I were settled on the sand in the sun, side by side, while the men, too restless to merely sit, went off exploring the seaside caves with the younger children.

Chloe returned from her walk a bit more upbeat. 'I told Tessa about you and Marizette,' she announced, flopping down beside me.

'Oh yeah? And what did she say?' I enquired.

'She says her aunty is gay.'

I turned to Patricia, 'Really? How come you've never told me?'

Patricia rolled her eyes, 'Well, there's never been any reason to. I mean you don't say: "Oh by the way, I've got a gay sister," you know?'

Indeed, but I could tell Chloe was pleased with the news.

Later, when the children are fast asleep and the adults have turned in for the night, Peter and I are sitting at the dying embers of the fire.

He lights up a cigarette, 'Michele, is this really what you want?'

'I want to be with Marizette,' I reply with certainty.

'Well, I think you're making a big mistake; the biggest mistake of your life. We're so good together, but you have no idea what things are going to be like with Marizette. She's not an easy person, I can tell you that now. And you're so in love with her you don't care at the moment, but you'll regret it one day.'

'Peter,' I reply, 'I know what you're saying is probably true. I have absolutely no idea what Marizette will be like as a partner. I know I'm being crazy, but I can't let a chance to be with her go; I just can't.'

Peter starts crying again and quickly wipes his tears away. Helplessly I take his hands in mine.

'Michele, just know, that if you change your mind, even if it's in many years' time, I'll always have you back.'

I laugh sadly, 'Peter, in a few years you'll have moved on, I promise you. You'll probably have a girlfriend, someone who can give you proper loving. The love you deserve.'

'Don't turn this into what I need, Michele. I want to be with you forever. I take my vows seriously.'

This comes as a blow. I've always believed nothing could make me break my marriage vows.

'Anyway,' Peter continues piously, 'I'm going to become a celibate monk, for at least ten years.'

I snort at this. 'That's how you feel now. One day I'll remind you that you said this.'

Chapter twenty-four

To: sara@naturalnurture.co.uk
Subject: De Hoop, The Last Family Holiday
Dear Sara
It's so peaceful here; beautifully untouched. Craggy mountains and cliffs bordering the sea, tiny hidden beaches, and enough flat land for the kids to race around on their bikes (which they are doing now, whooping and yelling to one another as the sun sets). Spring is my favourite time of the year. The ground is covered in an explosion of colourful wild flowers, wildlife everywhere, from buck to baboons, rare birds and lots of whales. There's a sense of renewal and hope, and every creature seems to be having babies.

Yet our own family is going through a far more painful rebirth. Here we are on this lovely family holiday, but when we go back home, Peter is moving out. That knowledge hangs over me; fills me with wretchedness, and I walk around with a lump in my throat that just won't budge. It feels so right being here with Peter and the kids. Mere months ago, filled with irrepressible, childish enthusiasm, I was so looking forward to this holiday. I would never have guessed it would fall on the cusp of my marriage splitting. Now I don't want it to end, I want to stay with Peter and be a family. I even miss sleeping next to him.

But at the same time I miss Maz like crazy. She's on my mind all the time – her face, her beautiful hands, how she touches me. I reel with mixed feelings. Part of me wants things to go back to normal, but the other half of me has tasted Marizette's love and now it's physically impossible to pretend I'm satisfied with the way my life was before she came into it. So I'm lost in a kind of madness: grieving for Peter; longing for Marizette. I actually don't know what the fuck I'm doing.

It's so peaceful out here in the middle of nowhere that it's difficult to believe there's turmoil at the core of our family. Or that we'll only be 'a family' for the time being. Peter told the children at breakfast this morning he'll be moving out when we get back. I didn't discuss it with him, although the current living arrangements aren't sustainable. I hoped he'd move into the cottage (Ian agreed to move out), and got quite excited by the idea. Peter would be near enough for the children to pop over whenever they wanted, I could still look after the cooking and laundry for him, and he could continue to tend to his beloved vegetable garden. He was considering it quite seriously, but immediately dismissed the idea when I couldn't promise that Marizette wouldn't move in with me. 'I don't want to see her on the property,' he spat.

Anyway, I must go. I want to phone Maz before Peter comes in with the kids. It's such a sensitive balancing act. She doesn't understand why I can't phone her all the time because we're not having an affair, and as my girlfriend she should be my priority. She says I hide her like some kind of sordid secret. But if Peter sees me talking to her he freaks out, telling me I don't care about the family and I'm highly insensitive, etc.

But bugger me, it's hard to make a switch like that overnight. Peter and I may be splitting up but I can't stop caring about him and loving him. So really, it's easier just to sneak-call her at every opportunity.

Hope all is well with you guys. Sorry to be so self-absorbed right now. All my love, Michi

◯

The trip home passes in silence, with no singing or games or merriment. We all know that Peter is moving out when we get home, and the gallows atmosphere in the car is almost unbearable. Personally, I think Peter's being a little insensitive in how he's addressing the decision to move out, but when I raised it with him last night, he exploded.

'I'm being insensitive? Ha! That's rich coming from you. Have you given the kids any thought at all? How sensitive have you been, Michele? Just remember, any suffering they go through is thanks to you, not me. This is your choice, not mine.'

I persisted, 'I just think it's very sudden and you haven't really prepared them.'

'Oh, like you prepared them for the bombshell that you're running off with their au pair?' he snapped back, his words loaded with sarcasm.

I turn around and look at the children seated silently on the back seat, staring out at the mountains, as they rush past in a blur, lost in thought. My insides constrict with guilt. I so badly want to make things right for them. And I can still do it; all I need to say is, 'Peter, I've

The Au Pair

changed my mind. Please stay. I can't bear to do this.' But then I'll have to tell Marizette it's over, and as much as I want to make things OK for my family, I can't do this. I have missed her so much. I can't wait to see her and the thought of being without her permanently is unbearable.

The bizarre thing is I'm not only sad for Peter and the children, I'm also sad for myself. Horribly, wretchedly sad. I can't believe I'm causing myself this amount of pain. I follow the children's lead and shut down for a while, watch the scenery rushing past. And every minute that passes draws us closer to the inevitable.

☾

To: sara@naturalnurture.co.uk
Subject: Peter moves out
Dear Sara
It's two in the morning again and I can't sleep. I'm still reeling from the shock of Peter moving out, which turned out to be extremely dramatic and traumatic for all of us. I think he played the whole thing up to make me feel as guilty as possible, so I could see all the damage I was doing to the kids. We arrived back in Hout Bay by nightfall and he started the emotional build-up at least ten minutes before we reached home.

    Peter: So guys, I'm moving out when we get home. I'm going to live in Sea Point.

    Chloe: Can't you stay and live with us?

    Peter: No, this is your mom's choice.

    Max: Can't you stay for a little bit when we get home?

    Peter: No, this is your mom's choice.

    Benjamin: Can I come and stay with you in Sea Point?

Peter: No, this is your mom's choice.

I wanted to scream at him to shut the fuck up about it being my choice. I'm not kicking him out; he's choosing to leave. But I was too emotionally wiped out to argue or explain that there were other options. And in the end, are there any other viable options? Is there an easier way of dealing with a break-up? Or any way to soften the blow to your children that their father is moving out?

Either way, I was totally unprepared for the children's raging grief when Peter did actually leave. When we arrived home, Peter helped carry all the bags from the car. Depositing them at the front door, he refused to cross the threshold, and dramatically announced, 'OK, children. It's time. I love you, now I must leave.' Everything was suddenly loud and chaotic. The dogs rushed to greet us, excitedly jumping up at Peter. The kids surged around him to say their goodbyes, tripping over bags and toys and holiday paraphernalia in the doorway.

Peter started crying when he said goodbye to Max and Chloe, but Benjamin refused to let go. Hysterical, he clung to Peter, his head buried into his father's shoulder, his arms locked around his neck and his legs wrapped around Peter's body, holding on with all his might. I begged Peter to stay and let Benjamin calm down but he was so hostile. This was all my fault and I could deal with it. So I had to disentangle a stubborn and struggling Benjamin from his father, prising his fingers one by one from Peter's jersey. Of course this forced extraction made matters worse and Benjamin threw his head back, roaring, with his mouth wide open, angry tears spurting from his eyes. Peter just turned on his heel and screeched off in the car, leaving me in the doorway with three sobbing children, and the mantra 'this is all my fault, this is all my fault' going round and round in my head.

My mom must have heard the commotion from somewhere on the property, because thankfully she arrived, seemingly from out of nowhere, and took a still-fighting and sobbing Benjamin from me.

Again, the most crushing thing is the overwhelming guilt eating away at me, and the sadness, so much sadness. Not just my own, but sadness for Peter and sadness for the kids. In spite of how angry I am with Peter for the way in which he left, I'm desperately worried about him living on his own, away from the heart of the family.

Shit, I must go to sleep. I wish that I could sleep and sleep and wake up when things are calm and more settled. I'm over-tired, over-sad, over-guilty and missing Marizette like crazy. I'm even too tired to play sudoku. Will write again soon. Love, Michele

Chapter twenty-five

'Hello, hello. This is a nice surprise,' says Marizette as I take her hand and slip it under my skirt. 'No panties, very nice.'

We're in her car outside the gates of the house on the dust road known as Mountain View Close, fuelling, I heard earlier today, a grapevine of gossip among the neighbourhood nannies.

It's just after five, home time for all the casual staff in the area. Nannies file past in twos and threes, talking animatedly, gardeners pass silently, and the woman from next door who runs a riding school rides past with a group of about six pupils, no doubt heading back to the stables. I barely notice her herding the children along as they pass our car.

The awkwardness of the gear stick between us doesn't hamper our passions one bit. And I don't care what people think. I'm so hot for Marizette right now I wouldn't care if people were standing at the window with cameras. I have, however, placed a picnic rug discretely across our laps.

After consulting the children's psychologist, Marizette and I have agreed to let the kids get used to the fact we're a couple, but to take things one step at a time.

The Au Pair

This means giving them six weeks before Marizette comes back on the property. Which is fine in theory, but in practice, with two people as crazy in love as we are, it's a nightmare. I'm hugely impressed by Marizette's commitment, though. She wants to see me every day, which means driving from work all the way to see me in Hout Bay, for what amounts to no more than half an hour, then driving all the way back to Sea Point again.

Now, like a couple of teenagers, we've been kissing up a storm and Marizette is delighted with my little surprise of missing panties.

'Oh God! You're so wet already,' she mutters, slipping her fingers into me.

'That's because you're near me,' I gasp in between kisses. And it's true. I need only think about Marizette and moisture gathers between my legs.

Marizette begins moving her fingers, not an easy task given the angle she's sitting at, and the awkward gear stick between us.

'Here, I'll take over,' I offer, slipping my hand under the blanket and sliding my fingers over my clitoris.

Marizette sits back and watches me, her lips shaking.

'Are you alright?' I ask.

'Oh yes, this is just the effect that you have on me. You literally make me tremble.'

I slide my fingers over and around my swollen clitoris, all the while looking into Marizette's sparkling brown eyes. I come so quickly I shock myself. I struggle to not scream and buck. My breathing quickens and the waves of orgasm explode from my clitoris into my belly right up into my neck and face, which I can feel reddening.

'Oh fuck, you're so fucking beautiful!' says Marizette,

leaning over to kiss me. Her kisses fill me with warmth and joy, and my whole body buzzes with post-orgasmic pleasure. We finally come apart and it's time for our goodbyes.

'I'll see you tomorrow,' she says as I gather myself, opening the door to leave.

'Same time, same place,' I reply.

'I can't wait, my love.'

I wander into the kitchen, lost in the waves of pleasure still spreading through my body after my dalliance in the car with Marizette. Lebo is sitting at the table, waiting for me. She looks uncomfortable.

'Michi,' she begins, 'what's going on with you and Marizette?' Before I can formulate a response she continues, 'Because the woman next door, she is very nosy and she says that you and Marizette are together. And all the workers, they know about this. I said to them I don't know; it is nobody's business. But, Michi, you are a sister to me. Tell me what is going on.'

I take a deep breath and tell her the whole story.

Throughout, Lebo shakes her head solemnly, and when I'm done, she adds: 'Michi, this is too sad. I am feeling very sad for Peter.'

Tell me about it, I think wryly. But right now I'm far more interested in the news that we're the subject of neighbourhood gossip. I'm dying to know what the nannies are saying. I beg Lebo to give me the details and after much persuasion she reluctantly agrees.

Apparently, the two-hour trip in a packed taxi from Hout Bay to Khayelitsha is the platform for the gossip. And it seems my relationship with Marizette has been the hot topic for the last few weeks, causing heated debate among the passengers. Initially I thought the comments would be amusing, but most of what Lebo told me is chilling and frightening.

Sadly, homophobia is present throughout every cross-section of society in South Africa, which as a whole is largely patriarchal. Unfortunately, there are many people who believe homosexuality is a disease that can be cured with the right treatment (or punishment) and Lebo's neighbours are no different. She says the men she travels with every day are unanimous in their belief that both Maz and I deserve to be punished for our actions, saying things like, 'If I was the husband, I would beat them both. By not doing this, her husband is being weak.' Or: 'They should both be raped, then they would see what it is to be with a real man and they will stop being lesbians.' For the women's part, they don't believe violence is necessary, but that in talking to me, Peter will be able to convince me that my actions are wrong.

The point is that nothing will stop me feeling the way I do about Marizette. I'm crazy about her. Of course, I've asked myself over and over again how it's possible at such a relatively late stage of my life to discover I'm a lesbian. And I don't have the answer to that. I can't deny I've felt sexually attracted to some men (especially Noel) and I know that I wasn't being deliberately deceitful about my sexuality when I married Peter. There were many telltale signs, but they were scattered across my adult sexual terrain. It's only now that those experiences (getting off with my brother's girlfriend, having a crush on my school friend) gravitate to the surface and gain power. And again I think: how could I not have known?

Chapter twenty-six

To: sara@naturalnurture.co.uk
Subject: Confessions and more guilt
Dear Sara
I made Marizette speak to her parents. She was extremely reluctant. Said they wouldn't be impressed. I insisted, saying I had to tell all my family and friends, not to mention the kids' teachers, that we're serious and am not happy to be kept as a secret. Anyway, Marizette finally plucked up the courage to phone them and her mom completely freaked. Said she had always thought Marizette couldn't shock her more than she did when she 'fessed up to being gay five years ago, but this was even more shocking. To be fair, your daughter running off with her married boss would shock most parents, so I do understand.

Talking of parents, Peter's mom is arriving soon and she's spitting mad at me. Don't blame her; actually very pleased she's coming to be with Peter at this time. She'll also be here for Max's birthday. I still want to have a party for him. We've always held a Halloween party for him, do you remember? And now it's become an annual event all our friends look forward to. But how do I go about it? There has been so much drama surrounding it:

The Au Pair

Marizette isn't meant to be on the property; Peter won't come if she's there and Max desperately wants his dad at the party. In the end I decided to go ahead with the party (without Maz) and Peter will come with his mom. I know Marizette feels terribly left out and Peter and his mom will feel awkward, but we've decided to put our differences to one side for the party, for Max's sake.

Poor Max is desperately miserable and angry at the moment. He competed in a judo match over the weekend. Peter and I took him – another thing arranged pre break-up. He's always been so keen at judo, but halfway through his first fight, Peter and I could see he lost the will to go on. He kind of went floppy, and was beaten in a hold down. He came off the mat tearfully and said, 'I want to go home. None of this matters any more.' Then as we approached the car, he turned to me and said, 'Mom, through any of this did you even once think of me and Chloe and Benjamin?'

Oh Sara, the pain! I can't tell you enough. Especially when all I've thought about over the last thirteen years has been my children and their well-being. And what could I say: 'Actually, Max, of course I've thought about you guys, and I know how much you're all hurting, but hey, I've decided to leave your dad anyway'? My guilt is so extreme at times that I hate myself. But on the other hand, since I've been with Marizette, I don't feel the deep, horrible shame coursing through my veins that I've lived with my whole life till now. It's as though being with her has cleansed me of that yucky feeling I reluctantly came to accept as part of me. And living without it is such a relief. So one awful emotion replaced by another – consuming guilt.

Would love to come to England for Halloween. It always seems weird doing trick or treat with the kids in broad daylight! Miss you lots, love Michi

PS: Our housekeeper, Lebo, who has been with us for years has left us and is working at the MediSpa. I think it was too weird for her to work for Maz and me after her and Maz both worked for me and Peter. We have a new cleaning lady called Princess.

○

Max's birthday party. The house and much of the garden is festooned with all the Halloween paraphernalia we've built up over many years. Walls are adorned with pictures of witches and haunted rooms. Spider webs hang in the corners; tables are decorated with pumpkins. Fake skeletons and plastic spiders dangle from the ceilings. As is compulsory, everyone is dressed up. Witches, ghosts and all variety of scary characters wander around the garden. It's a formula we've followed successfully year after year: a bonfire after nightfall, fire dancing from Max, a disco and even a karaoke. This year, however, there's a tangible awkwardness among our guests, less party cheer than usual.

The bonfire is going strong. People are standing around in small groups; smoking, drinking and chatting, while the children dash around the garden or jump on the trampoline, ignoring the no-more-than-two-at-a-time rule. The karaoke guy is setting up in the lounge.

Everyone has managed to be polite and pleasant so far, although Peter's mother is studiously ignoring me. Thank God for the endless bottles of wine! I go to the kitchen to get myself another glass. Peter is there before me, doing the same. I grab a glass and hold it out for him to fill up. He obliges and then drinks most of his in almost one gulp. I'm suddenly taken aback at how thin he looks.

'Michele,' he says looking at me seriously, 'you're making such a big mistake. You haven't thought this through. Look at the children tonight – they want us to be together. We're meant to be together, you know we are.'

I don't know what to say, so I say nothing. I just look at him, soaking up his suffering.

'I don't understand,' he continues. 'We've always been so good together.' Tears well up in his eyes and he covers his face with his hand as a sob escapes. 'I'm sorry,' he chokes. 'You have no idea how much it hurts.'

I place my arms around his shaking shoulders and the two of us cling to one another in the kitchen, the wine all but forgotten. Then Peter's mother walks in and strides over to us. She takes Peter gently by the arm and steers him away.

'Come on, darling. Let's take a walk around the garden.'

As she leaves, she turns to shoot me such a hateful look that it feels like a knife in my chest. But as much as I dislike her and her self-righteousness, I don't blame her for hating me. Peter is her son, and seeing him suffer breaks her heart, as it would break mine if it were Max. I reflect miserably that in fact Max's heart is also broken. His father has moved out of our family home, just a month before his birthday; a birthday we're celebrating with such a false sense of cheer. I swiftly drain my glass, enjoying the fuzziness that infiltrates me.

'Michele, quick,' Ian beckons from the door into the lounge, 'the karaoke's starting. Come watch.'

'Mom, come stand with me,' Chloe calls. She is standing, mike in hand, with Max, Peter and Benjamin. 'I've chosen this song for us to sing as a family.'

Almost the entire party is packed into our lounge and I panic. 'Um, I never sing karaoke,' I blurt out.

'Come on,' Peter says, 'you can share a mike with me.'

All eyes are on me, nervously wondering whether I'll make a scene and refuse. I take my place beside Peter. 'Alright,' I surrender, 'what are we singing?'

'I chose it,' says Chloe proudly. 'It's called "We are family".'

Hours later. Much singing has been done, much alcohol consumed. Several guests have left and those who've stayed are spread across the property: sitting round the bonfire, chatting in the kitchen, relaxing on the patio or cheering on the last few karaoke performers. I'm in the lounge, having been dragged there by Max to watch Peter sing. The handful of people watching is mostly our close friends. Almost all of them look teary-eyed. They have studiously not mentioned anything about us splitting. It has been the great unspoken tonight. But it's very much on everyone's minds as we watch Peter sing.

He's chosen The Beatles' 'Yesterday', an iconic, poignant tune that seems written specifically for a grieving husband whose wife has left him. Of course everyone has at last given up on the false party cheer and the atmosphere is miserable. Several of my friends have tears in their eyes and I can feel a lump forming in my own throat. Full emotion in his delivery, Peter's voice begins to choke, but he sings valiantly through it.

I am suddenly transported many years back to another bonfire evening of friends and music. Again, Peter is singing, this time the Irish folk song 'The Wild Rover'. Unlike Max's party and the melancholic mood, where everyone present bites their tongue about what's really on their minds, this evening was carefree, happy and filled with enthusiasm. The children joined in the chorus, belting out 'No, nay, never' enthusiastically and out of tune. I was so proud and so secure in my family.

But now, as Peter half-speaks the final words to 'Yesterday', I feel the colossal loss of never-agains: Never again will we be a complete family, sitting around a fire, singing happily, without a care in the world.

Chapter twenty-seven

To: sara@naturalnurture.co.uk
Subject: A long rant
Dear Sara

Max's birthday party was hugely sad. Pretty much all the children's friends and their parents know about me and Marizette by now, as interestingly the children haven't kept it a secret. In fact I think there are very few people who don't know about us. As well as my kids telling their friends and me telling mine, there's my mom, who is a fearsome networker. So it came as no surprise that she sent out a group text to everyone (including great-aunties I've never met), stating: 'Michele is now gay, and has left her husband for the au pair.' Thanks, Mom. Anyway, I'm grateful that my friends haven't stopped their children from seeing mine, and surprised by how unfazed the children's friends have been.

Oh God, Sara, talking of friends, I have to tell you a story that happened at school when I went to pick up Chloe a few days ago. While I was waiting for her to come out of her classroom, this little girl of about nine years old approached me and asked if I was Chloe's mom. I nodded, and then she says: 'Chloe likes girls, you know, she told me.' I was stunned! And I'm thinking, OK tread carefully, be careful what you say, maybe I'll broach the subject with Chloe later, etc. But also wondering why she hasn't told me, does this mean my daughter's gay or is she just trying to be like me?

All these thoughts raced through my head in a second. All I could manage to say was, 'Really?' Then she goes on, 'Yes, and so do I – lots.' Now I'm panicking. Although gay myself, I don't want to seem to be encouraging it in young children. Don't want to get into shit with other parents either, so I just smiled and said, 'Ah', knowingly. And she continued: 'Chloe likes girls with crossbones underneath. She drew a picture of one at break today.' And then it hits me. 'Chloe likes girls' is actually 'Chloe likes skulls'! Can't tell you how relieved I was.

My dad finally had his meeting with me and Marizette. He and Mom sat opposite us at the kitchen table and listed all the things that counted against us being together, laying it on especially thick about the damage to the children. He then asked Marizette how she planned to support me, because 'having been a full-time mother, Michele has no way of looking after herself'. Can you believe it? Poor Marizette, faced with this prospect at the age of just twenty-four, in the early stages of a relationship?

To her credit, she refused to be daunted, and told my dad she'd find a way. He firmly said he had no plans to support our relationship, which made me panic for a moment, I must be honest. The reality is that if Peter refuses to help out with the children and my dad decides to kick me off the property (which is in their name), then we're well and truly fucked. We can't exactly all move into Marizette's one room in Nico's flat.

Then my mom saved the day, saying she's got her

own money and she'll never allow me to be destitute: 'If Michele needs to be with Marizette, then I'm going to make it possible for her to make those choices herself.'

My poor dad looked crestfallen. He actually looked like he might cry. His chin wobbled and he blamed me, saying he and my mom never disagreed on anything regarding their children before all this happened. I felt so bad seeing my usually strong father so upset. Will I ever stop feeling guilty?

I also know in my heart of hearts that my dad would never allow me or the children to be destitute.

Peter is fuelling my wretchedness by sending me horrible texts, saying I ruined his life, that I'm a bitch, etc. Between the children and Peter's sadness and my dad's stern disapproval fuelling my guilt, coupled with the growing desire I have for Marizette, my nerves are trashed. My body feels too little to have so many conflicting emotions raging inside it. Sometimes I just wish I could just shut down for a while.

Sorry to sound so dramatic. Please let me know how you all are, especially the kids. All my love, Michi

Chapter twenty-eight

It's November, the month of the children's school picnic. Getting to this point has taken major negotiation and caused even more turmoil. I really didn't want to miss the Christmas picnic and I knew Peter would go as well, a fact that triggers Marizette's worst fears.

'I don't want you at the school with him there,' she insists in a heated argument. 'I don't see why I can't come. I do more for your children than that fucker does anyway.'

'Marizette, it's not about that,' I explain, trying to stay calm. 'He's still their dad and the kids really want him there, and if you're there he won't come.'

Silence.

'Come on, please. It's just that things are new; it won't always be like this. It's only a matter of time before we can all attend these events together,' I say soothingly.

'I can't see that happening any time soon,' she grouches. 'Peter hates me. And I'm not too crazy about him either – he doesn't see his own children nearly enough. What kind of father does that make him?'

Unfortunately, what she's saying is true. Peter hasn't seen much of the children lately, and on the odd weekend he has them over, he often phones to say he's in a bad space and can we fetch them.

I try to be diplomatic, 'Look, he's just trying to survive at the moment. Peter's still in shock. He's doing his best with his fragile state of mind.'

But I should've known better. I was entering dangerous territory; we've been over this issue several times.

'Why do you keep defending him?' Marizette demands, 'Loads of dads go through the same thing. And, yes, they're sad, but they still fulfil their responsibilities.'

I can see the anger in her eyes, and I should leave it right here, but something makes me continue. 'Really? And how many fathers do you actually know who've been through this? Because from what I've seen, many of them simply up and leave and don't come back. At least Peter's trying!' I say in frustration.

Marizette is incensed. 'I don't know why you keep standing up for him. You can hardly blame me for being paranoid.'

She's standing close to me and I can't help noting how unbelievably sexy she is, even in anger, with her dark eyes shining as they bore into me. I have a sudden urge to kiss her mouth, despite her venom for Peter.

'Alright,' she concedes, albeit reluctantly, 'you can go to the picnic with Peter. But I'm dropping you off and collecting you, and you're not to sit together like some happy family, chatting and laughing and shit.'

'OK,' I agree, 'you can take me and pick me up. Peter says he'll take the children home with him afterwards,' I say, leaning in to kiss her neck, 'so we'll have the night to ourselves.'

Marizette pulls away from me. 'No intimate chats, OK?' she warns, 'or this isn't happening again.'

God, how has my life gone from the relative peace and

harmony of a couple who understand each other, and are secure enough not to give each other this level of shit, to all this anger and insecurity and negotiation?

After fighting to go to the picnic, I'm now here, thinking wryly that if Marizette were the proverbial fly on the wall, she would be furious because Peter, the kids and I are sharing a picnic blanket. We're surrounded by other families. It would have been so awkward not to sit together. And in the end, it was actually down to the kids.

When we arrived, Peter had already set up. The children ran to him excitedly, dragging me along with them. They threw themselves at him and plonked down on his picnic blanket. 'Come on, Mom, come sit.' Chloe said, patting the space next to her.

'Yes, come on,' agreed Peter smiling, 'join us.'

What could I say? 'Sorry guys, but I'm not allowed to. Look, I'll just go and sit somewhere else and you can choose between sitting with me or Dad.' So we're sitting together and I decide to put all the tension this potentially causes to one side for now. It's a warm evening, which is a blessing, as traditionally the weather is appalling for the Christmas picnic. Chloe and Max have run off to join the hordes of children on the expansive sports field and Benjamin is snuggled up to Peter. A few parents have greeted us, but most families are sitting in their own little groups and we are pretty much left alone.

Everyone seems to be enjoying themselves as children dash around handing out copies of song sheets for the upcoming carols, after which the evening will end off with a fire dance by some of the older students. Peter and I are being surprisingly cordial to each other, and to be honest, I'm enjoying his company. It has been such a severance since he's moved out, what with Marizette's fears and with his anger, and I don't know when this small window of an opportunity will come by again, so I make the most of it.

A boy from Benjamin's class runs up to the picnic blanket. 'Benjamin, quick,' he says, grabbing Benjamin's hand breathlessly and pulling him up. 'Your brother's a monster and we're chasing him!'

In a flash Benjamin is off and Peter and I are left alone without the kids as a buffer. My phone rings; it's Marizette. I walk away from the sea of families, and find some privacy behind the aftercare centre. I sit on a swing and press accept.

'Hello, beautiful,' she purrs. 'How are things going?'

'Good, the children are running around and we're just waiting for it to get a bit darker so we can start the carols.'

'You're not sitting with Peter, are you?' she asks suspiciously.

'No …' It's not exactly a lie; I'm not sitting with him right now.

'OK, what time will it all be finished? When can I pick you up?'

'Probably about nine,' I estimate.

'OK, my angel. I'm missing you.'

'Love you,' I respond, hanging up, and return to Peter.

'Marizette checking up on you?' he teases.

'Yeah, she worries a lot. She's just insecure at the moment,' I reply defensively.

'She'll always be insecure. You're going to have such a hard time with that one. She's young and she's very jealous,' he remarks knowingly. 'And she'll have to follow in my footsteps, same as I had to follow in Noel's.

The difference is she won't have the same patience I did.'

I don't answer, but I suspect that he's right. I've already experienced the jealousy and anger that my empathy towards Peter causes in Marizette. I stupidly thought I'd be able to share my sadness and grief with her, and she'd help me through it. It's the same naiveté that let me think it was a good idea for Peter to live in the cottage on our property.

We sit lost in thought for a while, watching the children in the distance. Then Peter breaks the silence. 'I still don't understand how we got to this point.' He looks at me, 'Michele, we're soulmates; this isn't meant to happen. We have a special connection.'

'Look,' I reassure him, 'we'll always be connected. No one can take that away from us. We'll always love each other, and if we've been soulmates before then we'll be soulmates for always.'

Peter smiles, pleased. 'You're right,' he says, 'and that will never change. We'll always be connected.'

We sit in companionable warmth, not needing to say more, when I hear a noise coming from my pocket. It's my phone. I take it out and hold it to my ear. 'Hello?'

'So much for not sitting with Peter!' It's Marizette. And she's angrier than I've ever heard her before. 'You and your soulmate can go and fuck yourselves.'

In horror I realise that somehow the phone hadn't disconnected and Marizette had just heard our entire conversation. My heart sinks faster than a lead balloon. 'Marizette, please …' I beg, not sure how I'm going to explain this one.

'There's nothing to say. Get your stuff ready, I'm picking you up. Your soulmate can cope with the children for a change,' she snaps, hanging up.

'Domestic problems?' Peter asks, raising an eyebrow.

'Fuck! Shit! Fuck!' I explode, forgetting we're in the middle of a field full of children and families. 'Marizette heard our entire conversation!'

Peter laughs a spiteful, satisfied laugh, 'Oo hoo, karma!'

Filled with dread, I pack my few picnic items, still uneaten, and find the children to say goodbye. On top of my anxiety is a crushing disappointment that I won't get to enjoy the intimacy I was so looking forward to tonight.

Chapter twenty-nine

To: sara@naturalnurture.co.uk
Subject: The wisdom of children
Dear Sara

My mom has flown back to England. Dad's still here, and although still heavily disapproving of me, is helping out a lot with the children. Which is just as well since Marizette isn't working for us at the moment. Don't know what I'll do re driving the kids around once my dad goes back to England in January.

I'm struggling. Benjamin's full of questions. While having a bath earlier he said: 'Why can't you love Daddy like Marizette?' Then he asked when his dad is coming back to live with us and I said never, he threw his head back and sobbed, 'I don't want you to love Marizette, then Daddy can come home.'

Sara, I feel like such a bad person. I've always liked myself and now I don't any more. I can't believe I'm hurting my children. All I ever wanted was for them to have a happy childhood. And I made a promise to each of them on the day they were born to do everything in my power to achieve this. Childhood is hard enough as it is and those traumas stick with you for always. Now, out of the blue, my kids have to deal with a broken home and a gay mom. Max and Chloe have said they don't mind me being gay, but they're very sad about their dad moving out.

A major problem is that Peter hardly ever sees the children. He says he can't cope with it. So at the moment he only sees them for about three hours every Friday afternoon. I know he's broken, but think he's trying to punish me through the children. Also, when I suggested he see more of them, he replied: 'Why? So you can have more time to fuck that dog of yours?' Not helpful. I want him to see more of the kids because they miss him so much. As Peter keeps pointing out, it's all my fault. And he's right. But I can't leave Marizette.

Peter's living in the flat in Sea Point and Marizette has moved to a small cottage on a property in Hout Bay, where I visit her two nights a week. She's finally moving back into our home, which of course has Peter completely freaked out. It was getting ridiculous though, with her parking outside to visit me as she wasn't allowed inside the house. And then the children were running out to the road to see her when she came round. Although they're unhappy Peter's moved out, they miss Marizette, as she was a big part of their lives.

Max had a long talk to me about it the other day. He says he enjoys Marizette's company, but thinks it's 'really sick' that his mom's sleeping with her. Chloe, on the other hand, asks me all sorts of awkward and very specific questions. One such conversation went:

Chloe: Do you kiss each other?

Me: Yes, we do.

Chloe: Do you kiss each other with tongues?

Me: Um, no.

Chloe: Do you sex each other?
Me: Chloe!
Chloe: Well, do you? You used to sex Dad.

This line of questioning sends me into a flat panic. What do I say?! Never been at such a loss over what to say to my children – the right thing to say. So said absolutely nothing. The psychologist says Marizette shouldn't sleep over till after Christmas, to give kids a bit more adjustment time. But seriously, she should try living our life for a while before giving such prescriptive opinions. Marizette comes over straight after work. Helps with supper and school lunches, and putting kids to bed. Chloe is almost always tearful at bedtime and hangs onto me till she falls asleep. Maz and I then make love (normally for several hours, in spite of our exhaustion) and then she must face a long drive home, only to return early the next day to take the kids to school, before she goes to work herself.

I am awed by her sense of responsibility. I truly didn't expect it, especially at her age. I thought she'd still want to be a total party girl and see me in her spare time. I do worry though, as I think the relentless domestic grind will get to her in the end. I'm frightened her life with me is too different from the carefree time she shared with Hilary.

Peter has started sending hostile texts to me and Maz and I mean really nasty, which is so unlike him. And I've taken all these horrible text messages on because I feel so guilty. I know Peter and I know this isn't him talking – it's his grief. And almost every nasty text is followed by another where he apologises profusely for the messages and says he's just seriously messed up at the moment. Marizette is furious I'm letting him treat her so badly.

She says if anyone was that rude to me she'd put a stop to it. I don't think she realises how bad I feel about Peter; actually think he's justified in his anger.

Have started seeing a different psychologist, who specialises in gay and transgender issues. Found him through The Triangle Project. He says Peter's texts are abusive and I shouldn't accept them. Which is all good and well but he doesn't walk around filled with guilt, pain and mad passion all the time. It feels as though my insides are fitted with a blender but the off-switch is broken. Don't know how I'm going to get through.

This coming Friday, while the kids are with Peter, I'll meet some of Marizette's friends for the first time. One friend (Jo) lives just down the road and is having us over for a braai. Very, very nervous. Apparently all Maz's friends really liked Hilary. Hope they like me. Love, Michi

◯

It's past two already. We're parked in Jo's driveway; I'm rooted to my seat. I don't know why I'm so nervous, on the verge of tears. Again, I think: how has my life changed so suddenly? Until recently, weekends used to be family affairs with established friends, now overnight I'm attending a lesbian braai with possibly hostile friends of Hilary's.

I don't budge; I can't. Marizette starts running out of patience.

'Fine. You stay in the car, but I'm getting out,' she says, slamming the door and grabbing our cooler bag from the boot. She walks round to my side of the car and opens the door. 'Michi, come on,' she entreats, 'please. Nobody's going to bite. Look, here comes Jo. She's really nice, you'll like her.'

Reluctantly I climb out of the car and follow Marizette down the narrow path to the cottage. A woman I gather to be Jo waits at the gate for us. She has short blonde hair spiked up eighties-style. She's wearing shorts and a T-shirt, and her stocky legs and broad shoulders suggest she's done a lot of sport at some stage. I also can't help noticing she has the most enormous breasts. I mean huge, covering almost her entire chest. She looks close to my age, which surprises me, as I assumed most of Marizette's friends to be in their early twenties.

'Hey there, chicken! Give us a hug,' she shouts in a Cockney accent, wrapping Marizette in her arms.

'Hi there,' she says to me, all warmth and friendliness. 'Come on in.'

There's something about Jo that makes me feel completely at ease. I'm so relieved I could kiss her. The fenced-off garden is overflowing with people, mostly crowded around two wooden tables, which almost sends me running for the safety of the car again.

'Come on,' Jo says, 'let's introduce you to everybody.'

About an hour later I'm far more relaxed – after polishing off two glasses of wine – and sitting on Marizette's lap in a camping chair. Everyone's been very nice to me, with none of the animosity I expected. And surprisingly, not everyone is gay. In fact, Jo seems to have a large selection of straight friends.

Marizette and I are sitting opposite Kharli and Pam, a couple I've taken an immediate liking to. They live in Wynberg, but own a restaurant in Hout Bay, and have been together for six years, which apparently is pretty long in lesbian circles. Pam is tall and statuesque, with short, blonde hair, but she's not exactly butch. Kharli is petite and sporty, with shoulder-length blonde hair. They're both attractive, especially Kharli, who's also Cockney, and speaks really fast and laughs a lot. They're obviously good friends with Marizette, and keep referring to stuff they've done together in the past. Which of course means they're also good friends with Hilary.

I hope I'm making a good impression. Maybe I should tone it down a bit with Marizette. I've already been told to 'get a room' by Jo, who then went on to say, 'Aw, I wish someone was that crazy about me.' Marizette and I were pretzelled together on the chair at the time and I may have been covering her face in kisses. Oh my God, I'm turning into one of those people … Those in-love people who shouldn't be out in public, who can't keep their hands to themselves and who stare lovingly into each other's eyes while others are trying to have a conversation with them. I shudder unconsciously.

But I seriously can't help my actions – Marizette is so beautiful and there's no other place I want to be but curled up on her lap with her strong arms wrapped around me. For these precious moments, I can forget about the sadness of my broken marriage and simply wallow in the warmth and joy of being near this extraordinary young woman.

A couple of hours later I'm standing in front of the mirror in Jo's bathroom. It's a pretty bathroom; decorated in the eclectic style of the rest of her place. There are little naked statuettes, framed paintings on the walls, and a ceramic hand adorned with rings. Plenty of nice stuff, without it being too cluttered. I'm doing a mental inventory of the room and deep breathing, trying to calm down. All the warmth and security I felt earlier has been replaced by a little green monster, an entirely unwelcome companion. Over the course of the afternoon, I've discovered that Marizette has made out with no fewer than three of the women here. I'm beside myself with jealousy, and I hate this feeling.

At the beginning of our relationship, Marizette told me that after the break-up with her first girlfriend, she went through a stage of getting off with lots of different girls. She'd go clubbing and end up kissing several women in one night. In fact, one night very early in our relationship when we went out clubbing, an acquaintance of hers pulled me to one side and warned me I was dating a *los meisie*, translated literally as a 'loose woman', which didn't give me much confidence. Marizette, however, assures me it was just a stage she went through and that she's hugely committed and totally in love with me.

I believe her, but it doesn't take away this jealousy. And so, in the car on the way home from Jo's, I can't help but bring it up.

'Do you think your friends like me?'

'They think you're hot,' she grins.

'But do they like me?' I persist.

Marizette laughs. 'They do now that I explained your eye thing to them. When you went to the toilet, Kharli said: "I don't mean to be funny about your girlfriend, Maz, but she isn't half snooty. I smiled at her a few times and she just ignored me!" Then Jo said the same thing …'

'What? I was…' I begin, indignantly.

But Marizette shushes me with her hand, 'Then I

realised what happened. And once I explained that you weren't stuck up, you just couldn't see them, they agreed you were actually really nice.'

I pause. 'Marizette, how many women have you had sex with?'

'I don't know. I've kissed a lot of girls and I've had sex with quite a few women, but I haven't allowed them to have sex with me.'

Quite a few! Which means she's touched quite a few vaginas. Again, my insecurities start flaring up. I can't help it; I wonder how unfavourably I compare to these women whom Marizette has had first-hand experience with. From the start, Marizette hasn't allowed my insecurities to get in the way of how she makes love to me. Initially, if she wanted to go down on me, I would instinctively put my hand over my vagina in protest, and she'd gently move it aside, saying, 'Michi, please let me love you my way.' And then I'd forget about being awkward and literally melt as she kissed and touched me. Just thinking of her saying those words makes my belly contract. So, I no longer cover myself, but I still haven't shaken off my insecurities, especially if I think of all the other vaginas Marizette has experienced, which I imagine to be picture perfect, tucked-away neat affairs.

'Hey,' Marizette smiles, reaching over to ruffle my hair, 'are you jealous?'

'No! Yes. A little bit,' I admit. I feel so stupid, but I have to tell her what's bothering me. I take a deep breath, 'It's just … I don't know if my fanny is fine compared to the others you've experienced.'

Marizette takes my hand and pulls it to her lips, kissing each knuckle. 'Oh Michi, you have the most exquisite and sexy fanny in the whole world,' she says between kisses. 'And as soon as we get home, I'm going to show you just how much I appreciate it.'

I've always been self-conscious about my vagina, ever since I read my neighbour's secret porn stash. I knew from that day on that I didn't have one of those photogenic little vaginas, all neatly tucked away and pretty, where you can't even see a hint of fanny lips. Mine is very different from the ones in those pictures. As a teenager, I'd scrutinised myself with a hand-held mirror, and began to obsess about it. So, over time, I built up a massive complex. I never change or walk around completely naked in public change rooms. My friends were always surprised that, while I was otherwise quite daring and open, I would never join in skinny dipping or nude sun-tanning. 'Come on, Michele! You're not shy are you?' they would scoff. But in reality I was terribly shy, about my vagina, anyhow. Although I haven't discussed this particular issue with any of my friends (I've always been too embarrassed), I know there are many other women with the same problem (I've dubbed it *Playboy* perfect vagina envy); there must be, otherwise there wouldn't be operations to rectify the matter.

Anyway, before Marizette, I'd decided to live with my vagina even if I didn't love it. But now I have learned to love it, or rather, Marizette loves it. And I know she loves it, because right now she's lying on the bed, with all the lights on, while I stand (completely starkers) over her. I have one foot on either side of her head and she's imploring me to open my legs a bit wider.

'Oh God, yeah,' she moans as her fingers slip in and out of herself. 'Fuck, that looks so fucking gorgeous.' She reaches up and gently prises me open with her fingers. I am fretting and self-conscious, only having agreed to this unflinching view because Marizette wanted it so badly, and let's face it, I'll do anything for her.

Marizette's moaning becomes more insistent.

'Are you sure it looks OK?' I ask again, seeking reassurance.

Her reply comes out in gasps, 'Oh … yeah! Beau-ti-ful … uh … All … wet and pink and … ah, ah, ah, aah!' As her voice rises in a crescendo, she reaches up her free hand and pushes several fingers into me. 'You have the most beautiful fanny in the world! I love it so much; don't ever deny me.'

I look down at her beautiful flushed face against the white pillow and am about to lie down next to her, but she implores me, 'Please kneel down.'

'What? Right over you?' I panic, as the self-consciousness returns. 'But I'm all wet.'

'Exactly! Now sit on my face, dammit!' she demands, reaching up to grab my wrist and pull me down. The whole lower part of her face is concealed between my legs, so all I can see is the bridge of her nose and her gorgeous eyes; long lashes almost skimming my pubic bone.

She keeps her eyes closed, clearly revelling in the whole experience, as her tongue works its magic around my clitoris and in and out of my swollen vagina; her mouth sucking on my inner lips. I feel the incredible softness of her skin, as opposed to the sand-papery effect of even a cleanly shaven guy. I look down at her long eyelashes and again am blown away that I'm with a woman. Wow! And wow again, I think, as my vagina begins to pulse and my clitoris hits that incredibly tense, almost painful high. My heart starts beating faster, my head becomes lighter and it takes all my willpower not to writhe like a maniac and suffocate Marizette beneath me.

When I eventually stop coming, I swing my leg over Marizette's soaked face, and lie down next to her. I kiss her on her mouth and taste my own juices.

'Shit, you're good,' I whisper.

'And you're beautiful,' she replies.

I marvel at how much she loves all of me, even the parts I've always been incredibly self-conscious about. It's no small achievement that she's helped me overcome my hang-ups. Through her enthusiastic appreciation, my vagina has evolved from a shy and withdrawn vagina into a confident, joyful one.

'Thank you,' I murmur, snuggling into her armpit.

Later, Marizette is fast asleep and I switch on the bedside light to watch my very own Sleeping Beauty. I do this often, in the quiet of the night. She looks so vulnerable and it strikes me how much she has taken on at such a young age. The reality is that Marizette is only twenty-four. Less than a year ago she was dating a student; she's now with a woman who has three children, an angry ex-husband, and family and friends who are less than thrilled with our relationship. Sometimes I get so caught up in my own stress that I forget how hard it must be for Marizette. I run my fingers through her short, dark hair and am overcome with tenderness. I know we'll still face many more challenges, and I hope and pray we're strong enough to overcome them.

Chapter thirty

To: sara@naturalnurture.co.uk
Subject: The case of the parallel Michele
Dear Sara
Sorry to hear you're not feeling well. Really think the stress of suppressing who you are all the time is having an impact on your health. Just my opinion and I could be wrong. But I'm sure it affects you. Not that I would advise you to go the route of asserting your sexuality and leaving your husband for a woman either. Oh no! That is one way to send your stress levels off the charts, never mind your general health. Sorry, sounds horribly negative. Neither choice is easy. I sometimes feel so sorry for you, for not having the freedom to enjoy a woman you love, and other times I envy you for having the peace and stability of an intact family. At least you're not having non-stop dramas.

I feel weird and disjointed most of the time. Everything happened so suddenly. There are times that I have a strong sense of how things would have been if I had stayed with Peter, like a parallel life I get to glimpse every now and then. You know I don't believe in all that shit, but bear with me. In this parallel life, I never went to Lush that night and Marizette left us to live in Pretoria.

And it's weird, but I can sense this other Michele and I know what she's feeling. Is all this too confusing? Haven't spoken to my therapist as don't want him to think I'm going crazy. Anyway, this other Michele can watch me from her life, just as I can see her from mine. So parallel Michele is with Peter and mostly content, because her children are secure and have no idea there was ever a chance their parents would split. I'm envious of her peaceful and drama-free household. But then I feel sorry for her, because I know she's deeply unsatisfied and that yuckiness lingering inside her has been there for most of her life. When parallel Michele looks at me, she senses all the turmoil I'm going through, and she's relieved not to be caught up in the storm. Until she sees Marizette come up behind me to kiss my neck and then the parallel Michele is filled with an urgent and painful longing.

(God, Sara, have just read over that last bit. Thought of deleting it but decided I need to tell someone and you're the only one I know won't laugh at me, even if I do sound like a nutter!)

On a more normal note, Peter's still not seeing much of the kids and they miss him terribly. Marizette is making a real effort to try to rebuild her relationship with Max. She's taking him fishing this weekend on her friend's farm. Hope it goes well. Just can't wait for things to settle a bit.

My friends have been wonderfully supportive, but have confessed that the break up of our marriage has shaken them. Apparently they saw me and Peter as a great example of a solid marriage. The other huge problem is that they love both of us but can't see us together. Really hope they warm to Marizette eventually.

I've also got a whole new set of friends through Marizette. All seem nice, but it's not the same, you know? Takes time to trust people. Wish you weren't so far away. All my love, Michi

☾

'OK, Mama, I'll phone you later. Ja, bye, bye.'

'So,' I say, walking into the kitchen. 'You and your mom are speaking again.'

'Not only that,' says Marizette, cautiously excited, 'she's invited me up to Venda to her and my dad's wedding anniversary! All my mom's family are going to be there; her sisters and their children.'

'I think you should go.' I say firmly. 'Build bridges. It'll be good for everyone to see you, but most of all, it's important for you to spend some time with the rest of your family again.' I'm aware it's been years since Marizette has attended a family gathering, or visited her parents' home.

'Um, I asked if you could come.' She pauses. 'My mom says she'll speak to my dad and tell me later.'

'What? You're kidding me! Marizette, you've told me how incredibly homophobic your parents are. They'll never agree to having their gay daughter visit with her girlfriend. And not just any girlfriend, but her older ex-boss who is still married – with children. Or just any visit – an anniversary!' I babble. 'How's that for irony? We'll be celebrating your parents' long marriage, while our relationship has essentially ended a marriage.'

Marizette puts her arms around me, 'Michi, calm down. It'll be OK, really.'

But I'm not convinced. I know for sure I won't be welcomed into the Brink household. I'll bet Danie, family patriarch, won't allow people like us to infiltrate their family union. So there's nothing to worry about then, I reassure myself, feeling relief wash over me.

Chapter thirty-one

I can't believe I'm meeting Marizette's parents. And so soon! We've been together for only two months. How is it that we're driving to the back end of beyond in a rented car, to visit parents who are extremely hostile to the fact that their daughter is gay, let alone the fact that she's made off with her married boss, who is fourteen years her senior. It's very surreal.

After consulting with her husband, Helene agreed to the visit. A fact that has filled me with mixed feelings (no doubt it has the same effect on Helene). I think my overwhelming emotion is fear. However, I'm also grateful to be welcomed into their home, and dying to meet Marizette's parents, who are formed only in my imagination, based on what Marizette has told me. No wonder I'm scared! I gather they're an ultra-conservative couple, whose beliefs and lifestyle are reinforced by the ultra-conservative Afrikaans community in which they live.

Of course I desperately want to make a good impression, which isn't helping my nerves one bit. I met my friends for coffee on Friday morning and grilled them on how to impress an Afrikaans matriarch. Lisa, always looking for an excuse to mock me for being so outspoken, unhelpfully told me to just be myself (but less so), and to say as little as possible. 'In fact, maybe don't speak at all,' she laughed.

Luckily there was some more positive advice from Brandy, who is half-Afrikaans. 'OK,' she began enthusiastically, 'as Marizette's family is Afrikaans, being polite is everything. When her mom is working in the kitchen you must offer to help. And here's the important bit. She'll say, "no thank you", but you must help anyway. If you don't, she'll decide you're lazy,' she shrugs. 'And keep offering to make cups of tea, always offering Helene first.' Brandy thought for a moment before continuing, 'Oh, and whatever standard your Afrikaans is, if you want to make a good impression, speak it.'

My mother offered to look after the children so that Marizette and I could fly up to Johannesburg, then rent a car for the long drive up to Venda. It's our first trip away together, but it hardly counts as a romantic getaway. For starters, I'm sure we'll be put in separate bedrooms for the duration of our stay.

Peter is understandably upset about me visiting Marizette's family. He sent me a text saying: 'Meet the Fuckers. Enjoy your new family.' And then informed me his family want nothing to do with me. I texted him back immediately, saying if he sends me one more nasty message I'll change my number. Got a contrite reply seconds later, apologising: 'Sorry. Am just so sad. Am not myself.'

We've been driving for close on three hours now, through huge expanses of open, flat landscapes and I'm suddenly ravenous and bursting for the loo.

'I need to eat now,' I demand petulantly. My hungry monster is gnawing away at my insides, threatening to unstitch me.

'Look,' soothes Marizette, 'we're coming up to a service station now. We'll stop here.

It's sweltering as we get out of the car and a welcome relief to enter the cool air-conditioned fast-food restaurant. Heads turn to regard us curiously, and I immediately squirm self-consciously. Since coming out, I've prided myself on being openly gay, believing that lesbians and homosexuals need to be seen holding hands and displaying the same level of public affection that a straight couple would. 'People need to see that we are normal,' I've argued. 'The more we hide, the more barriers we create.' So we cheerfully hold hands in public, share a little kiss in restaurants and put up with the occasional stares or double-takes. By now I feel completely at home being open in Hout Bay, where everyone from the video shop to the local coffee shop knows us. But the whole point is that in Cape Town we get only the occasional odd look and most people have the decency to look away. But we're no longer in Cape Town. We're up north; we've crossed the boerewors curtain and every single person in the restaurant is staring at us – openly.

As we scan the room looking for an open table, I pull my hand from Marizette's. Confused, she gives me a what-the-fuck look. I glance at her apologetically and slide into a booth. I'm the one who's been so enthusiastic and vocal on the whole issue, after all. I look around. About five tables are full; mostly couples. The group that stands out the most is an Afrikaans family. I knew they were Afrikaans even before they started speaking. I am fascinated by Afrikaans families; actually, I have a fascination for all things Afrikaans, and lately my interest has been piqued as I'm dating an Afrikaans girl.

The family that's captured my attention is seated near us; they're all still staring at us, even though we've sat down and are pretending to scan our menus. Ma's face is fully made up with a solid layer of foundation dusted in powder, bright blue eye-shadow coloured in well above her eyelids, and maroon lip pencil emphasising the contours of her lips (currently pursed together disapprovingly). Her clothes are immaculately pressed; blue slacks complemented by a white, short-sleeved blouse, and her short, sensible hairstyle has obviously been blow-dried.

Pa, an imposing figure, dons the unofficial uniform of men in these parts: khaki shorts belted at the waist (under a sizable paunch, no doubt grown proudly after much *wors*, *brandewyn* and *koeksusters*) and a matching khaki collared shirt, lace-up hiking boots and long socks. I half expect to spot a comb peeking out from one sock.

The two children – a girl of about eleven and a boy about eight – are both eerily quiet and well behaved for young kids. They are also neatly dressed and pressed. While the parents try to get a good look at us in the most subtle way possible, their kids stare openly.

They're still gawking when we place our order, and haven't taken their eyes off us when our food arrives. Thankfully it looks as though they've finished their meal and hopefully they'll leave soon.

Finally I can't take it any more. 'Marizette,' I say in exasperation, 'why is that family staring at us? I mean we're not even holding hands or anything!'

'Michi,' Marizette replies somewhat wearily, 'they're staring because I don't look the way most girls do up here. In fact, I don't look like most girls full stop. So they probably started off trying to work out if I'm a girl or a boy. And now they're probably staring because they wonder why I'm a girl who's dressed like a boy.'

I glance across the room. 'They're still staring.'

'Fuck it! It's times like this I want to reach over and kiss you,' she mutters.

Impulsively, I lean over and do just that – just a little kiss – not even on her lips, but on her cheek. But immediately wish I hadn't, because the little girl pipes up at the top of her voice, '*Mama! Hoekom soen daai twee meisies?*' (Mom, why are those two girls kissing?)

Ma doesn't answer, probably because she isn't sure how to explain to her innocent child why two women are kissing. With the persistence so typical to children, so the little girl repeats her question, louder this time.

Marizette drops her head into her hands, ostrich style. She is puce with embarrassment. I'm so mortified I contemplate making a dash for the car, but we haven't paid our bill yet and I don't want to create even more of a scene. Then Ma jumps up from the table and drags her still-curious children outside. Pa follows, stately, and gives us one last once-over as he passes. By now everyone, including the waiters, cashiers and petrol attendants are staring at us. Marizette peers at me from behind her hands, then signals for the bill.

'OK, um … right. I know,' I stumble, 'let's just pretend none of that happened, OK?' I make a dash for the toilets to have yet another wee before the last long stretch to Venda. Sensing there won't be much opportunity for any real intimacy until we get back to Cape Town, I decide to give Marizette a little surprise. I take out my cellphone and press some keys.

'OK. On to Venda,' announces Marizette, climbing into the car. As she turns the key in the ignition, I pass her my phone.

'What's this?' she pauses. 'Oh my fuck! How can you do this to me? You bitch,' she says breathlessly, her attention locked on the screen of my cellphone. Pictured is a short video clip of my fanny up close, as my fingers work their way all over my clitoris before sliding inside. Marizette has gone pink, the most delightful giveaway that she's turned on. I'm thrilled with her reaction.

She hands me back my phone and with a smile, pulls off. 'You just wait till we get back to Cape Town,' she warns. 'I'm going to fuck you silly. You're not going to be able to move afterwards.'

I can't wait, but for now I have a family to impress. And just to be safe, I delete the latest footage on my phone.

At about midday we finally pull into the farm. The scenery over the last two hours has been breathtaking and has managed to ease a lot of my trepidation. Venda is beautiful; emerald green hills, with a mixture of traditional and modern dwellings scattered on the slopes. The soil is a deep rusty red. And children wave excitedly from the side of the road as we speed past.

Marizette's youngest brother Etienne is sitting in the back, happily tapping out a beat on the seat, and half-singing along to the music on the radio. We collected him on our way, about half an hour ago. He was delighted to see Marizette, and I keep losing track of the conversation as they flit from topic to topic in rapid Afrikaans. At sixteen, Etienne is a young man; an extremely handsome young man, actually. In fact he looks like a boy version of Marizette: same beautiful eyes, shapely mouth, and dimpled cheeks when they smile. They even have similar hairstyles; short dark hair, with a longer fringe.

I'm delighted to have him with us to break the ice. Although admittedly, nothing will be able to slow my rapidly beating heart right now. We've driven all the way up the long dirt road and have drawn to a stop in front of the farmhouse. We are here. I panic and wonder what form of procrastination I can use to put off the inevitable meet-the-parents for as long as possible. But it's too late.

'Come on,' Marizette urges, 'you can't sit here forever. Leave the bags in the car and I'll fetch them later.'

I breathe in deeply and exhale, trying to force myself to calm down. But my rapid heartbeat shows no signs of abating. Just do it; bite the bullet, I urge myself, following Marizette into the parental home. Chances are Helene will be fairly nervous herself.

Marizette knocks on the front door and an immaculately dressed, attractive blonde woman answers. Marizette steps forward and wraps her in a bear hug, before releasing her mother and introducing me. We shake hands formally. It's clear I'm not the only one suffering from a case of nerves. Helene immediately lights a cigarette and we follow her as she bustles into the kitchen. She chatters and smokes, opening cupboards and looking anywhere but at us.

Marizette excuses herself to bring in the bags, leaving me alone and completely panicked. Luckily Helene is still talking and so far doesn't seem to need a response from me, which is a good thing because with my frazzled

The Au Pair

nerves and her rapid Afrikaans, I'm struggling to follow a lot of what she's saying. I pick up bits here and there. Like when her husband will arrive home and how many guests are expected on Sunday.

I interrupt her monologue by offering (in Afrikaans) to make her a cup of tea.

I have established how many sugars she takes, and stored the knowledge away for future teas I'll be making over the weekend, when Marizette returns.

'I've put the bags in the hallway,' she says to her mother.

'Oh! Let me show you where your rooms are,' Helene says, leading the way down the passage.

Ah, rooms, plural. So I was right; separate rooms. I feel like such a teenager. Mind you, I probably feel less awkward this way.

Marizette pauses in the hallway to pick up our bags. I'm perfectly capable of carrying my own bag, but I've learnt by now that it's part of Marizette's chivalry to take on any heavy lifting or carrying. And interestingly, I don't mind. With Peter, I would've taken a bag from him to prove I was perfectly capable of carrying it myself.

My bedroom is the first stop. Marizette drops off my bags and follows her mother to her room. I half close the door and sit on the bed, which is covered in a pretty floral duvet cover. The room also boasts a freestanding wooden cupboard and a dressing table with a large mirror. Through the window, I can see the dense foliage of the forest and, to my amazement, I spot some small monkeys sitting in the branches on the closest trees. Gosh, we really are in the middle of nowhere; who knows what hostilities await us. I have been quite upbeat till now, but suddenly I feel trapped. There's no turning back, and the thought of meeting Danie completely terrifies me. I breathe in deeply and exhale, as tears prick my eyes.

Suddenly Helene's in the doorway. She must see the anxiety on my face because she says quietly, 'Michele, *jy is baie welkom in ons huis*', with those simple words, welcoming me not just into her house, but into her family.

I'm so grateful that, to my horror, tears start running down my cheeks. I nod, but remain where I am, stiff and wooden, unable to move. Marizette walks in and looks at me curiously, at which point Helene also starts to bawl; proper, loud crying. She throws her arms around Marizette, all sobbing and heaving shoulders. Poor Marizette, who has no idea what's going on, catches my eye over her mom's shoulder, as if to say: 'Yikes, what's going on?'

Outside a car rolls up over the uneven dusty ground of the driveway. Helene extracts herself from Marizette and wipes her eyes. 'Danie is here,' she announces, leaving to greet him.

Here we go. I try to keep my breathing steady. It's going to be an interesting weekend. Nervously I follow Marizette and Helene to the entrance hall. Helene greets her husband with a kiss. He's a big, solid man, sporting the farmer's standard khaki shorts and matching shirt, long socks and a big moustache. Marizette throws herself at her father and holds on to him for a long time. She is clearly overjoyed to see him. I would be happy for her to hold on forever, anything to prolong the point where I have to greet him.

Danie returns Marizette's hug with equal pleasure. They finally separate and Danie moves to greet me. In my imagination, based on the rocky examples of some of my

The Au Pair

Afrikaans uncles, older male cousins and a few Afrikaans acquaintances, I have created a (rather unfair) stereotype. He is stern, patriarchal and conservative. If he is friendly, it'll be in a sleazy, worrying way. Well, Danie is none of these things. His only stereotypical characteristic seems to be his dress code. As soon as he shakes my hand and introduces himself, I am at ease. Smiling genuinely, Danie welcomes me to his home, and his natural friendliness melts away my anxieties.

I am about to offer to make everyone a cup of tea, when Danie suggests he take us on a tour of the farm in his bakkie. 'It'll take about an hour. If you're interested,' he says.

'I'd love to,' I enthuse. And really, I would.

Marizette nods happily in agreement and we leave straight away. Helene elects to remain behind, so Marizette insists I sit up front with her dad, while she jumps into the back.

What follows is a fascinating introduction to the farm, delivered in detail by Danie, whose knowledge not just of mangos, the fruit he farms, but of the land and the area in general, is incredible.

○

Supper time. Helene has cooked up a storm with meat, salad and butternut both looking and smelling delicious. We're sitting in the TV room with our plates balanced on our laps and my mouth begins to water at the delicious aromas. I'm absolutely starving. I decide to start with the butternut, then work my way through the salad and finish off with the steak. I take my first mouthful and look over to Marizette, smiling. She winks at me. I wink back at her and take another mouthful. She winks again, well, not quite; more of a blink, with both eyes opening and closing exaggeratedly. I frown in confusion. She blinks again, this time twice in quick succession. Is she trying to tell me something? I look to Helene and Danie. And in horror realise that no one has touched their food. They're waiting for grace. I put down my knife and fork, swallowing the food left in my mouth in one gulp without chewing.

'*Oogies*,' announces Danie, and we close our eyes while he gives thanks.

Chapter thirty-two

To: sara@naturalnurture.co.uk
Subject: From behind the boerewors curtain
Dear Sara
This is going to be very outdated as there's no reception out here. It's our last night here, we leave tomorrow. I can't wait! Can't wait to cuddle up to Marizette again, hold hands without being self-conscious and kiss her when I feel like it. Not to mention fucking her brains out! Which I miss an obscene amount ... We've been in separate bedrooms, creating a very tangible sexual tension between us. Also, Maz may be amused but I suspect is a little exasperated by my reticence and shyness during our stay. Don't think she realises how nerve-wracking this has been. I'm so conscious of what her parents will think. If she comes into my room to say hello, I insist the door is open, lest Helene or Danie walk past and wonder what we're up to in there. I even struggle holding hands or showing any sort of affection in front of her parents. A couple of times, while watching TV, she has reached over to touch my hand and I quickly pull it away. She says she misses me, but the point is, I desperately don't want to embarrass her parents. Surprisingly, in spite of my trepidation, I've taken a genuine liking to both of them.

Looks-wise, Helene is the antithesis of Marizette. She's very attractive in a blonde, feminine, made-up way. Whereas Maz has dark hair, and wears shorts with flops more often than not. Yet, with all their differences, they're indisputably mother and daughter: they share the same smile and both have shapely calves. There's also the notorious temper, which I haven't witnessed with Helene yet (thank God!), but Maz reassures me she has one.

Helene and I have had many chats over the last few days and I've learnt just how incredibly passionate and vocal she is about her opinions. From a religious standpoint, she's torn that her only daughter is gay. On the very first evening after supper, Helene came to my room and sat on the bed with me. She asked me if I was '*die Here se kind*', meaning literally 'a child of God', or more broadly, Christian, I suppose. Of course I didn't know what to say so I mumbled, 'Um ...' and let it hang there. I didn't want to admit to her that I wasn't sure. For all I know, I could be, I just don't have the required faith to know for sure. I played it safe and told her I was raised Christian (and before you open your mouth, just let me finish!); it isn't exactly a lie. My family wasn't particularly religious, but my parents still sent us to Sunday school. Anyway, she seemed satisfied and then asked whether I planned to stay with Maz as she didn't want me breaking her daughter's heart! I was completely flabbergasted! Given her extreme aversion to the fact that her daughter is in a gay relationship, I would have expected Helene to beg me to leave Maz. It was a fascinating conversation and made me realise two things. Firstly, Helene is complex and can be completely contradictory. And secondly, in spite of her convictions, she truly loves Marizette and wants her to be happy.

Anyway, the reason we came up in the first place: the anniversary party on Sunday. It went incredibly well. I've now met most of Marizette's family on her mother's side, and luckily get on well with all of them. Everyone stayed over in various rooms and the guest cottage next door as the farm is too far away from anywhere to just pop over for the day. All three brothers were there too. Maz's older brother is a really nice guy, but very serious and almost too grown up (he's only twenty-six). He's the one who's done everything right. He went into farming and married a pretty blonde Afrikaans teacher. They own a house and are trying for a baby. Don't think they'll ever do anything to rock the Brink family boat. On the other hand, Juan, who's studying film, is very much like Etienne – fun, flamboyant and gorgeous.

I must say that in spite of my nerves, I actually enjoyed the day. It mostly consisted of perpetual eating, drinking and chatting, with music and dancing later. To the family's credit, everyone treated me respectfully. Maz and I mostly mixed with her younger brothers and teenage cousins, which brutally highlighted the age gap between us, and made me feel a million years old!

Must try to get some sleep. Long drive to Joburg tomorrow. Feel bad that Marizette has to do all the driving. Hope all is well with your family. Love, Michi

☽

Hotel outside Johannesburg.

Oh bliss; oh heaven! I'm exactly where I'm meant to be: naked in Marizette's arms on a double bed. Having driven for most of the day, Marizette was too exhausted to carry on, so we've stopped for the evening. There was a moment of awkwardness when the receptionist asked what kind of room we'd want. I toyed with the idea of requesting a twin room, but then thought, 'Stuff it, I've been apart from Marizette for long enough,' and requested a double. I've missed my beautiful girlfriend so much these last few days. All my senses are heightened. I revel in her delicious smell and exquisitely soft skin. My body responds instantly as she touches me. My hands run greedily over her breasts, her stomach, her thighs. I manoeuvre myself on top of her and take in her beautiful face, her strong shoulders, her pert breasts. I want her so badly it's like a gnawing hunger. And I can have her. There are no prying eyes; no disapproving parents, just the two of us. I lay my body on top of her, writhing my torso against hers. Breasts touching breasts; stomach to stomach; pubic bone on pubic bone.

Marizette kisses my face, my mouth, and whispers, 'I love you,' over and over into my ear. She turns me over onto my back and I gasp as I feel her fingers slip into me.

'I love you too,' I say. 'Oh God, I love you.'

Warm tears slide down my cheeks, and tenderly, Marizette kisses them away.

Then all of a sudden I don't want tender. I want Marizette to take me. 'Marizette,' I beg, 'can you fuck me?'

'I am fucking you,' she responds, confused.

'I want you to fuck me properly,' I demand. 'Hard, without holding back.'

She smiles, 'OK, prepare yourself. Or rather, let me prepare you.' She moves down to kiss my vagina, licking me inside and out, making sure I'm lubricated enough. 'Are you ready?' she asks breathlessly, kneeling between my legs.

'Oh yes.'

'Just tell me if you want me to stop,' she warns, before starting off with two fingers, building up speed and rhythm, going in deeper and deeper, faster and faster.

The sensation of her fingers sliding in and out of me is indescribable, but I'm worried I'm too tired to orgasm. 'Maz, wait,' I say. 'Wait. I'm loving it, but I'm so exhausted, I'm not going to be able to come.'

'Oh yes, you are,' she insists. 'There's no way you're going to sleep before you do.'

Rhythmically she pushes deep inside me, drawing her fingers out every now and then to expertly circle my clitoris, over and over. In and out. On and on. I don't know how long we've been at it, but I'm sure I'm taking an inordinate amount of time to come. Just as I start climbing the peak of an orgasm, I begin to worry that I'm taking too long. Is Marizette bored or getting fed up? A line of thinking of course which sets me back. I've never been one of those women who can come just like that, in about two minutes flat. I briefly wonder if I should fake it, but I don't have the confidence to pull it off, and besides, by now I'm on such a high I'm sure I'll die if I don't climax. I could almost cry with frustration.

'Maz, I'm so sorry,' I apologise. 'I'm taking so long. You can stop if you like.'

'You must be joking,' she says, still fingering me. 'Michi, don't stress. We've got all the time in the world. And I love making love to you. Besides, I was just warming up your clit for a bit of mouth action.'

Keeping her fingers inside me, Marizette places her head between my legs and I feel myself relax as her tongue works its magic over my clitoris. I start to tingle and I'm all fluid; cresting and ebbing, over and over, till finally my whole body contracts, from my vagina, a sea of bliss spreading through my veins and exploding in my head. And I'm screaming, a low primal scream I have absolutely no control over. Then it's over and Marizette collapses on top of me, as I wrap my legs around her.

'You're awesome. Now squash me flat,' I demand, pulling her closer to me, so I can feel the full weight of her body pressing down on me. Right now, I'm truly the luckiest woman in the whole world.

Chapter thirty-three

To: sara@naturalnurture.co.uk
Subject: Preparing for a tough Xmas
Dear Sara
It's holiday season in Cape Town, which means the city is literally heaving with tourists. Usually I love the vibe of Cape Town at this time of the year, but I feel so drained and heavy at the moment. I'm dreading the long festive season break.

Firstly, Marizette is being made redundant from her job in December. My dad, who is thankfully warming to Marizette, suggested she move in with me. That way she can help out with the kids and driving when my parents are back in England. So, in effect, she'll still do what she did before, but without being officially employed (it would be a bit weird to call my lover my au pair). Instead of paying her, we'll share a joint bank account. In the meantime Maz will have time to look for something else.

Before deciding anything I spoke to the kids about it. Understandably, they don't want more changes, and would rather Marizette look after them again. So she'll be moving in come the New Year, which to be honest fills me with trepidation. What if our relationship becomes bogged down with the relentless domestic grind? Right now, I love visiting Maz at her place; I love feeling that I'm officially 'dating' someone. But unfortunately we can't sustain living apart, especially when my parents return to England and I don't have the luxury of asking them to babysit when I visit Marizette. Peter has the kids over, but only every second Saturday night, so that's not much help either. Am kind of dreading my parents leaving, even though it'll probably be a good thing for Maz and me to have a bit of space to ourselves.

My mom's doing really well. Her tests have come up clear (yay!) and she's now on the drug Tamoxifan for the next five years. She hates it as it gives her hot flushes and makes her feel hormonal, but she'll do anything to keep the cancer at bay. It's such a relief she's stable and OK for the moment. I can't even begin to contemplate losing her.

Peter's still not talking to me and it's created a huge hole in my life. I don't think we'll ever be friends again. I miss him so much. Sometimes (often, if I have to be honest) I imagine we meet for coffee or bump into one another and I can chat to him about everything from the children and Marizette to how I'm feeling. It's a bit of a one-way conversation, as he doesn't really need to respond. He just smiles and nods. But he's all kindness and understanding. The weird thing is that this kind, loving imaginary Peter feels so much more like the real Peter than the bitter, devastated man who refuses to have anything to do with me.

I'm struggling being a split family. It doesn't fit in with any of the hopes or plans I had for us. The worst is seeing other families together, like on the beach, and thinking, 'that should be us'. And until very recently, it was us.

On a more positive note, Maz and I have been to a

few events together with the kids – a bit like a family. We all went to Lisa's year-end pottery party together and last weekend we took Benjamin to his friend's birthday party. So we are doing family-type things together, but not sure if we'll ever feel like a family.

In spite of the domestic worries, I'm still madly, crazily in love with Marizette. She's actually pretty romantic, which I didn't expect. She buys me flowers and organises surprises for me. Just hope we can sustain the romance when she moves in.

Oh God, Sara, I'm dreading Christmas. As you know I usually look forward to it with childlike enthusiasm. I love the mince pies and the secrecy of buying and wrapping presents for my family, filling the children's stockings, Peter playing carols on his guitar … But this year will be the first December without Peter, and I'm so down about our broken family that there seems little point getting excited.

Our main focus this year is that the children get to see both Peter and me, so we've decided to have Christmas Eve at our place, then the kids will sleep over at Peter's and open stockings with him, before joining us for lunch on Christmas Day. It's all so damn complicated. Hope it all goes OK. Give the kids a hug from me. Love, Michi

○

Christmas Day. The table is festooned with all the traditional garish and colourful decorations that we've collected over many years. My parents and the children sit at the table, while Marizette and I run backwards and forwards to the kitchen, carrying out the different dishes.

Marizette, desperately eager to impress the family (and Max in particular) offered to prepare the entire meal by herself. While the kids and my parents were at Peter's, she sweltered for hours in the kitchen. And I must say that she's produced a succulent turkey, complete with stuffing, crispy roast potatoes, two types of veg and homemade gravy. She even made an unusual nut roast for Ian and Chloe, the two vegetarians in the family.

Thankfully, the kids seem in good spirits. Marizette and I did as much as we could last night that I traditionally did with Peter. We left out a mince pie and some sherry for Father Christmas, and a carrot for his reindeer. My dad even dressed up as Father Christmas and asked Max to help him hand out presents. My mom and dad gave me and Maz a beautiful quilted bedspread. But the one thing that gave me a lump in my throat was when Benjamin asked why his dad couldn't be with us.

Marizette and I have finally laid out all the food on the table and we join the rest of the family. 'Please everyone,' I say, 'start dishing up while the food's still hot.'

Marizette looks decidedly nervous. I think the children can sense this and can see how much effort she's made. For now, they've let her off the emotional guilt hook and are being quite complimentary.

Max, being a foodie, loves the roast. 'Wow, Marizette, he says enthusiastically, 'this is really good!'

'Yeah,' echoes Chloe, 'I love the nut roast and the potatoes.'

Marizette is visibly relieved. Her shoulders, which have spent most of the day hunched up near her ears, relax and she smiles. 'It's my pleasure. Shall we pull the crackers?' She offers one to Max.

The Au Pair

There are screeches of delight and much joviality as we stretch across one another to tug open the crackers. I'm relieved, and so proud of Marizette. But I'm torn between mixed feelings. The most significant thing about splitting up a family and starting a new relationship is the firsts and lasts. There's the overwhelming feeling of loss: the breakdown of our family unit, our last family holiday together, the first Christmas without Peter. And then the budding enthusiasm of new beginnings: our first Christmas with Marizette, the special meal she single-handedly created for the children, and her officially moving in.

At the end of the day, I think, our first Christmas as a broken family didn't turn out too badly. Peter was missed, but ever the optimist, I nurture a glimmer of hope deep inside me that one day we'll all be able to spend Christmas together.

Chapter thirty-four

To: sara@naturalnurture.co.uk
Subject: Happy New Year!
Dear Sara
Happy New Year! Hope your New Year will be filled with peace and abundance. I already suspect mine will be filled with drama and turbulence. Maz and I spent New Year's Eve with the kids in Citrusdal. We rented a little stone cottage on a farm near a river, having decided to forego the usual mass-invite New Year's party I normally hold at our house. On one hand I've tried to keep as many family traditions as possible, so the children aren't too stressed out with all the change. But in the end, Marizette and I were so exhausted and wrung out, we opted for the peace of the Cederberg. The peace and calm of the place was good for all of us. Max and Chloe had the freedom to go exploring on their own and Benjamin made friends with a slightly older boy who took him under his wing. Mostly, all went well on our first family holiday. Even New Year's Eve passed without incident, and we were all in bed before twelve.

But it's never quiet for long in my life! Already this year has kicked off with an extraordinary series of events. Peter and Ian have become very close since the break-up, and they decided to go to this Vortex trance festival. Ian persuaded a woman called Tana to join them. (Quick note on Tana: female friend of Ian's from Joburg whom Ian had brief thing with a couple of years ago. We all liked her; very nice girl, unlike some of his crazier girlfriends. But the relationship didn't work out.) Anyway, to cut a long story short, Ian and Tana reconnected at the festival, and Tana and her daughter have moved in with Ian. Can you believe it?! And she moved in on the same day as Marizette did – how's that for coincidence?

But, the biggest surprise of all is (cue: drum roll): Peter has hooked up with someone too! He met Ingrid at the same festival (wonder what happens at these trance things?!), and she works as a dietician at the MediSpa where he works. Ian says apparently they connected during a yoga workshop. Ha! And just months ago he said he was never going to have another relationship again, and sulked about living the life of a celibate monk for at least ten years. Men are so funny, honestly.

Needless to say I'm thrilled about all of the above. Tana's daughter Rebecca is the same age as Chloe, and Ian's place finally looks lived in (food in the fridge!). And I'm delighted Peter has companionship because I've been dead worried he's lonely. Maz gets angry, saying Peter's well-being isn't my concern either way. If I make a mistake of pointing out to her that it is hard to not care about someone, having been involved with them for so long, then a big argument ensues.

Anyway, when I finally got to speak to Peter I asked about the girlfriend and he said: 'Not girlfriend; lover. Not ready to commit yet, have been too hurt.' Then proceeded to explain how she's a Tantric master and they have forty-eight-hour sex sessions! Said I'm very happy for him as he deserves to be loved like a man, which I couldn't give him. So of course he got all shirty and said it made no difference, he was still miserable and I ruined his life. Don't try to make myself feel better because he'd found someone. What I've done to him is still terrible, etc. Well, I'm still pleased. Want to thank this woman and beg her to take care of Peter and treat him well. Not so sure this would be appreciated though – either by her or Peter!

BTW: above phone call was conducted while Maz was out grocery shopping, otherwise would never have got away with what she'd have seen as an 'intimate chat'. Honestly, she is so jealous and insecure! Am only allowed to speak to Peter about the children and only when she's in the room. The few times I've spoken to him without her standing right beside me were the few times he's phoned me. Think she is still paranoid after the Christmas picnic fiasco where she overheard us talking about being soulmates.

So, Ian's new woman, Tana, is exceptionally sweet. Beautiful, Jewish, not particularly religious, but still honours Shabbat. She's into raw food and although she's ten years older than Ian, is bursting with health and vitality and looks about thirty. She's got two sons away at university, and Rebecca seems very sweet, if a little shy and withdrawn. A lot of adjustment for her, I suppose.

Anyway, New Year and many changes all around, with Maz moving in. She works for the family again but in a different capacity – more disciplinarian with kids. She's made me change cupboards, which is awkward, but it's more difficult for me to adjust to changing the side of the bed I sleep on. Doesn't want me to be on same side of the bed or have same cupboard space as when I was with Peter! In spite of many teething problems, passion's still very much there. Even if we argue, we have sex every day. Wish I could've had longer courtship. So sad our honeymoon stage was filled with stress.

It's Maz's birthday this week and I've organised some surprises for her. Hope she approves. Will let you know.
Love, Michele

○

'Oh Michi, you're the best girlfriend ever!' Marizette gushes.

At this moment I feel like the world's luckiest girlfriend, as Marizette is laid out on the bed in front of me, gloriously naked. We're cocooned in a cosy bed-and-breakfast in the coastal village of Noordhoek, in a cottage right on the beach. Tomorrow, for my third and final stage of birthday surprises, we're going to ride along Long Beach. But Maz doesn't know that yet. The first stage surprise was this morning at home. I organised a beautiful princess birthday cake, complete with tiers and a princess and even an icing dragon. The children (including Rebecca) decorated the outdoor table with pink napkins, gold paper plates and colourful balloons tied to the chairs.

We kept it a family-only affair this year, as Marizette said she's still too raw and stressed to have a big party. We all made her cards and read them out to her, before she blew out her twenty-five candles. It was lovely having

Tana and Rebecca with us. Rebecca is coming out of herself a bit and they already feel like part of the family. Marizette was so touched by everything that when she said thank you, she started crying.

And now, for the second stage of surprises.

'You just lie down and relax,' I murmur to Marizette. 'I'm going to make love to you for hours …'

She's lying on her back, naked, and as usual I can't get enough of her. 'Oh God, you are so beautiful! You are so fucking beautiful,' I enthuse.

We've spent the whole afternoon kissing, touching, and staring into each other's eyes. Normally at this point, Marizette whispers, 'Can you put your fingers in me?' Which I do happily, while she proceeds to bring herself to orgasm by playing with her clitoris. I then watch her cheeks reddening as I keep sliding inside her, till finally I am treated to that exquisite moaning, as I feel her tightening around my fingers. At which point I'm also dripping wet and ready to explode.

So when Marizette whispers in my ear that she needs to orgasm, I expect the same procedure. I manoeuvre myself on top of her and am about to slip my fingers inside her, when she announces, 'This time, you're going to make me come by yourself.'

'I am?' Panic explodes in my brain. I'm still so new to all of this. What if I can't manage it? Or I take too long to get her there and she loses interest? Marizette's told me many times how her first girlfriend managed to bring her to an orgasm every single time they made love. Which of course triggers my deepest jealousies, competitiveness and insecurities.

'Come on,' Marizette urges, opening her legs. 'You've

been a lesbian for long enough. Time to put in some effort. Besides, it's my birthday,' she smiles, teasingly, 'so you can do all the work for a change.'

I look at her glorious, inviting mound. All pink and lovely, with just a hint of her lips poking out ever so slightly and I don't need any further encouragement. In fact, just try and stop me! Without delaying any longer, I dive down between her legs.

'Hey, slow down, tiger! Remember: this is about my pleasure, not yours, so stay focused.'

'Sure, angel, just lie back and enjoy,' I murmur, all false confidence. Shit! What if I can't make it happen? But my stubborn streak of determination has decided I will keep trying until it does happen – however long it takes. 'OK, honey, prepare yourself,' I say, slipping two fingers inside her and placing my tongue on her clitoris.

In theory, bringing a woman off is relatively simple. Stimulate the clitoris and the vagina at the same time and she'll have an orgasm. But alas, it sounds much easier than it is. As I soon discover. Off I go, licking her clitoris and fingering her. I keep going for what feels like hours. In fact it's probably been only a few minutes, but I'm already getting a crick in my neck, which is at an awkward angle so I can slide my tongue over her clitoris in just the right way. To me this is highly challenging. You'd think you'd see results fairly soon, but no such luck.

My tongue is working overtime and Marizette makes all the right sounds, 'Mmm! Ah … oh God! That's good, oh, yeah!' And each time I think it's about to happen, she says, 'Sorry, babe, it's gone. You've lost the spot. Could you keep your tongue where it was?'

I pause, 'Uh, where was that exactly?'

'Just carry on. I'll tell you when it's right. Mmm. OK. Oh yes, there! Just there ... Could you keep your tongue on that spot? And move your fingers a bit more? Whoa! Don't speed up too much, just keep the same rhythm.'

Right. I've finally got it. Same rhythm, keep to one spot. No problem. I'm doing well, except now my forearm is about to go into spasm. And I've got another crick in my neck. I desperately need to change position, but I'm scared I'll lose the spot if I do.

A while later and I can't take it any more. I have to give myself a break. I decide to come up and kiss Marizette on the mouth, telling her I need to be close to her. Then I'll take a quick, sneaky stretch and get back to business.

As I'm about to carry out this plan she gasps, 'Oh. My. God! Don't stop! Please don't stop! Don't you dare stop!'

Am I humanly capable of carrying on? Then I feel her vagina walls tightening around my fingers and this spurs me on. Her moans become deeper and she begins to thrust her hips upwards, her pubic bone whacking me in the nose. But I keep going, because right now I can't feel the pain in my arm or the ache in my neck. I'm completely overcome by the sheer beauty and power of Marizette's orgasm. My own vagina is starting to clench, gathering moisture, and I'm so turned on I want to explode.

Marizette screams in her final throes of orgasm and I'm outrageously thrilled I'm responsible for making her thrust like this. When her screaming and clenching subsides, she stretches out and relaxes back into the pillows. I move on top of her and cover her beautiful, flushed face with kisses, keeping my fingers inside her to enjoy the gentle pulsing.

I have a new-found respect for men. Well, those who put in the work, anyway. I swear giving a guy a blow-job is a doddle compared to this. But bringing a woman to orgasm is so much more satisfying. I feel like such a stud. I want to jump up and shout, 'I did it! I finally did it!'

'Happy Birthday,' I whisper. 'How do you feel?'

'Amazing,' she replies blissfully, flipping me over in one move. 'Now it's your turn.'

'Oh yeah, baby …'

○

Brandy's birthday party.

The beat of the music is competing with my furiously thumping heartbeat, as Marizette and I approach the outdoor party table at La Med. This is the first straight venue I've been to since coming out and I feel strangely out of place. No matter how much people accept us, I know we'll be an oddity – the lesbian couple. Will they secretly criticise us? Will they expect us to behave differently from other couples? Defiantly I take Marizette's hand in mine. I don't see why we shouldn't behave like any other couple in public. I'm also incredibly proud of Marizette and am filled with pride to have such a beautiful girl on my arm.

I know Marizette is even more nervous than I am. On the way here, she was agonising over how my friends would receive her. 'What if your friends don't like me? What if they resent me for breaking up you and Peter?'

'Mazzie', I assure her, 'we've been invited, haven't we?'

I squeeze her hand, 'Come on, let's do this.'

We approach the bustling party group, mostly seated around three long tables, all pushed together. I freeze momentarily, scanning the tables and taking it all in. They're mostly parents from the school and a few faces I don't recognise. Ah, the relief! I spot Brandy sitting with the rest of The Group; a beacon of glamour in the crowd.

'Michi,' Brandy says with pleasure, standing up. 'It's so good to see you!'

Dressed in a plunging black halter-neck, she looks elegant and immaculate, as usual. She whispers in my ear as she leans forward to kiss me hello. 'Jack wants to talk to you. He's at the bar. We'll keep Marizette busy.'

Patricia, Anne and Lucy also stand to greet us. Big smiles and hugs. Dare I leave Marizette with them?

Brandy takes my arm, 'Come, I'll take you to say hi to Jack and the guys.' Then to Marizette, 'I'm just borrowing Michele for a minute.'

At the bar, Jack greets me with an enthusiastic hug. Very male body: muscular arms, hard chest pressed against mine. It seems ages since I've been so close to a guy. I'm taken aback by how different it feels from a woman's body. Not unpleasant. Nice, in fact, comforting even, but sexual, no.

'So, ask Michele,' Brandy says nudging her husband and looking amused.

'Uh, OK,' he begins awkwardly. 'Look, I don't want to do the wrong thing. I mean, how do I greet Marizette? Do I kiss her on the cheek like I would with you, or do I slap her on the shoulder like I would with one of the guys? Or, do I shake her hand?'

'Jack,' I say, swallowing my laugh, 'Marizette's a girl. Just treat her like the rest of us. Kiss her on the cheek.'

'Ah, yes. Yes, of course. I thought as much. Just wanted to check, you know, didn't want to embarrass her.'

Brandy cuts in laughing, 'You have no idea how much that was bothering him! He was so stressed about it!'

We both laugh as we head back to Marizette, who is flirting easily with Anne, Patricia and Lucy.

Hours later, it's almost midnight and inhibitions are gone.

'Michi,' Brandy shrieks, 'come dance with us!'

Everyone is dancing, but standing out among them are Brandy, Anne, Lucy and Patricia. Marizette and I are at the bar, chatting to the men.

'Michi!' Brandy shrieks again. 'Come here!'

'Go on,' says Maz, 'I'll stay here.'

Suddenly I'm among them. All of us bumping and grinding with each other. Patricia up behind me, hands on my hips, pelvis moving against my bum. I feel horribly awkward and unsure of my boundaries. Before Maz I would've just joined in. Done the sexy dance routine for fun; a bit of titillation for the watching husbands. But now suddenly I'm awash with panic. What if my friends think I'm being serious and trying to come on to them? What if one of the guys takes offence and gets paranoid that I'm trying to steal his wife? What if Marizette gets an attack of jealousy?

I decide to dance with my friends, but not too sexily, and to keep my hands to myself. I find I've been way more cautious lately, even in everyday life. I always used to be complimentary and easily affectionate with my female friends and acquaintances. Now I worry that if I say something as simple as, 'You look pretty today', they might get the wrong idea. God, being a lesbian is so complicated.

I look over at Marizette, chatting and laughing with the husbands. She slaps Jack on the shoulder as they both roar with laughter at something he's said.

I catch her eye and she winks, and my heart melts.

Chapter thirty-five

To: sara@naturalnurture.co.uk
Subject: Times of transition
Dear Sara

Maz has been living with us for a few months now and there've been huge adjustments all round. The kids complain she's way more strict than before, and isn't fun any more. They're right in a way, she's far more serious, but a huge part of that is the sheer responsibility she's taken on. Although, admittedly, she still behaves like a child sometimes, which often leads to conflict.

For instance, Chloe makes a point of keeping me with her as long as possible at bedtime, and starts crying when I do try to leave. Maz then becomes resentful, as it's often after ten by then and we haven't spent any time together all evening. Trying to point out that Chloe has been through major trauma and needs reassurance gets me nowhere and I often land up in the middle, with Marizette complaining that Chloe's being manipulative and Chloe saying I care more about Marizette than I do about her. Sigh!

Maz also hates the dogs being in the house and all over the furniture. She was raised on a farm, where dogs belong outdoors. So I've compromised by letting them in the house, but keeping them off the furniture.

I'm still very down about my marriage coming to an end. I miss Peter terribly, and often have moments when I think I won't be able to breathe as I'm so full of grief. Hardly surprising – I've known him since I was a twenty-year-old student and we've been through so much together.

Also struggling with not being able to express myself. Maz and I saw the shrink together as a couple for a few sessions, and he suggested that we take a break. Maz was horrified. Refused to see him again and pushed me to not see him either. Now she doesn't want me to see anyone, so I have no outlet. Her reason: 'If you speak to someone else then you won't speak to me. Also, I don't want you talking behind my back when I can't defend myself.' Seriously! So it feels like I'm bottling everything up at the moment. I know you'll want to know why I let her control things, but she's so determined it's not worth my while to argue.

And whenever I do get frustrated or stressed I remember her dedication to the family and all is instantly forgiven. I truly didn't expect so much from her. She helps make school lunches, drives the kids around, and helps put them to bed. I sometimes worry she's going to burn out and wonder what the hell she's doing at this stage of her life. I've mentioned it to her but she brushes me off saying she's committed herself to me.

Oh, and get this. In spite of the fact that we are domestically exhausted, Marizette desperately wants a baby. Of course I'd love to do this with her one day, but only once things have settled down – a lot.

For my birthday this weekend Maz organised a dinner party for me and some friends. Everyone was impressed and I was very proud and spoilt. My friends are definitely warming to her. Wish you could meet her, know you'd love her. As usual, I always miss you at the major events in my life. Wish you could've been at my birthday. All my love, Michi

◯

Marizette and I are standing within the stone walls of the crumbling fortress on Chapman's Peak Drive. We escape here periodically to get away from the children, animals, various adults, and casual staff who make up our bustling home. We leave the children with my mom or Princess, and make our way up the cliff. It's a breathtakingly beautiful drive; the mountain soaring on one side and the bay on the other, and I feel the stress seeping out of me as we ascend. We pull over as we reach the old fortress and find sanctuary within its walls. Then, as soon as we're away from prying eyes, Marizette pushes me up against the stone wall and kisses me; passionately, greedily. And I in turn submit to her touch and open up to her.

But today's different and Marizette is being quite reticent. She's chosen for us to sit on the grassy bank, where we can overlook the sea. I'm so happy to have her to myself that as soon as I note there are no cars parked nearby I start kissing her, pushing my hand up her T-shirt.

To my surprise, she pulls my hand out and moves away from me. 'Michi, not now!'

'Why not now?' I reply sulkily, unwilling to miss a perfect opportunity to get intimate with this beautiful woman.

'Michele, I need to talk.'

'Alright,' I say, slipping my hand back up her top and kissing her face, 'you talk and I'll touch.'

'Michi, stop! I'm being serious,' she says impatiently, removing my hand from her breast.

Suddenly I start stressing. It must be serious if Marizette stops me from groping her. Oh my God, what if she doesn't want to be with me any more? What if, now that she's been living with me and all the domestic stresses and strains, she wants to call it quits?

'Michele,' she says, startling me out of my reverie, 'I want you to close your eyes.'

Obediently I close my eyes and Marizette gently takes my left hand in hers. My heart skips a beat. Could it be? No, surely not ... I open my eyes and on my finger is a perfect gold ring with a square diamond.

Marizette is so nervous her lips are shaking. 'Michele,' she says quietly, looking into my eyes, 'will you marry me?'

There's no doubt in my mind. If the most beautiful woman in the world wants me to marry her, how can I possibly say no? I throw myself at her, pinning her to the ground, kissing her face all over.

'Of course!' I gush, 'Of course, I'll marry you.'

○

To: sara@naturalnurture.co.uk
Subject: Wedding bells!!!
Dear Sara

Marizette and I are engaged! She proposed to me and it was so romantic, I wish she'd do it all over again. The shadow over the whole thing is her parents, who are less than impressed and say they won't attend the wedding. Maz was so hurt and upset she spent a whole day in bed, unable to function. It breaks my heart when she's that upset, and makes me realise how protective of her I am. I want to rage at her parents, shake them to make them realise they have such a wonderful, kind, daughter, and should be bursting with pride. But all they can express to her is their shame. It makes me so angry. Think I'm going to write them a letter.

To add to our stress, Peter and I have met for mediation sessions so we can discuss divorce proceedings. That Maz didn't freak out about me meeting Peter is progress. Maybe now we're engaged she feels a bit more secure. In many ways it's a terrible month for me. It would've been my tenth wedding anniversary and it's Peter's fortieth. His birthday caused a huge upset with Maz, as I bought him a present from Benjamin. She didn't understand at all, even when I explained that Benjamin wanted me to help him choose something for Peter. Am I meant to tell him that I won't?

Whenever Peter is involved, Maz works herself up into a state. To the point where I think, 'What am I doing with this woman? And at the same time what would I do without her. Why have I complicated my life so much?' But then she makes love to me so beautifully and I melt and fall in love all over again. She also spoils me rotten. Seriously rotten. I mean, she warms up a towel for me while I'm in the shower. She gets my clothes ready for me in the morning, laying them out neatly on the bed. Of course she always chooses the sexiest, most plunging T-shirts in my cupboard, or little dresses I'd never normally pick out for myself. It's weird how much more feminine I am with Marizette than I was with Peter or any of my boyfriends.

Anyway, I'm happy to be indulged by Maz, just wish that things could be more peaceful sometimes. Peter sees far more of the kids now and luckily they all get on well with Ingrid. Although I miss them terribly, even if it's just a couple of days, it gives me some quiet time alone with Maz.

Pleased to hear your life's going smoothly at the moment and the kids are doing so well. Love and kisses, Michi

Chapter thirty-six

'OK, Peter, bye. Give Benjamin a hug from me,' I say, putting the phone down, only to be greeted by a sullen-looking Marizette, standing in the doorway, arms folded across her chest.

'So, that was Peter, was it? What exactly were you talking about?' she asks, each word clipped and hard.

I feel the knot tightening in my stomach. This is happening way too often. No matter how many times I tell Marizette how much I love her, she's still extremely jealous that Peter's still a part of my life and insecure about whether or not I still have feelings for him.

I sigh, 'I was just talking about the children and organising when we're going to pick them up.'

'Really, well that was a long conversation,' she snaps. And almost as though she can't help herself, 'What else did you talk about?'

'Marizette, it wasn't a long chat. We just discussed the children, that's all.'

'Well, I just wish we didn't have to have anything to do with your ex-husband. Except, oh, he isn't your ex-husband, because you're still married to the fucker!' she rants, raising her voice, her eyes blazing. And damn she's beautiful. I can't help but notice, even with my rising stress levels.

Marizette continues, 'When exactly are you going to get a divorce? Because if I'm not mistaken, we're meant to be getting married at some point!'

In truth I should have started divorce proceedings long ago, but I simply haven't the strength. Whenever I bring it up with Peter, he has a near-breakdown, saying he can't deal with it all right now and accusing me of being insensitive. The bottom line is he doesn't want to get divorced. And of course the fact that I care about Peter's emotional well-being drives Marizette to distraction.

I sit down on the bed. 'OK, Marizette,' I say wearily. 'I'll phone a lawyer and get the proceedings started.'

I still don't feel as though I've caught up with my current situation yet. It seems like yesterday I was a regular wife with a husband, a complete family and no major dramas. Now overnight I'm living with a woman, and dealing with distraught kids, an emotional ex and a highly insecure girlfriend.

Marizette sits down beside me and places her hand on my knee. 'Michi,' she says, her voice softening, 'I know it's been really difficult for you.' I feel my tension easing. 'Look,' she continues, I know there are a lot of changes in your life and I'm sure you're missing Peter. And that can't be easy for you.'

My suspicions are alerted. I mustn't say anything. Every time Peter is discussed, things become highly volatile.

But Marizette doesn't want to let things go, she wants answers. She puts her arm around me. 'You miss him, don't you, Michi? Just tell me.'

She's not going to drop the subject, so I sigh and tell

the truth. 'Yes,' I reply.

Like a wildcat, she turns on me, 'Why do you miss the fucker? I saw how things were. It was a marriage of convenience. Peter never spent time with you; he never looked after the kids. And you even told me you only got married because it seemed like the right thing to do, not because you were in love with him,' she pauses and I am about to add something, but she holds up her hand to silence me. 'I must have had it so wrong. If I'd known you were really in love with him, I'd never have destroyed your home.'

I want to defend my marriage; to tell her that as far as marriages go it was a good one. But I know better, especially not while she's this angry and emotional.

After what feels like hours later we're still talking in circles. She wants answers I can't give her. She wants to hear that I love her so much; that I'm not upset by the break-up of my marriage; that I have no feelings for Peter, and preferably that I don't care about him at all. I'm trapped in a corner. Nothing I say is the right answer and I have no idea how to get out of this nightmare.

'OK, Marizette, I don't love Peter. I never really did. I don't miss him at all. I'm only feeling sad because I miss the children.'

But she knows I'm lying and she won't let it go. 'You do miss him! I'm not stupid, Michele. Don't lie to me.'

And on and on it goes, till I can't take it any more, I feel like my head's going to burst. I get up and head for the door. 'Marizette, I need a breather. I want to be on my own for a bit. We can discuss this later.'

'Don't walk away from me!' she demands. 'We're not finished with this yet.'

'Marizette, we're not getting anywhere. We need a break, even if it's just ten minutes,' I plead, exhausted.

But as I open the door to the passage, Marizette shouts after me, hysterical, 'Don't walk away while I'm still busy! If you walk away from me then that's it between us!'

So I return and the whole conversation repeats itself, with no resolution in sight. By now Maz is tearful and angry, convinced I don't love her, because if I did, then I wouldn't be sad my marriage had ended. I'm exhausted trying to convince her of my love and commitment to our relationship. Everything I say seems to make it worse.

'Mazzie, I love you so much. Do you have any idea how difficult it is to leave a marriage? I would never have left if I didn't love you as much as I do.'

'Oh really? Was it so difficult to leave Peter? Why is that, Michele? Because you loved him so much?' She sneers, 'Because that's not the impression I got when you two were together.'

Finally I can't take any more. 'Marizette, I need a break. I'm going to the garden to be on my own for a bit.' And ignoring her protests, I turn on my heel and walk out.

Breathe deeply; calm down, the mantra repeats again and again in my head. I'm in the sanctuary of the children's tree house at the bottom of the garden, and am trying to unravel my frazzled nerves. Looking down, I can see where Peter's beloved veggie garden used to be. Once flourishing and abundant, it's now neglected and dying. Marizette has forbidden me to tend Peter's veggie patch. She doesn't want constant reminders of him and she certainly doesn't want me putting time into something that was once so dear to him. Looking down on all the wilted plants and shrivelled tomatoes, my heart breaks all over again and I wish I had the space to grieve. I close my eyes and breathe in, savouring these precious few moments alone.

'There you are!' says Marizette triumphantly. 'I've been looking all over for you.'

I open my eyes to see her head appearing through the trapdoor of the tree house.

'Why'd you run off? We haven't finished this discussion yet.'

Wearily I follow her back down the ladder and into the house. The conflict's still unresolved, going in circles. Marizette accuses me of missing Peter, of not loving her enough, and I try unsuccessfully to defend my position over and over.

And then I crack. I have no energy left to argue and we're not going to resolve these issues. I can't carry on, not for another second. I start to cry. Not heaving sobs, just quiet, hot tears. I lie on the bed and cover my face with my hands, as I feel the grief overflow uncontrollably. Once I start, I can't stop. And I'm terrified if I do stop crying the arguing will start all over again and I can't take any more.

Later, I run myself a bath. I've been sitting in it for ages and the water's going cold. I'm still crying; my head thick, my eyes swollen and my nose blocked. I hug my legs, burying my face in my lap. It feels like I could cry forever.

Marizette is sitting on the floor beside the bath, stroking my hair. 'Michi, please, stop crying. I'm so sorry.

Please stop crying.'

But I can't.

Much later, I lie on the bed, my tears soaking the pillow under my cheek. Marizette has wrapped her arms around me, as if she's holding me together.

'Michi, I'm sorry,' she whispers over and over. 'Please don't worry. We're going to be OK, I promise. We'll be fine, you'll see.'

I feel like a wrung out rag-doll. I don't know if we'll be OK. I don't see how, but for now I take comfort in her assurances. I snuggle into her embrace, enjoying the warmth of her body, feeling safe in her arms.

○

'You see, Jo?' Marizette says, her voice rising and eyes flashing. 'You see what I have to put up with?'

'What about what I have to put up with?' I counter.

Poor Jo is sitting between us, trying to be diplomatic. We came round to her cottage for dinner and it all started off well; good food and light-hearted bantering. But now, two bottles of wine later, the conversation has turned to Peter, and both Marizette and I are emotional and angry, each determined to get our view across.

Jo is in her element in counselling mode. 'Well Michele,' she says calmly, 'I can understand that you'd miss Peter. It's perfectly normal.' She turns to Marizette, 'And I also understand why that would make you feel insecure, Maz, but anyone can see from a mile off that Michele absolutely adores you.'

'But she loves that arsehole too,' Marizette shoots back. 'And he is an arsehole. Ask Michele about the texts he sends me – ask her. I can see how great a dad he is when I play his part every day, trying my best to keep everyone happy. Admit it, Michele. He's an arsehole.'

I don't want to call Peter an arsehole, but I know that if I appear to defend him, it'll only fuel her anger. 'Marizette,' I say, pouring myself a glass of wine (we've opened a third bottle), 'can we drop it?'

'Oh yes, let's drop it,' she fumes. 'Because that's how you deal with everything – we'll just not talk about it. How are we meant to sort anything out?'

'I don't want to talk about it, because when we do talk about Peter, absolutely nothing is resolved and we both end up hysterical,' I say, exasperated.

Much, much later ...

'Michi. Michi,' calls Marizette, shaking my shoulder. 'Come on, it's time to go home.'

I'm curled up on Jo's couch, hugging a cushion. I've had far too much to drink. The last time I was this drunk was at my penthouse birthday party ages ago. And that was cheerfully drunk. This time I'm weepy and maudlin. Marizette and I ended up having a full-blown shouting match, with me sobbing uncontrollably in Jo's lap.

Now Marizette is struggling to get me to the car so we can go home. She's been coaxing and pleading with me to no avail, so now she's trying the tack I used on the children when they were younger.

'OK, Michele,' she says heading to the door, 'you stay here if you want to, I'm leaving.'

'Thas jush fine,' I slur, slipping off the couch onto the floor beside Rocky Dog, Jo's beloved Jack Russell.' 'I'll jush sleep here with Rocky Dog,' I mumble.

Half an hour later we are home. Marizette and Jo

had to practically carry me to the car and once we got home Marizette somehow managed to haul me down the passage to our bathroom.

'Alright,' she says, 'let's get you to bed.'

I feel like I'm going to pass out, then a huge surge takes over my body and I heave, throwing up all over the bathroom floor. Oh God.

'I'll clean it up in the morning,' I mumble, my eyes already closed.

The last thing I remember is Marizette putting me into bed and covering me with the duvet.

Chapter thirty-seven

To: sara@naturalnurture.co.uk
Subject: It must be love
Dear Sara

Marizette really loves me! I know this because she cleaned up my sick when I threw up all over the floor last weekend ... classy on my part; just don't ask.

I'm also finally seeing a psychologist. He's an amazing guy called Jeffrey. Initially I was reluctant to see a male, especially a straight one, but he came highly recommended. Marizette was dead set against me seeing a therapist, but Jo had a word with her and explained it would be good for me to see someone. Where Jo got this insight and powers of persuasion is beyond me. Anyway, it's been invaluable having someone to speak to.

Another sign of progress is that my dad and Maz are getting on really well. It was his birthday recently and Maz went to a lot of effort to organise it. We invited his friends and family, and held it at the penthouse. My mom and I sat on the couch at one point, watching Maz and my dad laughing. We both marvel at how well they get on. Sometimes I think she gets on better with him than I do.

Then Marizette's mom, Helene, arrived a few days

later. I'm not actually 100% sure what motivated her visit. Obviously I'd like to think it's to see her daughter, whom she misses so much, but the truth is Helene hasn't visited Marizette once since she moved to Cape Town. Maz made a point of this recently, which may have something to do with Helene's visit. However, I think (rightly or wrongly), Helene's making a last-ditch effort to talk Marizette out of marrying me. In their last conversation, she begged Marizette to get out while she still has a chance, before she ruined her life.

When we picked up Helene from the airport she and Marizette were equally tightly wound and nervous. Both devoured three ciggies each on the drive home and Helene spoke non-stop about everything and nothing in particular. Maz and I are trying really hard to make sure she has a nice time. My parents have moved out temporarily to the penthouse so Helene can stay in the flat upstairs. Mostly it's going well, but on the couple of nights the kids have stayed with Peter, we've had these 'chats'. They start off well, but then end up as a mud-slinging session.

We were out on the stoep last night when Helene finally broached the fact that we're in a gay relationship, and of course it got heated. She says she truly loves me, but can't accept us being together. And that she and her husband will never come to our wedding, because it will be the saddest day of their lives. Can you believe it?! The saddest day of their lives. With all the possible drama and tragedy that can occur in your lifetime, how can your daughter getting married to someone she loves possibly be the saddest day of your life? Unless, of course, she marries a mass murderer or a rapist.

Then she went on to rant about the whole Christian thing and what a sin it is to be gay. At which point I had to speak up. I said if she wants to talk about the Bible and sinning then she's got to accept all of it, not just cherry pick some bits out. I made a comment about her smoking and how that was like sinning as the Bible states you must treat your body like a temple, not fill it with poison. She conceded I had a point, but still maintains what we're doing is wrong. 'Two women can't love each other like a man and a woman, and two men even less so' – words of wisdom from my mother-in-law-to-be!

She's such a mass of contradictions. One minute she tells me she loves me and she loves her daughter, and the next she wants nothing to do with our wedding. I suppose I also have mixed emotions about her. On one hand, she drives me absolutely crazy, where I get so angry and frustrated that I want to spit, and on the other I truly like her. As long as we don't broach the gay thing, we get on really well.

Anyway, she's not going to be able to talk us out of marriage, so we must just try to make sure she has a good time while she's here. Thankfully, my kids have been beautifully behaved. So far we've been up Table Mountain, and to Kirstenbosch gardens and tomorrow we're taking her walking on the beach. Whales have been spotted in the bay and Helene, like most land-locked people, loves anything to do with the sea. Will write again soon, once she's left. Love, Michi

'Oh my word! Quick! Let's get closer,' Helene gushes.

We're on the pier at Hout Bay beach and Helene has her phone held up high, camera mode on, trying to snap a photo of the whale we're watching breach in the calm sea. Her enthusiasm for nature is infectious, and is one of the things we have in common.

'I got it,' she beams, walking back to me and Marizette. She holds up the phone for us to see. The screen is filled with grey sea and a tiny dot – the whale's tail.

'Let's take a walk on the beach,' says Marizette, grabbing my hand. I don't pull away like I did in Venda and Helene doesn't seem to mind. As we step onto the sand, she kicks off her shoes. It's a beautiful evening. The sun's setting and everything is bathed in a golden glow. The mountains have turned a metallic pink and the sea is calm, dotted with kayaks. Hout Bay is a dog owners' paradise, perfect for strollers, where no one takes any notice of the leash laws (like so many flouted laws in this country). So there are lots of people and children out walking with dogs of every breed and size. A cute Jack Russell comes bouncing up to us, sniffing our feet. Marizette and I recognise him immediately; it's Rocky Dog, and where there's Rocky Dog there's bound to be …

'Jo! Jo, we're over here,' Marizette shouts waving her over.

Jo strides over. 'Rocky Dog, there you are! I was looking for you. Hi there, chicken,' she says giving Marizette and me a hug each.

'Jo,' says Marizette, 'this is Helene, my mom'

'Nice to meet you,' Jo beams, grabbing Helene's hand. 'Hey listen, I'm meeting a few friends at Dunes for a couple of drinks. Why don't you guys join us?'

The Au Pair

Marizette glances at Helene, 'Maybe just a quick one.'

Over an hour later we're still at the restaurant. Dunes is popular for its prime location and its child- and dog-friendly policy, rather than for its service or food. You can't go wrong with drinks though, and Helene and I have already worked our way through a chilled bottle of crisp white wine and Marizette has polished off two ciders.

Jo's usual selection of friends is here: Kharli, who has split up with Pam; her two straight friends Justine and Sonya; and Nicola, who's bi. Helene's surprisingly chatty and sociable. Jo has freely admitted she's gay and Nicola has divulged that she's bi. Jo's told Helene she sells sex toys as a sideline business and Helene astonished me by sharing with us that she'd love to go to one of those parties. She then proceeded to give us all some advice her mom had given her: In a long-term relationship, you must work to 'keep it interesting'.

Helene and Jo are getting on particularly well, which isn't that surprising, as Jo manages to connect with everyone. Marizette is offering us another glass of wine, when I hear a smooth male voice behind me.

'Hello there!'

I turn around. Shit, it's Herman, Jo's friend. Well, not really Jo's friend, but the ex-boyfriend of one of Jo's friends. I met him at a drinks party a few weekends ago. He's a creep. Dressed beautifully, as he was then, in ironed jeans and a designer shirt, with nice shoes. He's perfectly groomed, from his carefully trimmed facial hair to his manicured nails. But I don't like him. Partly from what Jo's told me about him being a major player and partly because the last time he crashed our drinks party he proceeded to flirt outrageously with Marizette.

After several drinks, he told her in front of everyone how gorgeous she was, and said he wanted to marry her.

'Sorry,' Marizette said, putting her arm around me, 'I'm already taken.'

'Pity,' he replied, shrugging. 'Well, if you ever change your mind …'

And now he's here. He greets everyone at the table. When Jo introduces Helene as Marizette's mother, he switches to perfect Afrikaans and greets Helene warmly, taking her hand in his, smiling, and meeting her eye. The smooth prick.

Helene looks impressed and intrigued.

'Look, I'd love to join you, but I'm meeting some friends,' he says politely, directing his comments at Helene. 'Hopefully we'll see each other again.' Then he nods at Marizette, pointedly making eye contact, and walks off.

'Oooh, he seems nice,' Helene enthuses.

'He's a jerk,' I say, laughing. 'And he wants to marry Marizette.'

'Quick! Call him back,' says Helene, making as if to rush after Herman. 'Sorry for you, Michele, but I think my daughter should marry him.'

I'm incredulous, 'You don't even know him!'

'I don't care,' Helene says, dismissing my concerns. 'He's a man. If he wants to marry my daughter, then I want her to marry him.'

Jo, bless her a million times over, jumps in. 'Helene, I know that guy. Trust me, you don't want him to marry your daughter. He'll cheat on her, smack her about, and steal from her. But that's OK I guess, because he's got a penis,' she quips.

'My daughter's strong. She can take care of herself.'

I can't believe this. 'Helene, you must be joking. Would you really rather have a guy who'll abuse Marizette than a woman who'll treat her like absolute gold? Because I will, you know,' I swear, passionately, 'I'll treat your daughter like gold. Better than any man could ever treat her.'

Helene shakes her head, '*Nee*, I would rather she were with a man,' she insists.

I'm about to respond when Jo jumps in. 'So, Helene, how are you enjoying Cape Town? Have you been up Table Mountain yet?'

I'm furious with Helene, but then I picture what she must have dreamed of so many times before: Marizette in a beautifully tailored wedding dress. She enters the church – a picturesque stone affair in Louis Trichardt – on her father's arm. Helene sits at the front of the chapel, glowing with pride. As mother of the bride, she's elaborately dressed. The 'Wedding March' begins and Marizette and her father walk down the aisle towards the groom, a handsome, young farmer, who smiles as he sees his wife-to-be approach ...

I so badly wish I could give Helene and Danie that happiness, rather than the shame that their daughter is marrying a woman. And not just any woman, but a much older, previously married woman, with three children. No matter how hard I try, how good a wife or daughter-in-law I am, Helene and Danie would rather Marizette marry a man, even if he is a complete arsehole.

Chapter thirty-eight

To: sara@naturalnurture.co.uk
Subject: The Tempest
Dear Sara
Wow, what a month! It was a big relief when Helene left, I must say. Not that I don't like her. It was just all so stressful. I haven't written for a while, so I'll give you a quick rundown of my life at the mo:

Maz and I. We've been together for over a year now, but it still feels like early days. I'm as in love with her as ever, but I have to be honest: things can be extremely stressful at times. And I'm not sure how much can be blamed on circumstance (it's been a year of adjustment for everyone), and how much can be put down to personality. I suspect it's a bit of both.

The main problem between us has been my sadness. Marizette can't handle it. She wants me to be happy to be with her, not mourning Peter and my marriage. Of course my grief for Peter in no way lessens the incredible love I have for Marizette, but you try telling her that. Where Peter's calm suited me, there are now times I don't know how to handle Marizette's storminess.

I'm especially sad at the moment, because yesterday she made me take down our hand-painted picture.

Remember, the one I did of me, Peter and the kids all in bed together? I painted it in England just before we left, and all my UK family and friends (including you and your kids) helped decorate it. Well, she made me take it down, as it shows me with Peter in bed together. Then she was angry because I was sad about it. I love that picture. Not just because it represents my family together at a happy time, but because all my close friends in England painted something on it. Plus it's so beautiful; all sparkly and glittery.

In spite of all her insecurities, Marizette is an extraordinary girlfriend and stepmother. She goes to all the parent-teacher meetings, helps the kids with their homework and, thanks to my rapidly deteriorating eyesight, does all the driving for us. So although she can drive me crazy, I'm hugely grateful to her.

My parents: Maz and I told my folks we want to get married next year and have a baby, and let's just say my dad was very unimpressed. He went on about how we're not financially independent yet, and what a bad idea having a baby would be for the kids, as they need our time and attention now more than ever.

The kids: What can I say? They hate being in between homes. Chloe especially hates having to take all her toiletries and school books from one house to another. She says she'll never get used to it. Benjamin doesn't understand why Peter can't move back home and we all live together. He even worked it out: 'You and Marizette can have a bath together in the evening, and me and Dad will bath together in the children's bathroom. Then we can all eat together. Then Daddy can put me to bed and you and Marizette can have some quality time together.'

He honestly said 'quality time together', can you believe it?! Anyway, Marizette asked him what would happen to Ingrid, and he went, 'Ah, I didn't think about Ingrid.' So I'm sure he's gone back to the drawing board to work out what to do with Ingrid in this perfect family solution.

Chloe just got back from school camp where Marizette went along as her parent. Chloe begged Maz to go with her, which I was thrilled about, as those two can bang heads sometimes. I was a bit put out she didn't ask me (but was told: 'Duh, Mom, we need someone who can drive.'). Think Chloe is secretly quite proud of Marizette, because all her friends think Maz is really cool. Benjamin even asked Marizette to run in the mothers' race at sports day last month because he thought she'd be faster than me because she's so much younger. My kids, honestly! Anyway, she crossed the finishing line metres ahead of any of the other moms, so Benjamin was delighted.

It was Max's fourteenth birthday last week. He spent the day with Peter and then had grown-up supper with my parents, me and Maz. He's still being home-educated, but we're going to have to think about what to do with him next year, as Marizette and I have to find a way to make more money. Peter isn't paying enough maintenance to raise the kids. Thank God my parents are helping, but don't want to rely on them forever. Maz is a qualified swimming teacher and we're thinking of starting up a swimming school from home, using the pool. Marizette has even written an impressive-looking business plan.

Peter: Although he's still angry with me, he and Ingrid are going strong. She's wonderful to my children, for which I'm extremely grateful. Chloe in particular adores her.

Well, that's about all my news for now. Oh wait, I almost forgot! I can't believe Gael is texting you again. I thought she was out of your life for good? Just think about what you really want. You'll probably need to make a decision one way or another. And, Sara, no matter what you say, I find it difficult to believe she just wants to be friends this time. Be careful! Remember what you've told me about her before.

Oh, and Ian wants us to help out at the Cape Town International Convention Centre tomorrow. He called me in a panic earlier, asking if Maz and I can come to the Organic Living conference with him, to help him sell some computer game called 'The Wild Divine'. Personally, I was hoping for a lie-in, but I can never say no to Ian. He gets this look on his face. It's always been like that, ever since we were children. Luckily, Tana is highly nurturing and doesn't have a problem spoiling him rotten. Oh well, I better sign off and try to get a good night's sleep. Lots and lots of love, Michi

◯

Cape Town International Convention Centre. Marizette and I are smartly dressed. She's wearing black trousers and a white shirt and I'm wearing a dress. I've even put on shoes with a heel. Ian has set up two computers, and so far there's been a steady stream of people showing an interest in or playing the game.

I enjoy watching Marizette do her sales thing. She's really good; confident and enthusiastic, without being pushy. I stand back perving, when two women with little girls approach the stand. My interest is immediately aroused as I study the little group. The women are standing close, side by side, with the children holding hands in front of them. The little girls are similar in age; I estimate about six or seven. One little girl is blonde and the other is mixed race, with gorgeous, long, spiralling curls. One woman has mousy brown, shoulder-length hair, and is wearing a long skirt with a baggy top. Nothing definable there. But the other woman. Ah yes, the giveaways, I nod knowingly. She has short hair. So short you can see her scalp where it's been cropped at the side. Her hairstyle accentuates her multiple earrings. Not just any earrings, but silver hoop earrings. And she has a thumb ring. Now, I could be wrong, but I feel my gaydar is becoming quite finely tuned already. And this to me looks like a lesbian couple with their two young children.

Marizette approaches them and takes one of the girls off to play 'The Wild Divine'. Deciding to investigate, I casually stroll over to the two women and the remaining child.

'Hi there,' I smile at the little girl. 'Are you going to have a go?'

'Yes,' she says. 'We're going to be better than our mommies. We beat them at everything,' she informs me proudly.

Oh my God! I was right; they're gay. And they're a proper family. I love the ease with which she said 'our mommies'. With longing, I think how great it would be for my kids to see Marizette as a co-parent.

I decide to pry a little further, so addressing the two women, I enthuse, 'I think it's amazing your kids are so open about you both being their moms.'

They look at me, but say nothing. The one with the

short hair nods, so I continue, 'I mean, I'm in the same situation, and my kids are still so embarrassed about us. I think it's amazing yours are so natural about the two of you being their moms; so unashamed.'

The one with the mousy hair frowns and says, 'Well, why should they be ashamed that we're their moms?'

'Oh no, I'm not suggesting they should. I mean, of course they shouldn't!' I stumble over my words. 'I just wish my kids felt the same about us,' I conclude.

The two women give each other a look.

This is so cool. They've obviously been lesbians for so long and their family is so established that it's not even an issue for them. And indeed, why should their children be ashamed? Still, I'm itching with curiosity. I'm pretty sure the little blonde girl is biological, and curly-haired one is adopted.

'So,' I persist, 'who do the children belong to?'

'Well,' says the short-haired woman, pointing to the mixed race girl, 'she's mine.'

'And this little one is mine,' continues the other woman, placing her hands on the shoulders of the little girl standing in front of her.

'Cool,' I enthuse. 'So, how did you go about having her? I mean, did you already have her before you got together, or did you go through a sperm donor? And,' I plough on, 'did you both adopt the other little girl together, or just one of you?'

I'm so curious about all this stuff because I know at some point Marizette is going to want a child of her own and we have to explore our options, it'll be fascinating if another couple can share their journey with me.

The mousy-haired woman's quizzical look turns hostile

and she snaps, rather crossly, 'My friend and I have not had the need to adopt or seek out a sperm donor, as there is nothing wrong with our husbands' fertility.'

Shit. Shit. Shit. Fuck! How could I get it so incredibly wrong? I can feel the heat rising from my chest and into my face. Now, I don't often blush, but I know for sure that right now I am a deep shade of burgundy. I'm mortified. I don't even wait around to make any apologies, which I'm certain will make things worse. What could I possibly say that won't offend? 'Oh, I'm terribly sorry, but I just assumed you were both lesbians?' So I turn on my heel and walk away without turning back.

I pass Ian, who tries to intercept me, 'Michele! What's wrong? You're the colour of a beetroot. Are you OK?'

'Ian, not now,' I hiss, barely slowing.

I make a beeline for the toilets and lock myself into a cubicle, where I start the whole laughing and crying thing, trying very hard to keep as quiet as possible. I can only imagine what it would sound like to some poor unsuspecting woman coming in for a quiet wee only to hear lunatic laughter coming from one of the cubicles. And I've been embarrassed enough for one day. Well, for a lifetime, actually. What will those poor women be thinking? I'm so ashamed. Why was I so sure? It's a major lesson to me – don't make assumptions. Don't stereotype.

But come on. She had such short hair and a thumb ring, for God's sake! I mean they can hardly be upset with me for so spectacularly getting the wrong end of the stick. The shocked looks on their faces when the penny dropped! I start laughing again, clutching my aching sides. I must pull myself together.

I phone Ian and tell him the whole story. 'And Ian,'

I continue, 'please tell me when they've left, because I'm not coming out till they have.'

Ian is also laughing out loud. 'Michele, you're hysterical! You've made my day. I was wondering why they left in such a hurry. Come on, it's all clear, you can come out.'

I gingerly come out of the cubicle, praying the two women haven't entered the toilets while I was on the phone. I splash my face at the sink and vow to never, ever, trust my gaydar again.

Chapter thirty-nine

'Michi,' Marizette says casually, 'do you ever miss penises?'

'Maz, where on earth did that come from?'

It's a Friday afternoon and we've just dropped off the kids with Peter. We're driving through the city and I'm filled with the usual mixture of relief and sadness at not having them for the weekend. Although, more often than not, we end up seeing them at some point, as one of them inevitably phones to complain they miss me.

Marizette sighs, 'I don't know. I've just been thinking, you know? You've been straight for years and you've had sex with guys for most of your adult life. You must miss them sometimes. Even if you don't necessarily miss the guy, you must miss his penis. I mean,' she says, matter of fact, 'I can't do that for you; fill you up, I mean. I don't have the right ... tools,' she trails off.

I take her hand and kiss her fingertips. 'Trust me,' I say, 'you already have everything you need to keep me happy.'

Minutes later, we're gobsmacked, standing in a shop enticingly named Whet, to search for a few tools. I'm not sure if Marizette was unconvinced by my insistence that I didn't need any more than the expertise of her fingers and tongue to keep me satisfied, or if she just wanted an excuse to do a bit of shopping, but as we drove past

Whet, she decided on impulse to pull over.

We could easily be in an upmarket clothing boutique. The store is tastefully and sumptuously decorated in hues of maroon and dark pink. The walls are adorned with oversized photographs of lingerie-clad models. And of course, instead of racks of clothing the room is filled to capacity with all manner of appliances related to sex. I'm fascinated, as I circle the store slowly, taking everything in. I start with the dress-up stuff. There are maids' outfits, police uniforms and nurses' outfits. I'm rather tempted by a nurse's uniform till I look at the price tag. Marizette loves me to dress up for her. It's a role I didn't assume as often with Peter, but with Marizette, I play far more on my feminine side. She encourages me to get dolled up in lacy lingerie, complete with suspenders and silky stockings, and I'm just too happy to oblige.

Having dispensed with the nurse's uniform, I move on to the various S&M and bondage gear, some of which are fascinating. There's all manner of spanking tools, from canes to leather straps, and of course restraining items, such as cuffs and other more complex-looking bondage accessories. In spite of myself, I feel a frisson of excitement as I pick up a leather strap with a little heart cut out. The words on the packaging read: 'Make my bottom pink, make me squeal.' Firmly I put the strap back on the shelf. We're here to find a few love toys not bondage gear.

But where to start? There's a sensory overload as we take in the various sizes and colours of strap-ons, love balls, dildos and the like.

'Can I help you?' offers a young brunette.

'Oh, yes please,' I say, thankful someone with a bit of

expertise will take us through the different merchandise. 'We're looking for a suitable strap-on.'

I feel a hard pinch in my side. It's Marizette. To my amazement, she looks furious, then to my even greater surprise, her entire face flushes red.

'We didn't need any help,' she hisses into my ear. But it's too late, our sales lady, oblivious to Marizette's embarrassment has enthusiastically started her sales pitch. Marizette turns on her heel and looks intently through the lingerie section.

'We're in a sex shop for God's sake,' I mutter under my breath, 'where you brought us. What's there to be embarrassed about?'

I should be used to Marizette's contradictory sexual nature by now. On one hand she's extremely adventurous and capable, and on the other hand, there's the conservative (Afrikaans), easily embarrassed side. A combination which I find extremely endearing, of course.

'This strap-on is particularly popular with lesbians,' our assistant is saying knowledgeably. She holds up a harness thing with straps and buckles. It has a triangle piece with a hole in it, which the woman explains is where the dildo attaches. 'And the wonderful thing about it,' she continues, 'is that it can be used with a variety of different sizes.' She waves her hand to indicate a display of multicoloured dildos standing upright on a glass shelf, like ornaments on a mantelpiece. There really is an incredible array of sizes and shapes; from eye-wateringly enormous, to a tiny one I doubt I'd be able to feel.

I select a purple one that looks thick and long enough to make an impact, but not so big it'll hurt me. Then I realise I'm not the only one who's going to be using it.

I wave to catch Marizette's attention and call out, 'Will this one be okay for you, Mazzie?'

Poor Marizette goes an even deeper shade of red. 'That's fine,' she says, quickly joining me. 'Just get it.' She gets out her wallet and walks to the till. I can tell she wants to get out of here as quickly as possible.

But, we're not free to go just yet. 'You're going to need a good-quality water-based lube,' our sexpert adds. 'You want to make sure you have a smooth ride.'

Marizette swallows hard and accepts a tube from the assistant. While the woman is ringing up our purchases, Maz discreetly adds an egg-shaped thing claiming to be a clitoral vibrator to our pile of purchases. We leave the shop almost two-thousand rand poorer. Being a lesbian is an expensive business.

○

'I hope you're ready for me,' I call out from the bathroom. 'Because I'm definitely ready for you.'

I've managed to get myself all strapped up, which if truth be told, was a bit fiddly, but I'm very pleased with the result. I'm walking, nay, strutting, up and down the bathroom having a good look at myself in the mirror. The black leather straps hug under the shape of my bum and, in front, my appendage pokes out rudely from my pubic bone.

It was a hard-won battle to be the first one to wear this gear. I nagged and pleaded, but Marizette always wants to be the do-er in our relationship. Given the chance, she would probably be perfectly happy to always service me, and that would be enough for her. However, I'm so enthusiastic in my desire for her that I normally insist on making love to her as well. I haven't yet worked out why she always wants to be the one going down on me, but I think it's something to do with being a stud, wanting to please her woman and all that. Which is great, but there are those times that I want to be the stud, so dammit, I was determined to wear the strap-on first.

I enter the bedroom and, if I was a guy, the sight of Marizette naked on the bed would be enough to give me an instant hard-on.

'Shit,' she says nervously. 'That thing looks really big.'

'Well,' I reply, kneeling over her on the bed to kiss her mouth, 'you should've paid more attention in the shop. You agreed to this one, remember? Now you're going to have to deal with it,' I tease. 'Look, I promise I'll go slowly and gently. To begin with, anyway …'

Shit, I love this being in control for a change! I take the lube from next to the bed and apply a generous amount to my appendage, coating the shaft in clear, cool gel. Then I slide some into Marizette's vagina. Oh bliss! The heat, the glorious softness, the slight contraction around my fingers as they slip into her. I don't think I'll ever feel anything but awestruck every time I go inside this woman. I start to kiss Marizette, enjoying the softness of her lips and the closeness of her body. Then, ever so carefully, I grasp my dildo and insert the tip inside her.

She gasps at the sensation, 'Please go gently.'

'Of course,' I whisper, 'trust me.'

Slowly I push all the way in, and start to build up speed and rhythm, spurred on by Marizette's sighs and moaning. I love the closeness of being on top of her, as I thrust into her, but I must confess my stomach muscles are really feeling it. A little while later and my abs are burning. And not for the first time, I feel a genuine respect for guys, especially those who manage to just keep going. How do they do it? I've only been at this for about five minutes and already I feel as though I won't be able to hold out for much longer. Of course, I can't let Marizette know this, so I keep my breathing steady and my rhythm strong ... until my stomach muscles can't take any more. Abruptly, I stop thrusting and pull out of her.

'What's wrong?' she asks.

'Nothing's wrong. I want you to turn over, onto your hands and knees. And get your buzzy thing ready; I want you to play with your clitoris while I'm busy,' I order.

Marizette obediently positions herself on her hands and knees. I rub one hand over her lower back and round her buttocks, and with my other hand I gently insert the dildo. Oh my, what a sight! I take in Marizette's broad shoulders and beautiful, long back. And most glorious of all, her vagina lips hugging my half-entered purple appendage. I grab onto her hips and gently push myself all the way in and slowly pull out again, hypnotised by my shiny penis, glistening with a mixture of lube and Marizette's juices. I have the most enormous case of penis envy. Maybe I always had a little penis envy, but it was restricted to not being able to pee standing up. But now, I'm really and truly envious. I imagine being able to feel her silkiness and experience her tightening with a real penis. Do guys have any idea how lucky they are? I start thrusting in earnest. Luckily being on my knees is far easier on my stomach muscles, so I feel as though I could keep going forever.

Marizette takes her buzzy thing and begins to work

it over her clitoris. 'Oh God,' she moans. 'Oh my God, that feels good. Deeper! Go deeper; harder. Don't stop,' she demands.

Of course, I'm more than happy to oblige, thrusting in and out of her, deeper and harder. I find the image of the purple dildo thrusting inside Marizette, combined with her moaning, so exciting that I'm fairly sure I could explode.

Then suddenly, Marizette is screaming, loudly, on and on, till eventually, she stops and I pull out of her. She rolls on to her back, and I realise she's crying.

I lie beside her, kissing her face. 'Are you alright, my darling?'

'Very much so,' she replies, her eyes still closed in ecstasy. 'That was awesome. Now it's my turn.'

Chapter forty

To: sara@naturalnurture.co.uk
Subject: The swimming coach & the tea lady

Dear Sara

I haven't written in so long I don't even know where to start! Max has started school this year, so for the first time in fourteen years, I don't have kids at home the whole day. I miss him terribly, but in the same breath I'll say it's given me some time to concentrate on what I want and need to do. Our swimming school is up and running now. It's fully heated and has an awning, so we can teach in all weathers. When I say we can teach, I mean Marizette can teach. I did a course recently, but I don't have the experience or confidence to teach young children to swim.

Marizette, on the other hand, is a phenomenal teacher and specialises in babies. She starts teaching them as young as four months old. We already have several clients who are delighted with their kids' progress. So, rather than even trying to teach, I let the parents in and make cups of tea for them while they wait. When asked what I do, I say I'm the tea girl!

And then there are the children. They're more settled recently, and each has a creative outlet that seems to help them cope with things. Max has his guitar, Chloe has her pottery and Benjamin (to my joy!) has started ballet, which he loves. He told me the other day, 'When I dance I feel happy.' Yes, I finally think my life is getting back on track, and I'm starting to feel more in control. All my love, Michi

PS: Maz desperately wants a baby. She's so broody she bought a whole bunch of newborn clothes on the Woolies sale (mostly white stuff that would suit either a boy or girl)! She wants to start fertility treatment ASAP. But between you and me, the last thing I want is a baby disrupting our lives, just when things are getting a bit easier. xxx

◯

I'm snuggled up in bed for a rare and much-needed lie-in. Lost in a deep and lovely sleep, suddenly Marizette is shaking me awake.

'Michi. Michi, wake up. Princess wants to talk to us. She says it's important.'

'Huh? What?' I'm bleary with sleep, trying to hang on to that last dream memory. 'Coffee, need coffee,' I mutter, mock-grumpy. 'Can't get up till I've had caffeine.'

'Come,' Maz urges, 'get up. The kettle's on. We can have coffee now. Mich, come on!'

Grumbling all the way, I follow her into the kitchen.

Coffee in hand, Marizette and I are seated next to each other, with Princess, our new housekeeper, sitting opposite. She fiddles with phantom crumbs on the table, then stops to wring her hands together. She doesn't look up.

'Princess,' I say, hoping to speed up matters, 'Marizette

said you wanted to speak to us.'

'Yes, Michi,' she pauses. 'It is my cousin. She is staying with me. And she is having a baby.'

Oh Christ, I think impatiently, why don't you just come out with it and say, 'I want a day off'? Why the long explanation? I know she's gearing up to ask for the day off, because she's done it so often lately, for one reason or another, and it always starts with a long explanation. I always give her the time off but it's been happening so much lately I wonder if I'm being taken for an idiot.

'So you want the day off?' I interrupt.

'She is having a baby,' Princess continues, determined to get the story in. 'And the baby, it is two months old. And my cousin is staying with me but she is drinking too much.'

Oh yeah? How come I've never heard of this cousin or this baby, my sarcastic inner dialogue continues.

'So last night, she leaves this baby in the location, on the ground outside her father's shack. Just there, on the ground, on her own and very late. At almost eleven, two women, they hear a cry and they recognise the baby, because they are neighbours and this, it has happened before. So they bring the baby to me. And I give it to my sister and I go to look for my cousin. I find her in a shebeen and I am so angry. I shout at her and I beat her. So now I must go to the social workers and the police, because she has done this thing before,' Princess finishes, her eyes still downcast, refusing to look at either of us.

What a story! She almost deserves the day off for the sheer effort she's put into manufacturing the whole thing. I mean, there are so many holes in it, it's unreal, I think, exasperated. I can't believe my lie-in was interrupted for this. For starters, why would two women be wandering around the township at close to midnight? Also, I can't imagine the mild-mannered Princess building up enough of a temper to give anyone a beating, especially in front of a bunch of her neighbours at a local bar.

I look sideways at Marizette, one eyebrow raised in a conspiratorial 'yeah sure' look. But she's ignoring me. She's looking at Princess with a strange, shiny look on her face. 'So who's looking after the baby now?' she asks.

I'm confused. What baby? There's no baby; Princess just wants the day off for whatever reason, I'm sure of it.

'It's my sister. She is looking after her.'

'Look,' says Marizette, I'll take you to the police station and then to the social workers.' She gets up to grab the car keys.

Of course. Marizette's going along with her story, not letting her off that easily. OK, if she wants to, it's her call. I shrug to myself.

In a matter of seconds Marizette is out the door with Princess close behind and the house is empty, which is extremely rare. A first, actually. The house is always busy. But for now, all the kids are at school, Marizette's pupils only start later, my parents are in the UK, and even Princess and Marizette are out. I stretch, smiling to myself. It feels great. I grab a book I've been meaning to read for ages, and jump back into bed. Ah, the life.

Then I hear the car pull into the driveway – they're back already. Although they've probably been gone longer than it seems, as I've already ploughed through several chapters of my book. I jump out of bed to meet Marizette at the front door. But she's already pushing it open with her shoulder. She's using her shoulder to open the door because in her arms is a baby, so swaddled in blankets in spite of the boiling weather, it's completely hidden.

Oh shit. Fuck. Shit! There is a baby after all. For a manic moment, I wonder if Marizette is playing a joke on me and has a doll in her arms. But then she looks at me, her eyes shining and her cheeks pink and I know I've seen that expression before. It's the same look, overflowing with love, that Peter had when he held Max for the first time. Oh shit, fuckity fuck.

I have to be the sensible one here. We're entering uncharted waters and in this moment, of all the possible outcomes, most of them will lead to heartbreak. I can see by Marizette's face she's already lost. I can only protect myself. I know instinctively I mustn't allow myself to become attached to this baby. Marizette pulls the blanket away, revealing a tiny head, topped with a mop of fuzzy black hair. And set in an ebony face, two huge, beautiful brown eyes.

'It's a little girl,' whispers Marizette. 'She needs some clothes. These are all wet. I'm sure we've got something among those things I got on sale.'

I reach out and touch her hair. A little girl! 'Well put them on for now, just until we can get her some proper pink clothes,' my resolutions to be the sensible one all but forgotten. 'Couldn't we get her just a couple of baby-grows?'

☾

On our way to school to collect the children, our newest ward is sitting in a car seat we managed to dig out of the garage. She's washed and dressed in clean clothes. Physically, she's in a shocking state, something we realised only after we peeled off three layers of clothes, which were soaked through and stinking. She's unbearably thin and malnourished. Her little body is covered in some kind of angry rash and the folds in her neck are filled with a kind of manky white fungus.

To my shame, I was quite squeamish, worried the rash was catching. But Marizette has no such qualms and I watched her wash and dress this baby with the utmost gentleness and care, while giving me a summary of the situation. The baby's name is Emihle, which is Xhosa for 'beautiful'. Her mother Tumeka is an alcoholic, who moved in with Princess shortly after giving birth to Emihle, or Emmy, as Maz calls her. The woman's given Princess repeated problems, and regularly leaves Emmy with strangers. Princess would sometimes return home after work to find Emmy lying on the bed alone, a bottle propped in her mouth with Tumeka nowhere in sight. And according to Princess, Tumeka was often rough with the baby, and would smack her if she cried.

I turn and look at Emmy. She's fast asleep and is yet to cry or make a sound. 'You're safe for now,' I think, biting my lip.

Marizette spoke to the social worker and offered to have Emmy for the night, as apparently all the foster homes are full and the children's homes are worse. Staying with Princess is not an option either, as Tumeka is theoretically still living there.

We arrive at the school. Chloe and Benjamin are waiting for us in the parking lot. They clock Emmy straight away as they jump into the car.

'Oh my gosh,' says Benjamin, wide-eyed. He sidles up to the baby seat and touches Emmy's hair. 'She's so beautiful. Are we keeping her?'

'No,' I say firmly, 'we're not.'

'Oh, Mom, please, please!' Benjamin begs with surprising urgency. 'She can be my sister.'

Chloe looks at me. 'Whose baby is it, Mom?'

'Long story. I'll tell you on the way home. And we're just looking after her for tonight. Just tonight, mind you. Tomorrow, other arrangements will be made for her.'

Chapter forty-one

To: sara@naturalnurture.co.uk
Subject: You're never going to believe this
Dear Sara
Prepare yourself. Get a cup of tea and sit somewhere comfortable. This is a long, long letter. Have so much to tell you. Enjoy the read. Am so exhausted and busy right now that you might not get another letter for months. So here goes.

We are fostering a baby! Can you believe it? Her name is Emihle ('beautiful'), but we all call her Emmy for short. She is our nanny's cousin's baby, and was abandoned by her mother. The mother has been tracked down, but because of the seriousness of her neglect, she's not allowed to have Emmy back for now. You have no idea how much this beautiful baby has opened up people's hearts. Shortly after we first got her, we took her with us to pick up Chloe and Benjamin from school, and all the moms literally swooned over her. We've been given clothes, blankets, a car seat and a crib. I'm overwhelmed by everyone's kindness.

Emmy is so tiny she's like a doll. Although she's two months old, she's still wearing newborn clothes, as she's so undernourished. Marizette and I are exhausted, as she can only take small amounts of milk at a time, so needs to be fed more often than regular babies. Honest to God, breastfeeding is so much easier than bottle-feeding. I had no idea how time-consuming all the bottle washing and sterilising is. We're also giving Emmy vitamin supplements as she's seriously deficient.

The children adore her, especially Benjamin, who's quite overprotective about her. I was in the kitchen cooking this afternoon when he came running up to me to tell me Emmy's crying. I told him I was just about to go get her. And he turned on me: 'You must get her straight away, or she'll feel like you've abandoned her.' Kids, honestly.

So basically we are long-term fostering Emmy. Her mother, Tumeka, has no family of her own to help out, and Princess's home is filled to capacity. Tumeka seems to have no desire to give up drinking. We organised a visit where we met at a coffee shop, so she could see Emmy. She reeked of alcohol, held Emmy briefly and handed her straight back to Marizette as soon as she started crying. Of course by now Maz, the kids and I are desperately in love with this little girl and we asked Tumeka if we could adopt her. She said yes, so we're in the process of formally applying through Social Services in Hout Bay.

It's been a major mission, I can tell you. In order to adopt Emmy we have to get permission from both parents. And the dad, who is Angolan, is mostly away at sea. The social worker assigned to us was meant to track him down, but because Emmy's no longer on the critical list, she did absolutely nothing. So Marizette took it upon herself to find the father. And this is where I've learned a lot about Marizette's incredible determination, especially if she wants something badly enough. She found out from Princess when the father was back home and she went into the township on her own to search for him. To understand what a feat this is you need to see a township yourself. Also, remember there's a lot of white fear about townships, and most white South Africans have never put foot into a township, fearing muggings or worse.

The only times I've been into the township is when I take Princess home and it's always during the daytime. Imizamo Yethu is built on a mountainside, where the houses nearer the road at the base of the slope are mostly nice, solid homes, with shacks attached to them, like add-ons to the main property. The higher you go up the mountain, the less formal and more dense the shacks become. So near the top, where Emmy's dad lives, the shacks are packed one on top of each other, a mishmash of accommodation made from bits and bobs of anything from corrugated-iron sheeting to plastic bags to cardboard billboards. It's so dense there are only narrow pathways between the shacks to squeeze through. And by the time you get to these upper shacks, there's no road system to speak of, no water supplies (only a shared tap), no power lines or any kind of sewerage system. The narrow paths serve as a rubbish tip and stink like open sewers.

When Marizette went to search for Emmy's dad, this was the terrain she had to negotiate. There's no proper road, so she had to go by foot. She started at the dad's home (well, shack, really) after Princess pointed it out to her, and then moved on to the neighbours' homes, asking questions as she went. Finally, she trawled all the shebeens in the area. She did this relentlessly, for several days in a row, till finally she tracked him down. They went to the police and then to the social workers. He was initially reluctant to sign anything as he's in South Africa illegally. But once the social workers convinced him it was a completely separate matter and they wouldn't report him, he agreed to sign. Now it just has to go through court and then the parents still have sixty-eight days to change their minds. It's been the most stressful, mind-numbing process. And we all love Emmy so much and are so attached to her that the thought of losing her is truly terrifying.

My parents are dead set against the idea of us having a baby in our home, for different reasons. My dad, ever practical, worries about the financial strain of raising a fourth child and the impact she'll have on the other three.

My mom, on the other hand, was frightened of getting close to Emmy and then having to give her up. Initially she tried to pretend Emmy didn't exist, then a few days ago I was trying to make supper and asked my mom, who was in the kitchen with me, if she'd hold Emmy. She refused so I just walked over to her and plonked Emmy in her arms, saying, 'Even if we don't get to adopt her, we'll still be fostering her for the next two years and you can't ignore her for that long.'

And my mom took one look at tiny Emmy and immediately burst into tears. I'll never forget her face; all blotchy and red, her eyes welling up and every fibre of her bursting with love for this little girl. Now my mom's our staunchest supporter and is willing to do anything in her power to make sure we adopt Emmy. Another thing my poor dad and mom don't agree on. Mom reckons he'll come round, but I don't know when.

However disapproving my dad is, it's nothing

compared to the reaction of Marizette's parents. When we decided to adopt Emmy, Maz said she'd have to tell her parents. As expected, their reaction was fairly horrible. She spoke to her mom a few days ago and Helene said if we adopted 'that child' it was the last straw. She and Danie would have nothing to do with Marizette ever again. God, Sara! Just writing about it makes my heart rate go up. It makes me so angry – Marizette is one of the most compassionate people I know. I can't believe that her parents would turn their backs on her.

So the last few days Maz has been in a cloud of depression. She even briefly thought about not going ahead with the adoption. She says I don't understand the fear of losing your whole family. She's been through it once before, when she told them she was gay. And it's taken her years to win back their trust and affection. She reached over and touched Emmy, who was asleep next to us and said, 'If I give her up and she goes to a children's home, how will they comfort her at night? They won't know how to rub her back when she gets stomach ache. How can I give her up? But my parents expect me to, or they'll give me up.' And she started crying.

I get so angry; I can't tell you how much I rant and rage about their stubbornness and intolerance. My mom has tried to get me to understand Marizette's parents, their upbringing, the years of racist conditioning, etc. She says they're just scared. My mom has also tried to speak to Helene, but to no avail. So I've decided against everyone's advice to phone her and speak to her myself.

My mom says I'm way too emotional and angry. But I've promised to keep calm. I want to find out where Helene really stands. And if she never wants anything to do with Marizette if we adopt Emmy, then there's nothing left to salvage. Anyway, I've decided; I'm phoning her tomorrow. Think of me. Love, Michi xxx

○

I'm alone in our bedroom. I've told Marizette I have to do this without an audience, as it's nerve-wracking enough. To my surprise, she agreed without arguing. It's only midmorning and I've already downed three strong coffees in a row, which has done nothing for my frazzled nerves.

I pick up the phone and replace it again. Pace the room, breathe deeply. There's nothing to be afraid of, I mutter to myself. I pick up the phone again, urging myself to be calm and collected. I will ask Helene to explain her concerns about Emmy. And then I'll try to reason with her. Tell her how sad Marizette is. Appeal to her mother to mother. It'll be fine.

I dial her number. The phone rings; maybe she's not home. My heart's beating unbelievably fast and feels like it's in my throat.

'Hello?' It's Helene.

Oh God. Shit. I can't speak. My mouth's gone dry.

'Hello?' says Helene again.

'Hello, Helene. It's Michele.'

'Yes?' her voice is cold.

'Look, Marizette's very upset and I just want to get my facts right. I, um, want to know what it is you mean when you say you don't want anything to do with Marizette if we adopt the baby ...' my voice trails off.

'I mean exactly that,' her voice is hard. 'If you adopt this baby I want nothing to do with either of you again.

Neither of you will be welcome in our home and if you ever try to visit you'll be turned away at the gate,' she says clinically, without emotion, as if she were talking to a stranger.

And then it happens. My resolve to remain calm dissolves in an instant and all that's left is red-hot anger. Fury at the unfairness of it all; that taking in an abandoned baby desperately in need of a home is leading to Marizette's abandonment by her own parents. I'm frustrated that Marizette is being hurt and there's nothing that I can do about it. I start to scream at Helene, the words flowing from me in a torrent of anger and pain, without pause.

'Well, Helene, you don't deserve children! You don't deserve to have any of your children, because any mother who's capable of turning her back on her own child has no right being a mom. And I'll tell you this, Helene, from one mother to another. I know I could be a drug addict or a whore or any number of atrocious things, but my mother will always be there for me and my daughter knows she can expect the same love from me.' I pause, my tirade over. The line is silent. I'm stunned Helene hasn't hung up on me yet.

'I don't want a black grandchild,' she states simply. 'Marizette has the right to make her own choices and I have the right to make mine.'

'Well, Helene, you might be a white woman, but you have a black heart. And you know what? One day God will judge you!'

Click. Finally I've gone too far and she's hung up on me.

I look at the phone in my hand, shocked at my

outburst. Where did all that come from? I certainly hadn't banked on a screaming match with Helene. Well, it wasn't exactly a screaming match, as the screaming was pretty much one-sided. I sit on the bed and try to compose myself before telling Maz the outcome of my call.

☾

Midnight. The house is silent, except for Emmy's breathing, which is surprisingly loud for such a tiny person. Marizette is fast asleep beside me and Emmy is lying on my chest. I've tried to put her down next to me, but each time she becomes fretful and starts to cry. Normally Marizette is on night duty. Actually, Marizette has enthusiastically carried out almost every duty concerning Emmy. She's so besotted with this baby and is an awesome mother. But now Maz is simply exhausted, so I'm looking after Emmy tonight.

Marizette has always said if we ever have a baby of our own, that we won't make the same mistake as Peter and I did by having the kids in bed with us. But Emmy is so restless at night, it's far too exhausting to get up and down to tend to her. We also can't bear to let her cry, as she's had such a rough start to life, we want her to feel safe all the time. I can feel Emmy's little heart beating and I'm overwhelmed by love. When did I come to love this little girl so deeply? I can't pinpoint the exact moment. Was it when we decided to apply for adoption? Or was it when she first arrived? I don't know, but I do know I feel as though I've loved her forever.

An ice-cold fear runs through my veins at the thought of losing her. What if Tumeka changes her mind? What if she's taken from us and placed in a children's home? I make a silent promise to Emmy that as long as she's with us, we'll treat her like gold and never handle her roughly, but I can't promise that she'll always be with us. It's an awful, disempowering, helpless feeling. I fight off images of police and social workers having to forcibly remove her from my arms. I'm not religious, but for once I pray fervently. 'Dear God or Goddess or any higher being who might have power over these things. I beg of you, please, please don't let this baby be taken away from us.' I repeat the words over and over in my head, as though through repetition they will become reality. I'm wretchedly tired, but right now, I'd put up with ten years of sleepless nights to keep Emmy.

Chapter forty-two

To: sara@naturalnurture.co.uk
Subject: A mother-in-law's wrath
Dear Sara

The phone call to Helene was a complete disaster. I got so angry I ended up shouting at her and she's basically said she wants nothing to do with us ever again. Oh, and get this: when Maz heard how I spoke to her mom she was furious! She couldn't believe I'd be so rude and disrespectful to Helene. God! I only lost my temper with Helene, because I'm so protective of Marizette.

So it's been a time of sadness and joy. Sadness because of the silence from Marizette's parents, and joy because Tumeka has given us permission to adopt Emmy. She's signed papers and now has sixty-eight nail-biting days to change her mind. After that waiting period, we'll have a naming ceremony. We asked Ian to facilitate the whole thing – you know how he loves that kind of important family occasion stuff – and he said he'd be honoured.

I haven't even told the older children we stand to lose Emmy if Tumeka changes her mind. They love her so much. Benjamin plays with her endlessly, even though she can't be much fun to play with as she doesn't really do anything yet. Max is the ultimate big brother, and very responsible and careful when she's around. She adores him too, often crying if we take her from him. When Chloe plays with Emmy, her face brightens up the way it used to, which is lovely to watch. Marizette has already started teaching Emmy to swim.

By the way, can't believe you've met someone else. Does Graeme know? You sound completely in love with this girl! I must say, that the master/sub thing sounds very intriguing. Let me get this straight ... She is the master, right? So she writes you letters detailing requirements of where to meet, how to dress, even what colour nail polish to wear, etc. Sounds sexy. Especially the bit about meeting you in public, you with mini skirt and no undies. Wow, must try it with Maz. Will ask her to write me a list of instructions. Can't wait. I wish I could spice my sex life up a bit. I miss being intimate with Maz – she's so in love with Emmy I feel horribly left out and neglected. Walked around the bedroom in sexy undies earlier, which would normally have Maz gagging for me. This time she barely noticed and then told me to look how gorgeous Emmy is. Now I understand what new dads feel like, utterly sidelined, after children are born. No wonder they have affairs.

Are you ever going to let Graeme know about the new woman in your life? You sound serious about this one. Just be careful. Don't want you to get hurt. Love, Michi

PS: Forgot to tell you: Benjamin's birthday party is coming up. He says he doesn't want any presents. All he wants is for the whole family, including Maz and Emmy, to be together. He's been so insistent and pleading about it that, between us, we've decided to put our differences to one side and just do it. Was amazed Peter and Maz agreed ... We're having a little party for him at Peter's flat, as he still finds it too hard to come to our place. Desperately hope all goes well.

○

'Alright, let's do this,' Marizette exhales the long breath she's been holding all the way up the stairs. We're outside Peter's front door; Marizette's holding Emmy and I'm clutching a bottle of wine. Both of us filled with nerves.

I knock loudly.

'Hi! Come in, come in,' Ingrid greets us warmly. She is also clearly nervous, her smile too wide, talking too fast. 'Your parents and Tana and Ian are already here. Would you like a drink?' she asks. 'Some juice, a cup of tea, a glass of wine?'

'A glass of wine' Marizette and I say in unison.

'Oh thank God,' Ingrid laughs, 'then I can also have one.'

The flat's small lounge is crowded with family members.

'Mom!' Benjamin says, rushing over to us. Emmy shrieks with delight when she sees him, throwing her arms wide open.

Benjamin takes her from Marizette and announces, 'Everyone's here.' And then, mischievously, 'Now I can open my presents.'

Hours later, just the four of us; Ingrid, Peter, Marizette and me are alone in the flat, sitting outside on the balcony. As Benjamin's party wound down, we were about to gather the children and get ready to go home, relieved the afternoon had played out peacefully, without too much awkwardness.

But my mom and dad gave each other a meaningful look, and my dad spoke up, 'Michele and Marizette, uh … you stay on a bit. We'll take the children home and put them to bed. You two just relax.'

And I thought, relax a bit? What's he talking about? Surely by now my dad must know Marizette and Peter are deeply uncomfortable being in the same space. But of course my dad is always the peacemaker and I can just guess what he's hoping for. It's not going to work, though, I think, sighing. We'll likely have a last quick drink together, a brief and stilted conversation, and then Marizette and I will be on our way.

I glance at my watch. Unbelievably, it's just after nine and my parents left hours ago. During the first bottle of wine, Marizette and I sat slightly apart, trying not to be all over each other, out of respect for Peter. He, on the other hand, was very affectionate to Ingrid; holding her hand, rubbing her shoulder, touching her leg. In fact, spontaneously doing all the things I used to beg him to do for me.

Two bottles of wine later, our conversation became progressively more familiar. Ingrid and I have moved indoors and are chatting companionably on the couch, while Peter and Marizette share a cigarette on the balcony. Actually it's probably about the third cigarette they've had in quick succession, and Ingrid and I are doing far more eavesdropping on their conversation than our own chatting. Through the glass doors, we've heard an entire confession, an opening up of hearts.

'Peter, I'm so sorry. I never meant to hurt you …'

'Look, Marizette, I know you love Michele. And I can't pretend it doesn't hurt …'

'I know; I'm so sorry. I never wanted to split up your family.'

'I know … I just want you to know how much I appreciate everything you do for them.'

'I really do love them, you know.'

Then there's silence, and Ingrid digs me in the ribs – Peter and Marizette are hugging! I'm astounded and thrilled at the same time. I would never have imagined it was possible. The two of them move apart and Peter offers Maz another cigarette to defuse the emotional tension, no doubt.

'Ingrid,' I say, deciding to get my piece in before they come back inside, 'I want you to know I'm extremely grateful to you for being so good to my children. They really love you, you know.' Oh God, alcohol plus me equals over emotional ramblings.

Luckily Ingrid is on a par with me, 'Well, Michele, I don't have children of my own, and I love your kids. They're such special people. I have to tell you, you've done a wonderful job with them. You can be really proud.'

'Aw, thank you,' I pause. 'I also want to thank you for being there for Peter. I really appreciate it. I will always love him, you know, and never wanted to hurt him. And I know you've had to deal with all his sadness and you've been so kind and patient. I really appreciate it.' I'm being stupidly bold and personal. I should just stop talking. But I don't.

'And Peter says he's had the best sex of his life since he's been with you. Apparently you're a Tantric master,' I giggle, then realise what I've just said. 'Oh fuck, I'm sorry! I'm being highly inappropriate.'

'No, it's fine,' Ingrid laughs. 'Actually, I'm flattered.'

'Yeah, well, I always said to him he needed to be loved by a woman in a way I couldn't, and it looks like he's scored in that department. And that makes me so happy,' I gush.

'Well, what I'm happy about is that those two are talking,' Ingrid gestures to Peter and Marizette outside. 'It just makes things so much easier.'

'Not just talking, hugging! Who would've thought? Let's hope it lasts.'

'Yes,' Ingrid agrees, 'at least longer than it takes for the alcohol to wear off.' She sighs, 'He's still so up and down about everything, you never know how he'll be tomorrow.'

Chapter forty-three

'Good afternoon, everybody. We're gathered here for a sacred and joyous celebration. As you all no doubt know, we're here to welcome the beautiful Emmy into our lives and our hearts.'

Ian is standing in the centre of a circle of our friends and family, looking handsome and mystical, with his shoulder-length hair and flowing white shirt, worn over loose-fitting white, cotton trousers.

It's been raining all morning and I was so worried we wouldn't be able to hold the ceremony outdoors. But luckily parts of the sky have cleared and the rain seems to be holding off for the moment. There are about thirty of us surrounding Ian in three consecutive circles, inside the waist-high lavender maze, all holding hands, except Marizette, who's holding Emmy in the centre. I look around at the various people who want to share in the joy that is Emmy. Only Ian could succeed in getting such a diverse group to hold hands.

The Group is also there, with some of my other straight friends, as well as family and children; my very religious aunt; a few of our lesbian friends; Tana, Rebecca and Tana's son Jonathan; Princess and my parents; and of course all my children, including Emmy, who's now officially ours. The sixty-eight days have passed and we're beside ourselves with relief.

Cupped in Ian's hands is a small brown clay bowl. 'In this bowl,' he says, 'is *imphepho*, a type of African incense, traditionally used in special rituals. It was specially given to us by my sangoma friend. When it burns, it's believed to summon our ancestors to ward off negative influences and any obstructions to peace. It's also used to gather Ubuntu, the energy of interconnectedness we all share.

'"*Umuntu, Ngumuntu Ngabantu*" literally means I am because you are, and so our journeys to happiness, peace and joy as individuals and communities are bound together. Thank you, Emmy, for reminding us of this truth,' Ian kisses Emmy on the forehead and lights the fragrant herbs in the bowl.

'Now I'd like everyone to pass the bowl around the circle of love, and to offer a blessing to Emmy, either aloud or silently to yourself, as we welcome her into our circle and are accepted by her into her circle.'

He passes the bowl to Benjamin, who says, 'Emmy, I'm so happy you're my sister. I wish you a golden life.'

The bowl travels slowly around the circle, with most guests holding it for a few seconds and then passing it on; a few people wish Emmy a wonderful life. When it reaches Princess, she says something in Xhosa. I have no idea what her words mean, but I know her intention is positive.

My mom of course is too choked to speak when the bowl reaches her and after a few seconds she passes it to Tana. Tana looks so beautiful with her long, wavy, blonde hair, emanating gentleness and goodness.

'I would like to offer Emmy a Jewish blessing,' she begins. 'Hashem bless you and safeguard you. May

Hashem illuminate His countenance for you and be gracious to you. May He turn His countenance to you and establish peace for you.'

Finally the bowl has travelled around the three circles and back to Ian. He's about to say something, when my aunty suddenly pipes up.

'Um, I'd like to say a prayer for Emmy.' She closes her eyes respectfully, 'Dear Lord, please bless Emmy and guide her. Please keep her safe. Amen.'

'Amen,' a couple of people echo.

I'm incredibly moved by this multicultural outpouring of love for our little Emmy. Though not at all religious, I am grateful for the blessings. At least we have all the angles covered, I think.

'Look,' Chloe shrieks, pointing to the mountains, 'a rainbow!'

And she's right; a brightly coloured rainbow spans the garden. I feel a bubble of laughter. It's the perfect end to our ceremony. As the circles disperse, Marizette comes over and wraps me in a big hug, squishing Emmy between us. I call the other kids over too and suddenly we're all enveloped in one big cheesy family hug.

☾

To: sara@naturalnurture.co.uk
Subject: The rainbow naming ceremony
Dear Sara
Had such a beautiful naming ceremony for Emmy. As part of the rituals, we circulated a blanket with a blank piece of white material sewn to one side. Gave everyone fabric pens to write with. There were plenty of beautiful

messages and wishes for Emmy. At end of the day, Maz and I snuggled up in bed together with the blanket to read the different messages. We were stunned when we came to one that read: 'Dear Emmy. Hope your life is filled with good things. Love, Oupa'! I couldn't believe he signed it 'Oupa'. Since the naming day, my dad has done a complete turnaround. He picks up Emmy to cuddle her and plays peek-a-boo with her. In return, she absolutely adores him. Her face lights up whenever he walks into the room.

BTW: I mentioned that master/sub fantasy thing to Marizette. She was quite excited and we decided to give it a go. I told her to write down things she wants me to do. But days passed and nothing! She says with Emmy and swim school she doesn't have any time to think up anything, let alone write it down. So we quickly discussed a couple of instructions – all quite simple – involving shaved fanny, sexy undies and doing a suggestive dance for her. Anyway, when the kids were at Peter's, I managed to shave, and once Emmy was finally asleep, put on sexy undies and prepared to perform for my master. It was all going well until Emmy woke up demanding a bottle. Once she was settled, we'd lost the mood and just went to bed. Will I ever get my sex life back?!!!

You're going to have to tell me about all the wonderful things you get up to so I can live vicariously through your sex life!!

Unfortunately, there's still often a lot of tension between me and Maz (almost always over how I feel about Peter). Things seem fine for a while and then suddenly flare up again. Also, after our cautiously successful evening after Benjamin's birthday we're back to square one with relations with Peter. With our wedding coming up, he's renewed in his hostility towards us, especially Maz. Sorry to end on such a downer. All my love, Mich

Chapter forty-four

I'm sitting in the car with Marizette; always the passenger, not the driver. We're on our way back from town after a gruelling morning. I place my hand on my stomach, silently forcing myself to slow down my breathing. The car is stuffy even with the air-con on and I can't seem to get enough air into my lungs. Breathe into your stomach, I command. Our day so far has been stressful and tiring. We spent at least two hours at Home Affairs, thanks to the incompetence and disorganisation of the staff, just to collect divorce papers. Then had to rush across town, in traffic, to the lawyer to have our pre-nup drawn up. Then we had a quick haircut before we had to leave again to collect the kids from school. And of course all of this with Emmy in tow, who gorgeous as she is, just adds to the general stress.

Shit. It really is stuffy. I open the window, gratefully breathing in the air whipping my face. Deep breath, I tell myself. Our wedding is coming up soon and suddenly everything feels like such a rush. Why are we doing this in such a hurry? I feel so pressured suddenly. I just want everything to slow down. There's no need to rush, I think. But Marizette feels differently. She's thrilled at our upcoming wedding. Although, admittedly, she's far from thrilled at the moment; right now she's furious. The cause of her anger: me. Her intended. Her wife-to-be. The nature of my crime: Candy, the hairdresser cut my hair shorter than she wanted. And she's still going on about it.

'I can't believe you just went ahead and told Candy to cut your fringe so short. It looks horrible!' she rants for the umpteenth time. 'And we're getting married soon! There won't be time for it to grow out properly,' she says accusingly.

Just breathe, I tell myself. Then, aloud, 'Marizette, it's just a fringe. It's not something to be so angry about,' I appeal. But I can feel my own anger rising, 'And besides, Candy liked it.'

'Well Candy's not the one who's going to marry you, is she? And you actually asked my opinion first. Why ask my opinion if you're going to go ahead and do whatever you want anyway?'

I can feel a lump forming in my throat. My eyes start tearing and the wind blows the wetness across my cheeks and into my ears. My heartbeat gets louder and louder; I can actually hear it thumping in my eardrums. I grab a tissue from my bag and blow my nose, trying to clear my sinuses.

Marizette is still going on, '... I don't understand why you don't get it. You should know why I'm angry!'

And I'm tempted to scream, 'It's a fucking haircut for Christ's sake! There's so much more to be worried about. This nightmare of a morning for a start; your parents refusing to come to the wedding; the children's sudden reticence; Peter's hostility, the list goes on.' I think all these things, but say nothing, and keep breathing deeply in through my nose and out through my pursed mouth.

We're home, thank God. The kids have been collected and I can lie down for a bit. I feel decidedly strange and a bit light-headed, but put it down to hunger. I get like this if I don't eat often enough. I make myself some toast and a cup of tea, and take it with me to the bedroom, where I lie down for a moment, gratefully.

But it's not for long. Chloe and Benjamin walk in, bombarding me with questions at the same time. I try to concentrate, but I lose focus. Then Max comes in to ask if he can bath in our bathroom. He runs a bath. I feel as though part of my brain has been removed. I'm not passing out, but it feels very unpleasant, like being smothered with a pillow without actually dying.

Suddenly, without warning, I feel my body shut down. I have no control but I know I'm in big trouble. I heave, gasping for air. I try to stand, but my legs give way and I collapse on the bedroom floor. I try to shout for help, but it's like those nightmares where you try to shout but nothing comes out. I manage to force out Max's name, 'Get Marizette,' I gasp.

He recognises the desperation in my voice because he immediately jumps out the bath, takes one look at me and runs screaming for Marizette. 'Marizette! Quick! Help, Mom's having a heart attack or something.'

Oh my God, of course. I must be having a heart attack. By the time Marizette gets to the bedroom my organs have shut down and my arms and legs have seized up. My hands are paralysed claws. Marizette tries to pick me up, but struggles with my dead weight and falls to the floor.

'Max!' she shouts, her voice panicky. 'Go get Oupa and Ouma quickly.'

Why isn't she giving me mouth-to-mouth? The questions float in and out of my mind. I know she's done CPR and I'm clearly dying. Surely she should be trying to save my life.

Then somehow I'm in the car with my parents. My dad's driving and holding me steady at the same time. My mom is sitting behind me rubbing my shoulders, making sure I don't keel over. They decided it would be quicker to drive to the hospital than wait for an ambulance. Marizette has stayed home with the kids, who are in shock, especially Max.

My parents are discussing me as though I'm not there.

'It could be a stroke.'

'Or a heart attack.'

This worrying dialogue makes me realise I don't want to die. But if I'm going to, I want to die quickly, because dying like this is a nightmare. I had no idea it was possible to feel this awful. And if I die, I think, strangely out of touch with the emotional meaning of those words, I want Marizette to know how much I love her. And Peter too. I want him to know that even if I'm not able to love him in the right way, I still love him. I want them to put their differences to one side and raise the kids with as much love as possible. I want to relay these thoughts to my parents, but I can't, because tears are gushing out of my eyes and I'm gasping for breath.

We arrive at the hospital and two nurses come out to help place me in a wheelchair before whisking me into the foyer. Things are attached to me; a mask over my face and clamps on my fingers. A nurse forces my jaw open to put some pills under my tongue. My breathing slows. I stop gasping, but I can't stop crying. Loud, heaving sobs

I feel will go on forever. I hold my hand over my face because I don't want the hospital staff to witness my face twisting into the horrible contortions I seem to have no control over. The nurse places another tablet under my tongue. Slowly my sobs start to subside.

My parents hover nearby as a doctor begins asking me a series of questions. 'So, are you feeling dizzy?'

'Yes, very.'

'Do your arms and legs feel numb? Possibly a bit tingly?'

'Yes,' I nod. 'Yes, they do.'

'Mmm ...' He checks my blood pressure and the reading from the oxygen mask. 'You've had a panic attack. Have you been under a lot of stress lately?'

'What? It can't be a panic attack,' I say confidently. 'I've been under a lot more stress before, and I've never had an attack. Shouldn't you run some tests?'

But he ignores me, and continues writing on the clipboard.

I seriously doubt his diagnosis. Doctors have been known to make mistakes before. The nurse places another pill under my tongue and my breathing becomes more even.

'She has been under a lot of stress lately,' my mom says eagerly. 'She's meant to be getting married to her girlfriend soon, and it's been terribly difficult, what with her ex-husband's reaction and everything.'

The doctor frowns, 'Um, right. Uh, I'm going to give you the name of a psychiatrist. If you want, you can stay overnight or you can wait here till you feel stronger and go home later.'

'I think she should stay,' my mom decides, before I

can say anything. 'She'll be better off here for the night.' Then to me, 'Stay, my darling, and get some rest. We'll pick you up in the morning.'

The doctor leaves. I don't think that he can get away fast enough, and I'm left alone with my parents. They're visibly relieved it's not a stroke or a heart attack. I should be relieved too; I'm not dead or dying. But instead I'm mortified – a panic attack! I can't believe it. I've seen people have panic attacks in movies. It's usually a bit of heavy breathing, nothing like what I just experienced. I can't believe it. I'm glad I'm not dead, sure, but something more life-threatening, not so embarrassing would be nice. Something that would justify a hospital stay. Possibly a spontaneous coma. But one that wouldn't leave me brain damaged. Serious enough to require a hospital stay for a few days. I'd emerge from my coma rested, possibly a few kilograms lighter, and everyone would've worried about me so much, they'd put their differences aside.

I'm broken out of my reverie by Marizette bursting through the door from the car park. I'm still laid out in the hospital foyer; clearly I wasn't serious enough to be rushed off somewhere.

Maz rushes to my side and grabs my hand, 'Oh baby, how are you?' Her face is pale, her eyes wild. She looks completely traumatised.

'She's going to be OK,' says my mom authoritatively, 'it was just a panic attack.'

Maybe it was just a panic attack, but it felt horrible. What if it happens again? The fact that I had no control over what just happened terrifies me. And worst of all, what if it happens in public or at the kids' school? I'm never leaving home again. Well, once I get home that is. Although being at home is hardly conducive to not having another panic attack. Just the thought of the general chaos of my home with all the kids, animals and general clutter, is enough to start me hyperventilating again. Maybe I can just stay in hospital. I can even put up with the food; just be grateful I don't have to cook it.

'Who's looking after the kids?' I ask Marizette, trying to slow my wild train of thoughts.

'Peter. They wanted to speak to him and tell him what happened. Then he asked to speak to me, and offered to take the kids for the night, so I could come be with you,' she explains.

I'm incredulous. 'You and Peter spoke to each other?'

'Yes. I think he could hear how worried I was and he felt sorry for me. He says he hopes you're going to be OK.'

I squeeze her hand.

My dad comes back from the reception desk, 'Mom and I are going home. I've given them all your medical-aid details. We'll see you tomorrow.' He hugs me, 'Now you get better, you're getting married soon, remember.'

I'm surprised. I would've thought my dad would use this attack as good reason to try to persuade me not to get married.

My mom leans over to give me a kiss. 'Have a good rest. I'll see you tomorrow, OK? I love you.'

And with that they're gone and I am left with Marizette who stays with me, holding my hand till I'm wheeled away to a shared room, and hopefully, a good night's sleep.

To: sara@naturalnurture.co.uk
Subject: Diagnosis: Adjustment Disorder
Dear Sara

I had the most excruciating and embarrassing panic attack the other day, which has left me feeling very fragile. The whole experience came out of the blue and I couldn't understand why I got one at this stage in my life. I think I've been though a lot worse. However, when I look over the past few years, I suppose I can see why it happened.

I spoke to my therapist about it, and suggested maybe I was suffering from something similar to postnatal depression, and that maybe I was struggling with having to look after a young child again. But he said it's not postnatal depression' it's 'adjustment disorder'. What a brilliant term! And it makes so much sense. In a short space of time, I came out as a lesbian, split up with my husband, started a new relationship, adopted a baby, got divorced, and am about to get remarried. And throughout all of that, I've dealt with Peter's grief and hostility, my children's sadness, my girlfriend's insecurities, and my own depression plus all-consuming guilt. No wonder I had a panic attack!

Now I have this fear hanging over me that I'll have another one, especially in public. I've had to force myself to go out. I sometimes feel the people around me don't realise just how debilitating the experience has been. Although, my family has been very supportive. It's made me realise how lucky I am to live with my family so nearby. Ian is going to give me Reiki, and Tana is the ultimate nurturer, always opening her home to me if I need an escape and plying me with smoothies and kind words. Marizette still gets angry with me very easily' which keeps threatening to set me off again.

But perhaps the most positive outcome is that the ice has broken between Peter and Marizette. Peter phoned to see how I was afterwards and said it's clear Maz truly loves me. He also realised there are going to be times when we all have to be there for each other.

Later this month Maz and I will have been together for two years. We're going to a cottage in Churchhaven, in the nature reserve on the West Coast, and my mom will have the children for three days. After the panic attack, she reckons we desperately need the break. Hope things are smoother on your side of the world. Love, Michi

Chapter forty-five

Marizette and I are snuggled up in the hammock facing each other, our legs entwined. The lagoon stretches before us, shining golden in the setting sun. Adding to the surreal beauty, a flock of pink flamingos has settled on the sand. Further out, a pelican floats past, lazily. And the peace, oh the glorious peace! A stark contrast to the relentless and noisy bustle of our home. I want to weep with the pleasure of it. We are here midweek and it seems we're the only people in the entire reserve.

'Ah, this is the life,' Marizette sighs in pleasure.

'I think I want to stay here forever,' I add.

However, the day after tomorrow we'll be returning to reality. Back to the stresses and strains of daily life. And we'll be getting married soon; making vows to love each other and be with each other for always.

'Mazzie,' I begin tentatively.

I'm so reluctant to do this. I don't want to spoil the peace we've had since we arrived. Yet, at the same time, I need to discuss some things with her. I want to be on the right track from the onset. I look at Marizette, her brown eyes shining bronze in the sunset, and my heart aches with love for her. I don't want to lose her; not now, not ever. The thought of not having her in my life fills me with a cold, hard fear. Which is why I need to raise these issues, even though I know she won't want me to. I'm risking ruining our whole evening. If I just left everything, we could bask in the fading sunlight, finish a chilled bottle of wine, and make love in front of the crackling fire …

But then nothing will be resolved. So here goes, 'Mazzie, we need to discuss some things.'

She is alerted by my tone. 'Michi, please let's not talk about heavy stuff and ruin our time here.'

But I'm determined. 'My angel, we're getting married soon and I really think we need to work on some things.'

'Oh for God's sake, Michele! We shouldn't be working on things at this point. We should be getting on with things,' she snaps impatiently.

'Mazzie, if we're going to be together for a very long time, then different issues will always arise and all marriages need continual work to be healthy. All I'm saying is I want to try to break the negative patterns we keep repeating,' I pause. 'Especially involving Peter. Even though the two of you are communicating, you still get so angry about the fact that we ever had a relationship and you flip out that I was so sad about my break-up.'

Marizette climbs out of the hammock and begins pacing, an indication that she's upset. She can't be still when she's emotional.

'Do you know what the main problem is?' she asks accusingly. 'It's that I want to make you happy. It's what I've always wanted. I want it so badly. And I've tried so incredibly hard, right from the very beginning, to do just that. I did everything in my power, Michele. Everything!' Her eyes fill with tears. 'I tried to be so much more than

Peter. I was more attentive and affectionate to you than he was. I'm more involved with the children. I work my butt off in this family! I have so much love for you, and it hasn't been enough to make you happy and stop you being sad. And that breaks my heart.' Her last words are muffled by tears, 'I feel so unappreciated.'

'Mazzie, listen, please. I do appreciate all you do for us, I promise.' I climb out of the hammock and take her face in my hands. 'I'm sorry if I don't show you that often enough. I know you took on a huge amount at such a young age.'

'I don't mind the responsibility, or the hard work,' she cries, 'but I do mind you grieving about Peter. My love for you should be enough to stop you from being sad.'

'Maz, my reaction was normal,' I say quietly.

'No, it wasn't. Other women wouldn't have been like that if their new partner gave them as much love and commitment as I give. Do you have any idea how hard it was for me? All I wanted was for you to forget your life with Peter and start a new one with me. One we could be proud of. How is that possible with you sad and grieving all the time?'

'OK, Marizette, see, this is exactly what I'm talking about. Right now, we're repeating a pattern and if we keep going we're both going to be hysterical and nothing will be resolved. If we don't deal with it we'll still be having these conversations in ten years' time and it will kill our marriage.' I pause, trying to find the right words. 'I can't do this forever; I don't want to be having these same conversations when I'm fifty or sixty. Marizette, I love you more than you could ever know. I would walk to the ends of the earth for you. But your issues with

Peter … and,' I add cautiously, 'your anger, send my stress levels sky-rocketing. Yours too. And that's not good for us.'

'But, Michi, it's the way I am. You have to get used to it. And there are a lot of good things about me.'

'Oh Mazzie, there are a million good things about you,' I reassure her. 'But I can't deal with these ongoing dramas forever. We're getting married. And we'll vow to be with each other for always. I want to make sure that we do everything in our power to make that possible.'

Marizette sinks into a chair and lights a cigarette. She takes a few puffs. It looks like she's run out of the energy to fight back. 'Michi, I never want to lose you. I feel more for you than I've felt for anyone in my whole life. I never want to be without you, otherwise my life will be meaningless and empty,' she pauses and takes a thoughtful puff of her cigarette. 'OK, what do you want me to do?'

'I want you to see a therapist. Jeffrey's suggested someone.'

'Oh, great so you discuss me with Jeffrey,' she says belligerently.

'Look, he believes therapy can help us move forward.'

I sit down on the chair next to Marizette and take her hands in mine. We look at each other, not saying anything.

'Michele, you know I hate the idea of therapy. We should be able to sort things out ourselves.'

'But we're still going over and over the same stuff and it's not resolved,' I protest.

'It'll be a waste of money. I won't have anything to say.'

More silence. We look into each other's eyes, mine imploring, hers defiant.

'Alright! Alright! I'll see someone,' she concedes.

Relief washes over me.

'But only because you want me to,' she adds.

I smile and kiss her on the mouth, 'That's a good enough reason for me. Now,' I say, pulling her closer, 'I think we have a fireplace to get naked in front of.'

She smiles, 'Remember the time we came here and I slept up in the loft with all the kids?'

I nod.

'Well, I got up in the night to go to the toilet and I stopped at your door. I stood there for ages, desperate to slip in and seduce you.'

'No way!' I laugh; she's never mentioned this before.

'Yes, really. And it took all my willpower to tear myself away. I wanted you so badly.'

'Oh my God, I had no idea you had any feelings for me back then. Well, now you have me.'

'I know, but maybe can we pretend that I don't. You go get into bed and then I'll come in after a bit and seduce you.'

Marizette loves role-play, and it usually involves first-time scenarios.

'OK,' I smile. 'Give me the setting. What am I wearing and what am I doing in bed all alone before you come knocking on my door?'

୨

To: sara@naturalnurture.co.uk
Subject: Breakthrough!

Dear Sara

Since November, Marizette has been seeing a therapist, which has been invaluable. After the second session, she sat me down and told me she wants to apologise for not being more understanding of my grief in the beginning, and that her therapist has helped her to understand the feelings of loss and sacrifice a woman experiences when leaving a marriage. She's also helping Maz deal with her anger, which has made such a difference. Honestly, I'm so proud of her for taking such strides, especially since she was so set against therapy. I know it's still a long road ahead, but we're on the right track.

Now, it's full-steam ahead for wedding arrangements. Although it's my second wedding, I desperately want it to be special. We're having it at home with a big pink Bedouin tent! We don't have a huge budget, so will be doing a lot of stuff ourselves. I've been making ceramic hearts to hang from the trees in the garden. Brandy has offered to do our make-up, and Anna's husband, Edward, will be organising the music for the walk down the imaginary aisle, which unfortunately my dad won't be doing with me this time around. He said there's no way he's making a speech and he hopes that I don't expect him to walk me in. I replied I was just happy he was going to be there. Luckily, I will be accompanied by Benjamin, Lucy's twins and Brandy's little girl, who will all wear matching bridesmaid and pageboy outfits.

With Marizette's parents … I keep hoping they'll change their minds and turn up at the last minute. They've already surprised me by contributing a lump sum to the wedding. Her brothers, Etienne and Juan, will be coming.

We've invited about eighty guests, which sounds like a lot, I know, but at least thirty of them are under eighteen, as most of my friends are parents. And it's the usual eclectic mix. Ian and his hippie family, the religious branch of our family, lesbians ... Wish you and Graeme and the kids could come over. Anyway, better go. Have hundreds of ceramic hearts to paint and decorate. Will write again after the wedding. All my love, Michele

PS: Although I'm not religious, we're having a reverend marry us (one of the few who officiate at gay weddings). Have met with him and like him a lot. Also, Marizette has decided to take my surname! Am hugely honoured.

Chapter forty-six

I recite the opening line of Katie Melua's 'Bicycles' song for about the millionth time. I'm so nervous about singing to Marizette, and I'm trying to get the tune into my brain parrot fashion, through sheer repetition. I'm fully made up in my wedding dress, and have been banished up to the loft by Brandy, who insists Marizette shouldn't see me until we walk together to join the minister.

It's a welcome break having nothing to do but wait to be summoned downstairs. This morning was a mad rush. The pink tent was set up yesterday and looks glorious, offset by all the fuchsia pink and purple gazanias flowering all over the garden at this time of the year. Unfortunately, the pink tent was the only thing that was ready this morning. What I hadn't realised was that our budget didn't cover the setting up of the tables, and the delivery guys dumped the huge, heavy round tables on the grass next to the tent and promptly left. With everything that still needed to be done, this was most unwelcome.

But thanks to my own personal fairy godmothers, almost everything was ready to go by the time I came upstairs to get dressed. My cousin Carina and Lucy took the delegating upon themselves: Carina motivated Max, Matthew and Marizette's brothers to do the heavy work of setting up the tables and chairs, and Lucy got Chloe and her girl cousins to hang the hearts in the trees and decorate the tables. They were still busy when I climbed the stairs to the loft, and I could hear Lucy shouting, 'Come on, girls! We've only got half an hour left. Come, come, this is no time for resting!'

Then there's Brandy, fairy godmother number three, who is single-handedly doing everyone's make-up. She originally offered to do Marizette's and mine, but by the time she banished me up here, she'd already waved her magic wand over Chloe, my mom, Kitty, her own daughter, and now Marizette.

Anna's husband Edward has promised to surprise us with the music for 'The Wedding March'. I'm not sure what he's bringing, but I trust him completely. And of course Ian, who's MC.

I switch off the CD player as the song comes to an end. That's it now, if I don't know the words then I'll never know them. I go over to the full-length mirror and regard myself critically. I look good. I'm delighted with my beautiful sparkly dress and Brandy has done wonders with my hair and make-up. I can't wait for Marizette to see me; I hope she approves.

There's a knock on the door and my dad enters with a glass of Champagne.

'Ah, Dad, thank you,' I say, pleased to see him. I take a quick gulp of Champagne and bombard him with questions. 'How are things going outside? Is everything ready? Is the minister here yet? How do I look? Can I quickly sing you my song?' My heart starts to do funny, fluttery things.

'Everything's fine,' my dad soothes. 'The tables have

been set, people have started taking their seats and the minister has just arrived. Ian's seeing him in. You won't have time to do your song now, but I heard you sing on the way up and it sounds fine. Also, you look beautiful.'

'Thank you. God, I'm so nervous!' I breathe in and blow out a long whoosh of air through my mouth.

My dad hovers for a bit, walks to the door, then seems to change his mind and stops. 'Um, Michele. If you like, um, I'll walk you to Marizette.'

'No, Dad, it's fine. Marizette and I are already planning to walk towards the minister together.'

'OK, right. I'll see you downstairs then.' And with that he's gone.

And then it hits me. My dad just offered to walk me. I must stop him! I run to the door to call him back, but the staircase is empty. My phone, where's my phone? I search frantically and find it next to the CD player. I need to let Marizette know, see if she's happy with the change in plan. Instead I try my mom.

'Mom!'

'Yes, my darling. Are you OK?'

'Yes, yes. Possible change of plan. Dad's offered to walk with me,' I squeal, 'but you have to speak to Marizette and see if it's fine and then inform the minister and tell Dad to get up here as soon as everything's ready.'

Fifteen minutes later, I step out on to the lawn on my father's arm. Behind me are my two beautiful little bridesmaids and two gorgeous pageboys. The wind has died down and the sky is a glorious blue, the mountain a picture-perfect backdrop. Hundreds of pretty ceramic hearts sparkle in the trees. Marizette is standing with the minister, beaming. I know she wanted us to walk together and didn't want to stand with the minister like a guy while I approach her, but I'm so happy to be on my father's arm and she looks so gorgeous waiting for me in her smart suit with smoky make-up. Happiness bubbles up in my chest, threatening to burst out of me. I'm smiling so much as I reach Marizette that my cheeks hurt.

Two hours later, I'm still smiling. So far it's been the most incredible wedding. The ceremony was suitably moving, and Maz and I pouring our glasses of sand into a shared vase was a lovely touch. At the start of the ceremony, I did a quick scan of the guests. I still hoped Marizette's parents would turn up at the last minute, Hollywood style, and surprise us all. Although I knew in my heart they wouldn't be there, I was still disappointed.

The younger children have been bouncing on the jumping castle we hired for the day. The teenagers have been mingling together and many of the dads are openly drooling over Kharli and her new girlfriend. Both are dressed in micro miniskirts. In fact, everyone is dressed up for the occasion, and looks fabulous. The dress code was 'summer elegance'.

When the wedding pictures were being taken, I tracked down the girls in The Group for a photo. Of course we all looked gorgeous. Even Patricia made a concession, and although her skirt is still crotch-swimmingly short, she has a long swathe of transparent material layered over it.

After supper it's time for the speeches. Marizette, Kharli, Jo and I have spoken and Lisa is wrapping up her speech, which I begged her to do for me, as I knew my dad wouldn't. As she comes to the end of her speech, she hands the mike to Ian for the toast. Everyone claps and

Ian is about to speak when my dad appears behind him and taps him on the shoulder. He takes the microphone and Ian takes a seat. This is completely unexpected, as my dad has refused from the onset to make a speech. There is an expectant pause.

'I wasn't planning on making a speech,' he begins, 'but looking around me today, I feel inspired to say a few words. When I courted my wife all those years ago, her Afrikaans family were none too thrilled with her English-speaking boyfriend. They were even less happy when we got engaged so soon after we met. In fact, her grandfather spent the best part of an hour trying to talk her out of marrying me. In spite of their disapproval, we did get married and more than forty years on, I've never had a day's regret.' He pauses.

'So then I must say that in spite of the disapproval from many corners that Michele and Marizette have had, looking around today, I can see they've also had a lot of support. And from a variety of different people. There is my daughter, who is gay, and her mixture of friends, my son's Jewish partner and her family, Christian family members, and my black granddaughter. Michele and Marizette have so much love, acceptance and support from you all, without which a difficult journey would have been even harder. So, I would like to raise a toast to everyone here in what my son reminds us is called the true spirit of Ubuntu,' he finishes, raising his glass, as everyone cheers and claps.

'Fuck me,' says Jo, who's sitting next to me. 'That was beautiful.' She takes a napkin from her table and roughly wipes a tear from her eyes. 'Now look what he's done, I don't do crying.'

'Thank you for that, Dad,' says Ian, retrieving the microphone, 'Now, let's drink a toast to the two beautiful brides and we can move on to the karaoke, which Marizette would like to open with a rendition of Katie Melua's "The Closest Thing To Crazy".'

Many, many drinks later. The karaoke has been a huge hit and mostly hogged by the teenagers. Almost everyone has danced non-stop, with a few of the show-offs predictably using the central pole of the tent to gyrate around. The music is a mix of standard dance stuff, South African favourites, including plenty of Afrikaans *lang-arm*, where Marizette has whirled me round the floor, and some instrumental, typically African music, in which Princess and the rest of the casual staff have knocked off work and given us a lesson in dancing to the African beat.

I love partying with my family on this special day. Mostly, my heart is exploding with pride and joy as I watch my beautiful children. Benjamin, who looked so smart in his pageboy's suit earlier, has spent most of the evening on the jumping castle or playing with Emmy, whose little bridesmaid's dress matches his waistcoat. And Max and Chloe look so grown up. Luckily, there are other teenagers for them to hang out with, and they've had plenty of fun dancing and singing karaoke. Max and his friends sang a song dedicated especially to us, and at one point Chloe came up to me and whispered in my ear: 'You know, Mom, I just want to say I love you and I'm really proud of you.' Which is the only time in the whole night that I got teary-eyed.

A slow song comes on, and Marizette takes my hand, leading me onto the dance floor, pulling me close to her.

My body melts as I press against her and feel her strong arms wrapped around me. This is the person I'm meant to be with for the rest of my life. I snuggle my head into her and think back over the long, rocky road that's led to this moment. And as I feel her lips on my neck, her hand in the small of my back, I know I would go through it again to be with her.

She kisses my cheek and whispers, 'I can't wait to get you into bed to consummate our marriage.'

I gently press my pelvis against hers and fantasise about the things I'm going to do to her later.

Several more hours later and we're pretzelled together in bed. Marizette is on her back and I have my head tucked into her armpit.

'Hey,' she says sleepily, 'what about all those promises you made me earlier?'

My limbs are so weary I can hardly move. 'Oh Mazzie, can we do it tomorrow? I promise I'll make it up to you …'

But she's already asleep.

☾

To: sara@naturalnurture.co.uk
Subject: Here comes the bride!
Dear Sara
The wedding was such a success. Most of our guests said that it was the best wedding they've ever been to. It was such a pity Marizette's parents weren't there; I'm sure one day they'll regret having missed her special day.

Our honeymoon was spent on the farm in Citrusdal. Although in fairness it wasn't exactly a honeymoon, more a family holiday, as we were joined by the kids, my cousins and their children, my aunt, Marizette's brother, and my parents. So Maz and I spent most of the week preparing food for everyone and running around after children. Not exactly conducive to romance. We don't have any money left to go away again just yet, so we've decided to try to get away on our own next year sometime. Marizette has her eye on a rainbow cruise (meant to be gay-friendly).

Everything has settled down immeasurably since we got married. I think it's mostly because Marizette feels so much more secure now. She no longer stresses over Peter or the possibility of me leaving her. Peter has recently moved to Hout Bay and lives less than five minutes away from us, which is much better for the children. At least now if they forget stuff at his place, or they want to see him for a while, it's not a huge mission to get them there and back.

The three older kids are all doing well at school and never hide the fact that their mom is gay. Chloe even wrote an article entitled 'My Gay Mom' that was published on a local website. Max is very protective over us and extremely vocal and defensive if anyone makes homophobic remarks. And Benjamin says he can't remember a time when Marizette wasn't in his life, and refers to both her and me as 'Mom'. Little Emmy of course will be facing her own challenges one day. Not just because she has two mothers, but because she's adopted and looks completely different from the rest of us. For now though she is the happiest little toddler around. She's adored by everyone who meets her, especially her three siblings, and so much love has to count for something.

Oh! Amazing news: Mazzie's parents have invited us up to Venda ... with Emmy. Yes! Unbelievable. Just out of the blue, they texted Maz and said they were missing her and could she please visit, and that we were welcome to bring Emmy. Not sure of their reasons for such a change of heart, but I suspect they don't want to lose Maz. And, whatever the reason, if they're extending the offer, then we have to go. Being an eternal optimist, I hope they fall in love with Emmy (how can anyone not?) and accept her as their grandchild.

Anyway, I must tell you about Christmas this year. Just picture it: a beautiful, sunny day and the table on the stoep, plus the vines overhead, all decorated with Christmas decorations. Sitting around the table were Marizette, me and the kids; Lucy and William and their kids; Ian, Tana, Rebecca and Jonathan; my parents and ... Peter and Ingrid! Amazingly there was no awkwardness at all. We had a proper Christmas lunch which everyone contributed to, complete with Christmas pudding and brandy butter. We pulled crackers and wore silly hats. Benjamin made a little speech saying how happy he was that everyone could be together on such a special day.

After lunch (which went on for ages) most of us swam while Peter and Chloe played the guitar and sang for us. The party went on late into the night and by the end everyone was well fed and happily exhausted. When Peter and I first split up, I never imagined we'd ever be comfortable in the same room, let alone spend Christmas together. As my mom has always said, 'Time. Just give it time.' Who knows, maybe next year the Brink family will join us.

I must say, Sara, I'm proud of you for finally telling your kids about being gay. I know how hard it is. Also, just be aware, they may seem fine with it now, but Graeme still hasn't moved out yet and it's only when that happens that the shock and reality kicks in. I know I'm on the other side of the world but I'm here for you. It's not an easy decision to make and if I look back at the last few years, I'm so relieved to be on solid ground again. I wouldn't want to put my family or friends, or Marizette and mostly myself, through that level of stress again. Anyway, give my love to your kids and Graeme, and tell them I'm thinking of you all. Take care, and remember, however stormy things are at the onset, they will settle eventually. Just try to hold on to your sanity; I almost lost mine. Lots of love, Michi

Epilogue

Things have come a long way since Marizette and I got married two years ago. The two of us are in a good space right now. Marizette is no longer so quick to anger and I don't fall apart so easily if she does.

Unbelievably, Marizette and Peter have become friends. Peter's gone as far as saying that he's grown to love Marizette and truly respects her as a co-parent. Part of me can't believe we've reached this level of peace and cooperation.

I'm writing this epilogue from my parents' farm in Citrusdal. Marizette, me, Peter, his girlfriend, the children and my mom are all here to celebrate my dad's birthday. That we are able to do this together is testament to each one of the members of my extraordinary family.

My last words must go to my in-laws, Helene and Danie, whom I feel have made the biggest adjustments. Marizette and I did take Emmy to visit them in Venda. We were all put up in the same room in their home and well cared for. There were gifts for each of us, including Emmy. Helene knitted her a gorgeous pink jumper.

Marizette's two younger brothers joined us for the weekend and we went to the Kruger National Park for the day, and stopped to have a picnic lunch. If Marizette's parents felt any embarrassment at having a black baby among them, they never showed it.

Later when we returned to their home, I stood staring at Helene's wall of pride. Among all the family photos is a picture of Marizette and me on our wedding day, and a picture of Marizette holding Emmy.

I have no idea how my in-laws made the enormous shifts that must have taken place to host the three of us in their home. I can't imagine what conversations would've taken place between them. I do know they've had to overcome a lifetime of conditioning to get to this point, which is truly commendable. There are many parents in the same position who would not have been willing to do the same.

Whatever Helene and Danie's reasons for accepting Emmy, I am enormously grateful. Marizette adores her parents and it would be tragic not to have them in our lives. One day, I hope they'll join us and the rest of the extended family on the farm in Citrusdal.

Michele Macfarlane, 2010

Acknowledgements

Firstly, I must thank Linda Nel at Exclusive Books, for helping me get my foot in the door, believing in my writing and passing on my story to Jacana.

To everyone at Jacana, especially Bridget Impey, thank you for all your enthusiastic support and for making this a reality.

A huge thanks goes to my tireless editor Gemma Harries for her gentle yet thorough edit, and for somehow managing to always be a cheerful and uplifting voice on the end of the line.

Thank you to Etienne, for taking the beautiful cover photo of me and Marizette.

To Renaissance coffee shop, where I sat and wrote this book, thanks for supplying me with the best cappuccinos in Cape Town.

To Lara Aucamp for her belief in this story and her constant promotion of the book. To Jeffrey Rink for keeping me focused.

To my friends Anita, Jason, Theresa, Pam, Wayne, Elena, Lisa, Lee, Brenda, Nathan, and Rita for enduring my many readings throughout the writing of the book. Your encouragement and feedback is much appreciated.

To my brother Ian, thanks for coming in with your

trademark energy and enthusiasm, and to his lovely wife, Dawn; thank you for all the nurturing and support.

To my four exceptional children: thank you for urging me to complete the book even though you know there's sensitive material in it and that it meant me being so much less available.

To my dad: you've helped out more than you know. Especially with the children. Thanks for being so involved with them. It's taken a huge pressure off me while I was writing.

Mom, words cannot begin to describe how incredible you've been throughout this journey. I don't know what I would have done without you, thank you.

To my beautiful wife, Marizette: I'm not exaggerating when I say that without you I wouldn't have been able to complete this book. You made it possible by single-handedly running the household, being my PA, buying me a laptop and making sure that I had the time to write. Thank you, my angel. I love you with all my heart.

And finally, to my dearest friend, Sara, endless thanks for your love and understanding.